The Slow Disappearing

Some things you lose. Some you surrender.

Also by P. A. Chawla

The Shenanigans of Time
Mumbai Mornings

The Slow Disappearing

Some things you lose. Some you surrender.

P. A. CHAWLA

Pen-N-Mouse

The Slow Disappearing
Some things you lose. Some you surrender.

For information contact: info.pennmouse@gmail.com

First North American Edition: January 2022
Not for sale in the Indian continent.
Cover artwork created by TheBookBakers@gmail.com
Printed on acid-free paper.

Library of Congress Control Number: **2021925809**

ISBN: **978-0-9888221-5-3**

To those who try.
Every day.

This being human is a guest house.
Every morning, a new arrival.

A joy, a depression, meanness,
some momentary awareness comes
as an unexpected visitor.

Welcome and entertain them all!
Even if they're a crowd of sorrows,
who violently sweep your house
empty of its furniture,
still, treat each guest honourably.
He may be clearing you out
for some new delight.

The dark thought, the shame, the malice,
meet them at the door laughing,
and invite them in.

Be grateful for whatever comes,
because each has been sent
as a guide from beyond.

Rumi
Translated by Coleman Barks

1

Annika

It arrived yesterday, a little travel weary, worn at the edges, and with a faint cinnamon scent. As letters go, it is benign enough.

My sister, Malavika, after an absence of nearly twenty-two years, wonders, on paper, if I am well. She wishes to reconnect, she says. There is also something she needs to share, in person, if it is at all possible. Is there any chance I might be visiting this year? I recognize the letterhead. It's the first one I designed before I moved away. She has squeezed her initials onto the right-hand corner, between my name and old address, claiming a space for herself, both in our parents' home and on the beautiful onionskin paper with the embossed quill.

Is she dying? I wonder.

The world opens its eyes outside my window. The curtains rustle in response to an uncertain wind. It is not a warm day, nor is it unseasonably cold.

I cock my head like a retriever. Ma too is rising. I know I must go to her, but Malavika buzzes above my head like a mosquito.

The first time she broke my heart was when she left. The second time was when she returned.

The slow shuffle, the sound of her bedroom slippers slapping the tiled floor, is followed by a low groan and *unhunhunh*–the minutiae of activity, that keep me informed of the condition of her bowels, the minutiae around which my world turns.

I fold my sister's letter and slip it into my bra. Duty calls. I stand outside, listening for the tug at the flush tank, the piddle of the faucet and her muttered imprecations before I turn the handle to help Adi's ma back to her room.

Ma

I need sturdier shoes, to latch on the floor. As always, the girl ignores my needs. Perhaps she is right. There is something a little extravagant about spending good money on two useless feet.

White shoes, paler than white, the color of eggshells. That is what my heart desires. How humiliating to ask again and again!

The ground slips like sand and shifts beneath my feet. I need new shoes!

If your two little toes don't touch the ground, you will lose your husband. Everybody knows that. I wore closed-toe shoes until the day I was married to cover my defects. Joined at the base, one little toe rides on the back of its brother.

My husband. The first time I saw him, he held a cigarette between his lips, a plume of smoke clouding the air. All the turbulence in my head grew silent and settled, instead, in my heart. Has it really been twenty-five years since his soul moved on? Ah! Even time shifts like sand.

I told him it was an unseemly thing for a grown woman, almost sixteen, to reveal her ankles in a public place! But he went down on one knee, lifted my foot and removed my slipper. Then he cupped my foot with his hand and put it down gently. I pressed my entire foot into the sand to hide the deformities. The sand felt ticklish. And warm. And comforting as a blanket. He removed my other shoe. This foot too, I sank in the sand, and I let him lead me toward the waves.

The water sucked away the grit exposing my pink and

wrinkled, new born feet. The waves grew bigger with every step. The sun dropped down in a rosy heap. His hand covered mine like a promise to protect. A promise he would not keep.

Lunch arrives thirty minutes past my usual time; my daughter-in-law gives me rice with watered-down lentils. She brings the food on a tray. Under the napkin and spoon is a gift - the Macy's catalogue. A little splash of color to fill the drab afternoon. The new dentures cut into my gums. If I take them off, she calls for my son. He insists I shove them back in my mouth. He says I must get used to them - *get used to pain!*

Old age is about getting used to and getting more used to.

I want to tell her to take the plate away, feed it to the dreadful creature pissing and whining underfoot, putting me in danger, all day.

Animals in the house bring money troubles. Everybody knows that. Somehow, I manage to swallow what-passes-for-lunch in this house.

Now it is almost time for her always-tepid tea. Shall I remind her?

Malavika

Will she? Or won't she? For twenty-two years, I have ignored her. Now, I ignore everything else as I dwell on my sister. It is imperative that she writes back. Imperative that we establish a connection. No. It is not her forgiveness that I seek. It is a practical matter that cannot be ignored. Perhaps she will write back. Perhaps she will get past the fact that I abandoned her. But it was never about her, you see.

I was tired of being the poor cousin. I wanted to live *their* lives. Their rich, gaudy, extravagant lifestyles.

They drove around in fancy cars - Chevys, Plymouths, and Ambassadors. My parents rode the bus everywhere. Mother covered her head with a scrap of her sari, her eyes watering in the afternoon sun as we waited for the public bus, that juddering monstrosity, and then fought through the greasy crush to climb into a vehicle already overflowing with foul creatures rubbing their puny pricks against our bums.

Telling ourselves *it* did not actually happen, even as the smell of semen stuck like shame, we debarked a mile away from family festivities and walked in with a nonchalant air, pretending to the doorman, as if it were *he* we had to impress, that we'd arrived in a cab.

They had bathtubs and hot water on tap and pastries just for the heck of it. We had a leaky faucet, a temperamental showerhead and pound cake once a year, if we were lucky, on our birthdays. And most of all, worst of all, I was fed up with seeing her so tired all the time – my underappreciated, overwhelmed mother. Fed up with the burn marks brandished on her wrist, from boiling Father's bathwater, ironing his undershirts and cooking on an open flame. I was sickened by the piece of charcoal she used to touch up the proliferating grays on her temples; nauseated from the pathetic mewling sounds leaking out of the bedroom as *the one who had no right to call himself a father* grunted on top of her and then snored until dawn.

In the end, when her eyes looked like two dead nails, and she stopped humming, stopped using hand cream and stopped asking about homework, I knew it was time.

Yes. I admit it. For years, I never gave her a thought –my little sister, exactly half my age. But you see, I was only sixteen. Then, years later, Samir, my son, fished out this old album and said, 'Is that your sister?'

She must have been six or seven. All legs and ropey black hair. In the photograph, she is sandwiched between Mother and me, but it is my skirt that she holds on to. From the creases visible in the thigh area, you can tell it was not a casual hold, more like a clutch, as if she was afraid to let go. In her black eyes burns a question. It took me all these years to realize she must have known then, little as she was, that I would run. I do think of her now. I feel her hands tugging at my skirt. *Why, Malavika didi?* She wants to know.

First, it was Anika, and then, it was my son, Samir, with always a question in those woeful, wild eyes. *Why do you leave? Why do you return? Why don't you love me?*

As if I have all the answers. As if love is easy.

Samir

My earliest memory of boarding school is lying naked, in a knee-chest position, on a thin cotton towel spread on the bathroom floor, to gather the leaks. My head is between my hands and my arse pushed high, for penetration.

A warm soap and water solution sucked out the waste and the streaming evidence gathered in a rubber bag. Mildly nauseous, somewhat lighter, I was then led to the bidet.

A weekly appointment in the bathroom behind her office was Principal Spencer's cure-all for rude behavior or poor marks.

Then one day, she came to visit. My mother. Of course, I hid behind a door to listen outside the Principal's office.

'Is my son a dunce, Principal Spencer?' A chuckle.

'He is smarter than he lets on, but perhaps not overburdened with gray matter...'

My mother's laughter sounded strained in the formal environment.

'Don't worry, Mrs. Captain...'

'Malavika, please!' I imagine her eyes fluttering out of habit, as if Spencer were a man.

'Don't worry, Malavika, nothing is so hopeless it cannot be rectified,' Principal Spencer guffawed.

Rectum is synonymous with rectified, and gray matter is the same as waste matter, I remember thinking, as I listened in, from my spot behind the door.

Suddenly, my book bag dropped with a thud. Principal Spencer turned her head sharply. She knew I was eavesdropping.

'Come here, Samir. Your mother is leaving. Give her a kiss goodbye.'

I went to them, scraping the floor with my shoes, lowered my head to my mother's rouged face and feigned a kiss. Then, I made myself a promise: *When I grow up, I will feed you both to the dogs.*

Why am I thinking about Mother now? When am I not? Through all my small triumphs and failures, obsessions and ordeals, she hums and buzzes madly around me. She is the bane and the mainstay of my life.

2

Annika

'How was your day?' Adi asks when he comes home, his eyes bright with decision making, his stiff white shirt unruffled by workday trials, until he draws closer, and you see the grays poking through his sideburns, the crescent-shaped circles under his eyes and the pleat of flesh as he lowers himself into an armchair.

'Great, thank you. We did not have any fires today.'

Sarcasm. The rusty, trusty weapon of housewives. Sometimes, it draws blood, and sometimes, it barely nicks the skin.

He goes up to his room, fake whistling. The smell of his cologne lingers like an illicit kiss on the first stair, where I still stand.

Out of the corner of my eye I study the terrain of his mother's face, the furrows, folds and sags that give her the air of a simian, oblivious of its surroundings. She focuses on the grime on the tip of her nose, picks each imaginary speck and flings it like birdseed into the air.

Perhaps she senses my eyes on her, because now she is bending away from me, sweeping the floor with her hands and pretending to find a missing hairpin or a length of string escaped out of her button box. But she can't help herself, you see, for her finger finds its way back to another area, this time at the base of her nose and works its way inside her nostrils. And we are back to picking at the face. I look with disgust at her nostrils and jaw, both dotted with blood.

Underneath her bed is a pullout drawer filled with miscellanea

9

she has collected from hospital visits, pharmacies, hotel rooms and so forth. I rifle through the keepsakes that chronicle her days - the worn socks, sleeping masks, salt and pepper packets, knitting yarn and prayer beads - and find at last, the tube of ointment, its surface a grimy yellow, the mouth crusted with dried medicine. I rub off the rheum-like crud with thumb and index finger and squirt a little on my index finger. I lean forward and hold up her chin lightly. She slaps my hand away.

'I will wait for my son to approve of this medication,' says the Queen Mother and covers her face with a shawl, suggesting an end to the discussion. I'm infuriated at her adamant refusal, but do my best not to show how I feel.

Behind the shawl her hand sneaks up to her face. With renewed energy, she picks at her skin. She thinks I can't see what she's doing, but it's obvious from the way her hand squirrels about.

Stymied, I watch. Finally, I Google "Obsessive picking at skin."

SPD, Skin Picking Disorder, it spews out - (people) repetitively touch, rub, scratch, pick at or dig into their skin, often in an attempt to remove small irregularities or perceived imperfections. *Wow! It's a real disorder.* She is collecting ailments like gourmet salts!

I can no longer stand it. I call out to Adi for help. He comes down in t-shirt and shorts, takes the tube out of my hands and massages the ointment into the crannies of her face. Her fingers reach out to rub off the cream. He holds her hand down firmly and does not let it go until she falls asleep, still twitching with discomfort.

How I long to laugh. Play. Live.

I once knew a man who laughed with his belly. One day, he laughed so hard his gum went the wrong way, making his face turn dangerously purple. Someone performed the Heimlich maneuver. When the gum flew out, he took a deep breath. Then, shielding his great big heart with his hands, he continued where he left off - convulsing with glee. His wife looked on with tender pride, and the room lit up with their shared joy.

I think I have lost the ability to laugh out loud.

I find old reruns of "Friends" and snigger soundlessly. Usually that is entertainment enough. But today, today I am filled with restlessness. I'm cold. Gloom settles over the house like a shroud.

She used to call me Ana-banana. The thought floats in unwelcome, making my heart flutter. Why has she written? *Malavika.* Do I not have enough going on in my life? *She will disappear as she always does and not once look back and wave.* Just then Old Coot jumps out of my lap to bang his head urgently on the front door. I ignore the hint. He bangs it again.

'Okay! Okay! Jeez. It's only music from the house across the street, and we are not invited!' I scold. He continues to pound, adding a low growl for effect.

It is a party, all right! Longing rises from the pit of my stomach and spreads upward, like flame. I admit it. I spy on the soft silhouettes swaying like a gentle breeze in my neighbor's great room, illuminated only by crystal buds. I shut my eyes in the amorous darkness and sway to the rhythm of the music, my arms crossed over my chest. With senses so heightened, I have no need for vision to read the invitations pressed between wet lips, nor do I need sound to hear the rustle of silk and chiffon or touch to feel their bodies burning. I am lost for what seems like moments or hours, transported to the incandescent world of dancers playing out their seductions, each to each.

I open my eyes again; I realize I've been found out. A white face, framed in curls, is glaring my way, her fingers curled around the delicate stem of her glass. I draw back, flustered, and with my sleeve, swipe the breath, forming a cumulus on the window.

I get a drink of water, and still flushing with shame, climb back into our bed. Ignoring Adi's rule, I let Old Coot flop between the two of us, his tail a drumbeat of happiness.

Ma

I did not sleep well at all. My room faces the street, and last night, it was especially noisy. At first, I tried counting the number of cars driving slowly past, headlights glaring, perhaps looking for the right address. Then I lost interest and shut my eyes, but the shock of light filtering through the blinds every few minutes, made it hard to doze off. For the old, night is about saving your strength. Not so, for the young. They are like night owls. In the silence of the night, drunk on the sacrament of the moon, they lose their morals and renew their lust for life.

Having been up most of the night, I am hungry. I want food. Real food. Why do they not leave? They should have left hours ago. The girl, Anika, won't allow me in the kitchen. Thirty minutes is all I need. I know exactly what I'll do:

Let one yellow onion brown in *real* butter.

Grind in two, maybe three, cloves of garlic and a green chili pepper.

Do I dare? I know it does not agree with me. But I will. I will!

I will toss in some tomatoes, at least two, and watch them burst out of their skins. Let the juices flow. Stir in some smoky cumin. Cilantro. Do we have any?

Wild mushrooms. Baby potatoes. Green okra. Long-grain rice. Pigeon peas. I can smell them now! A medley of vegetables, singing and sizzling and waiting to be cooked the way they are supposed to be cooked - not the boiled mush that passes for a meal in this house.

Why can they not leave?

She brings in a tray laden with buttered toast and more of her watered-down lentils. Prison food for one whose body is a prison. She waits for me to put a morsel in my mouth.

'I'm not hungry,' I tell her, polite as always.

She gets into a huff. 'But you always eat at noon.'

'I don't want it.' I slide the tray away, just a few inches. I don't want to seem too rude, you see.

'You…why won't you eat *now*? I *need you to eat now* so we can *leave!*'

She's grinding her teeth. Her face is so close I can see the blood vessels in her eyes. Resentment swirls in the air.

'What does my eating have to do with you? I can cook for myself,' I retort at last, losing patience.

She glares at me. 'Not exactly overburdened with charm, are we?' She mutters. But I hear every word.

So disrespectful! I was her age once, was I not? Twenty years I spent taking care of *my* mother-in-law.

Is this what you are giving me for lunch? Do you want me to starve? Answer me! Do you want me dead? She would slap herself. It took six people to restrain her.

Her face, a rash of color. The floor, a rash of lentils. Neighbors swooping down like vultures to pick at my shame.

I press my fingers to my temples. Yes. That is how it was, back in the day.

She is still here, that girl.

'I'm sorry. Darling. Forgive me,' I tell her, gently. I take a bite of my toast. Then, dutifully, a spoonful of lentil soup.

She looks chastised like a child.

'No. No. I'm sorry. You don't have to eat. Whatever you want is fine.'

They leave at last.

I go to the kitchen to make some real food. I turn the stove on. Nothing happens. I smell gas. Maybe there's water or cleaning powder trapped down there. When the knob won't do the trick, that girl sometimes uses a match. I bet she's hidden the matches. I hate the little shrew! I find a box of matches at last. Stuck behind bottle openers, pressure cooker valves and other rubbish. I strike a match and hold it close to the burner. The flare makes me jump. The pans! Where are the pans? My heart is pounding. I find a clean stainless- steel saucepan in the dishwasher and set it on the stove. I open the refrigerator. Where is everything? Random objects, sauce congealing in semi-open cans, tubes of something. Eggs. A gallon of milk. No onions. Tomatoes. Cabbage. My head is swimming. The draft from the refrigerator is making me shiver. What am I doing here? I go back to bed. I'm not sure whether it's time to change into my nightclothes. *There is a smell. What is that smell?*

Something's happened, I'm not sure what. People everywhere. Then they are gone. She brings me some tea, lays it gently on the coffee table, her head bowed. I think she's been crying. My son comes in, stands around helplessly, but like her, he won't look me in the face. He won't smile.

I ask him, if he smells smoke. He does not answer. His frown deepens. Is it something I did? To dispel the anxiety buzzing in my ears, I conjure up images of food:

Potatoes sliced thin, fried and crisped at the edges.

Snow peas green like summer, scattered in white basmati rice, a spoonful of ghee and whole cumin seeds for tempering.

A platter of *pakoras* – onions, eggplant, cauliflower and cheese.

Gram flour pancakes with cilantro and mango powder.

Spinach with *paneer* (made from cow's milk).

Button mushrooms loaded with onions.

Yogurt dotted with *boondi*.

A simple salad – onions, tomatoes and cilantro with fresh squeezed lemon.

Vermicelli pudding with skinny bits of almonds and a hint of cardamom.

Hot golden *jalebis*...fried to perfection.

My lips smack on nothing. My stomach is a raging lion. *A woman must never admit to being hungry.* Everybody knows that. Still, I lust for potatoes! Where is that dinner? Old age is about deprivations.

I asked her to drag my chair to my spot in the kitchen. I think it is the next day. Sunlight streams through the window, licks my face like a cat. She has the radio on. I hear her puttering about near the stove. The backsplash looks murky. The steel sink, too, looks like it needs a good scrub. Was there a fire, or is she just too careless to clean? I must have nodded off. Minutes, or hours, later, I am on the floor, moaning in pain. It appears I have broken my wrist. She says I slid off the chair. She is wrong. This morning I could not find my slippers. She gave me a pair of mules instead. They were not skid proof, you see!

She calls 911. Perhaps my fall is not a real emergency, because the EMS people do not come for a while. Not given to complaining, I sit huddled on the floor, and she kneels by my side, her face expressionless. Time ticks on. She's given me a painkiller. I did not want to take it. I don't like taking pills from her. *Who knows what she might give me? After all I am unable to read the fine print.* I take it at last with a cup of tea. It will not do to let her know of my suspicion. Soon, I feel better. A little sleepy. I need to use the bathroom, but I don't want to ask.

When the paramedics come, I'm sure they will tell her I need to be hospitalized. The thought that she will send me off with them, by myself, makes me wet my pants. She makes a tchk sound and brings me fresh pants. It is hard to get them on without disturbing my wrist. When we are finished, we are both breathing heavily. As she mops the floor, she tells me she has called my son. Thank goodness! He comes almost at the same time as the 911 people.

They are going on and on about something I need to do. My body is being pushed and pried and wheeled around without rhyme or reason. My wrist hangs limp, and there is a buzzing in my ears. I let my mind drift to my brother. When this matter is behind me, and I am back in a few days on my chair, a towel spread under my damp hair, a cup of tea in my hand, my prayers done, I will recount the day's events in great detail. He loves hearing from me! It is about time I let him know, these accidents seem to occur only when *she* is about. *Why are my ears buzzing?*

Malavika

She hasn't replied to my letter. Little Ana-banana. She is so like our mother, absorbed in the daily grind, not raising her head once, to look at the changing landscape.

I'm told it takes a certain amount of courage, even nobility of mind, to perform those thankless, mundane tasks that guarantee nothing but repetition and grayness of the bones.

As it happens, my mother's final act of courage was to end herself – the irony is not lost on me.

In a shambolic household such as ours, a husband never out, a daughter never in, it was all our mother could do to apportion her life into manageable chores. If there were pots to be cleaned, she cleaned them. If there were clothes to mend, she mended them. If there were noses to be wiped, she wiped them. She was a diligent little worker bee who had no use for existential questions. Then again, had she done so and asked herself the important questions, I mean, could she have bought herself a happy ending?

I guess, we will never know.

Personally, I have no such ambition. Find a benefactor and let someone else do the backbreaking work, I say. Courage. Nobility. Karma. Fate. Dress it up any way you like, what they all amount to is a failure of imagination.

My first benefactor was my math tutor. He was not a teacher by profession, but an electrical engineer. How I met him. A colleague invited him to a get together at the home of one of our close relatives. I found myself seated next to him after I walked over from my seat nearest the balcony to the dining table to ply my plate with fritters. When I returned, my chair was taken. I glared around, until I found his eyes on me. He patted the empty chair beside him.

We sat side by side, our knees almost touching in the close quarters. I was already bored by this quiet, although congenial-looking, stranger. Politely, he asked my name and my relationship with the host.

'He is my uncle,' I said abruptly. I wanted to get back to my younger cousins, not get stuck with some bespectacled engineer. He asked me what grade I was in.

'Ninth,' I muttered.

'Do you like math?' he wanted to know. I sighed. What an incredibly dull question. What a hopelessly dull man.

'I do,' I told him, 'but I would like it more if I was good at it.'

'Maybe you just need some practice,' he said.

Ass!

'No. My math teacher hates me, and I hate her,' I said, viciously kicking the leg of a stool, making the plates convulse. He tried to hide a smile.

'Why do you hate her?' he persisted. As if the reason really mattered to him. As if *his* fate rested on the answer.

'She's ... condescending. She's made up her mind I won't improve, and she doesn't even know me that well!' Now I was irate both with the math teacher and by projection, with all adults, but mostly with this man, burrowing into my life like a bespectacled rabbit and talking about school on my day off! He was quiet for a few moments, letting my anger billow into the space between us.

Then he said, very softly, that he could teach me math. I looked at him as if he'd lost it.

"I could make it fun," he iterated.

I shrugged and went to pour myself a fizzy drink. By the time I was seated again, I had a math tutor. For free.

His last name was Captain. At the time, I found that hilarious.

Every image the name conjured, he contradicted. Later, I called him that in the throes of passion. It was the magic word, if you know what I mean. I neglected to mention, he also asked me my age at that first meeting. When I told him I was almost fifteen, his pupils widened a little. He removed his glasses and wiped them carefully with a pocket-handkerchief. I never did ask him why he was so keen on teaching me math. A girl always knows.

Samir

As a child, I was often shuttled from our home, located in one of those teeming, narrow streets, behind City light Cinema, to my grandfather's home. In addition to grandfather, there was a girl there. Skinny. Dark-haired. I was under the impression she was either dumb or possibly a deaf-mute. Recently, I discovered she was my aunt. With all her faculties, intact. 'She was playing a game,' my mother said, when I questioned her, and added, 'and probably carried it too far.'

'What kind of a game was that?' I persisted.

'Hmmm. Dumb Charades?' Mother lifted her brows up and down, comically. More like Looney Tunes, I thought, but left the matter at that.

'What about Grandfather?' I asked, while we were on the subject of family.

'What about him?'

'He was always home. How did he support himself?'

'By translating a dead language into a foreign language for a bunch of old bores,' Mother said. She sounded pissed.

'Translating what?'

'Scripture. Philosophical arguments. Rules of grammar. Whatever they needed.'

'How many languages did he know?' I persisted.

'None that you would understand,' she said, and wandered

off moodily.

I remembered then how he muttered darkly to himself under his breath or read *shlokas* from dusty old books that sounded, ironically, like threats, and made me question his sanity as well. Sometimes, I found his eyes on me and was reminded of a snake. Seething, biding his time. But he did not ever speak to me. So, despite the fact that we could hear the ocean, rushing and roaring in the distance, mostly, it felt remote and cool in the apartment, as if we were parked like turtles under water or settled inside a tomb, and the hiss from the pressure cooker was really the walls, slowly exhaling.

My mother would put me on a mat on the balcony with some Legos or crayons and drawing paper while she swept and dusted and cooked for them. I did ask her once why Grandfather did not have a maid. She laughed maniacally and said, 'Why, when he has me?'

3

Annika

I decided to take a few days of personal days, with the understanding that I would make myself available for emergencies.

Now, as I stand guard, watching her like a hawk, as she wanders in and out of the kitchen, I grab a moment to check my emails and read the important ones first. It's obvious that my boss is trying to get into the Guinness World Records for sliminess.

Email one:

Do I have to call a "come to Jesus meeting" to receive the final version of the corporate brochure?

Email two:

While you are working "virtually," I just noticed there are two typos in a message sent out to 230,000 employees. Please resend – without mistakes, this time.

Email three:

If you could "grace" us with your presence tomorrow, we have something to discuss, namely, a meeting with the Foundation you did not update me about.

I don't know what was more nauseating, his use of air quotes or his malice sprinkled like bird droppings all over his emails. *I'm officially off and only working virtually to help you out in a pinch, dickhead!* It would be a while before I gained a measure of equanimity.

What with putting out fires at work and putting out fires in the kitchen, I am not exactly brimming with the milk of human kindness. I was often rude and insensitive with Adi's mother, but told myself that in her current state, she was probably oblivious to my dour mood. It is a pity I could not be a bigger person. I chafed like a child, aching to go outside and play, but I had to finish her homework instead, despite the glorious weather. On some days, although not often, I matched her, sulk for sulk and tantrum for tantrum.

'We need to do something about this situation,' I said, one day, throwing up my hands when she clogged the garbage disposal with banana peel.

'She's not a *situation*. She's my mother,' Adi retorted sharply.

'I know very well who she is.'

'I'm just saying, she can't help her confusion, she's *old*. You don't have to always be so ...'

'Be so ... what?'

He walks out, slamming the door with just the right amount of force, underscoring his disgust without being overtly rude.

'Yeah, well, I'm not getting any younger, either,' I mutter angrily, to myself.

We'd scarcely recovered from the kitchen fire, installed new smoke alarms even though the old ones still worked, hid matches and lighters on the top shelf, and generally idiot-proofed the house, when I found her on the floor, unable to get up, her twisted wrist, brittle as a twig, about to break off. Of course, I called 911.

'What's your emergency?'

'My mother-in-law's fallen off her chair. I think she's broken a wrist. I'm not sure whether I should move her to see if she has any other injury.'

'Is she conscious?'

'Yes. She is. But she is in pain.'

I gave the operator, my particulars. She told me to let her stay still. We were to await the first responders.

Then I called Adi. I made her some toast with a sprinkle of powdered sugar and sat beside her on the floor. We sipped our tea out of the large red mugs she seemed to like. She did not say much, silent as a Trappist nun. She accepted the Tylenol without a fuss. It must have helped, because there was a marked change in her demeanor. The lines of disapproval I thought were permanently etched on her face softened visibly, and just for a while, we were two friends sitting companionably, dipping bits of sweetened toast into black tea, regarding each other with quiet affection.

When she winced, I became nervous. I started babbling a little.

'Can I get you something else to eat?' I asked.

Her eyes twinkled with rare humor.

'A little *pani puri* would be nice.' She knew she wasn't allowed to have any.

'Mmmmm!' I said. An image of my old friend, the *pani puri* vendor, rose sharply in my mind.

He was a slender man, nondescript except for a mustache that seemed to cover most of his face. A poor, illiterate man, who spoke in a guttural dialect, had vanished long since from the gentrified suburbs of Mumbai. On his head, he wore a turban. And on the turban sat a metal trunk loaded with sweet, savory, tangy treasures such as *bhel*, *pani puri* and other hot and cold snacks guaranteed to explode in your mouth and whisk you off to a gastronomic heaven.

In his high-pitched voice, he sang out the list of his wares. More often than not, he had to cut short his aria and follow the gesturing servant or my equally high pitched '*Puriwallah*, come, *Puriwallah*, come!' urging him upstairs from our balcony.

Slowly, he climbed the three floors to our apartment, the trunk on his head flattening his turban. He laid his box on the floor, wiped his brows and asked, 'What will it be, today, baby?' Then he opened his box. It was the best part of my day.

He gave me an extra *puri, that final exquisite bite*, because I paid him the compliment of kneeling before his treasures and, with shining eyes, breathed in the heady scents of coriander and tamarind, cumin and mint, as he, smiling shyly, wiped his head with a corner of his turban.

Now, as she looked so peaked, I tried distracting Adi's mother, telling her all about the *bhel and pani puri* man and those countless moments of street-food bliss.

She grunted and asked for a cup of water.

The first responders arrived soon after, followed by Adi. They took in the situation at a glance and were pleased, I hadn't moved her. 'You will not believe the complications that could be prevented if people just left the patient alone,' confided the pleasant-looking aide. With astonishing speed, they had Ma in the ambulance and on her way to the hospital.

We were there all day. The medical staff had seen their share of elderly-abuse, so I had to explain the circumstances of her fall in great detail to the orderlies, the nurses, the doctors and several administrators. By the time we were done, I felt wrung out and irrationally guilty.

While we waited for her personal physician, her X-ray tech, her orthopedics doctor and her MRI, in case she had suffered a TIA (transient ischemic attack), she looked deathly afraid. Her eyes sought her son and followed him down the hall, where he paced. More than once, she needed to pee. The male nurse's aide looked at me with ill-concealed hatred. Briefly, I wondered if he found this task degrading because of the color of our skin. I shrugged. I decided it was easier to take her myself than to suffer his aloof care.

I had to pull down her drawers and make her sit. She seemed a little disoriented and used the toilet paper before she had done her business. When she stood up, she lost her grip on her pants and watched helplessly as they slid to her ankles. We bent down simultaneously and knocked heads. She grunted in annoyance and tried to reach for them a second time. They slipped off her fingers again. After the third try, she gave up and let me help. I pulled them up and helped her to the sink. She thrust me away with her shoulders.

'I can wash my own hands,' she mumbled. I decided not to feel hurt.

A nurse asked me if she was my mother. 'No. His.' I pointed to Adi with my chin.

'She loves you very much. I can tell by the way she follows you with her eyes.'

Love! I think of Gone-Mother. She never once told me she loved me. But like Ma, her eyes followed me everywhere as well. Until Malavika came in through the door and ruined everything.

Naturally, I think of my sister and the letter burning a hole in my jacket.

The nurse was still smiling and nodding. 'Beautiful family,' she said. Her hands were rough from scrubbing toilets. Her eyes were kind. I passed a hand across my face to hide my surprise. It had been a while since I'd given the word "family" any thought. In-laws are part and parcel of the baggage one brings into a marriage. We lived under the same roof for a few months each summer, and when she was completely healthy, we often went on day trips to the temple and the Indian section for vegetarian meals and food shopping. But, despite our daily interactions, we co-existed like tenants in a multi- family dwelling. I felt excluded from her circle of love, and not because of something she did, but the small confidences and intimacies she withheld, reminding me that dutifulness was less than love.

The stories she stitched together were dedicated to her children and to those she held as children.

Certainly, there were days when she did cut through the icy wall of politeness and reach for my hand, gasping out her need. But that was in a moment of urgency that neither of us mistook for tenderness. Emotionally we were two islands separated by a gulf of indifference, lost in private yearnings.

But still.

'We can sign the release form, tomorrow, barring any more emergencies,' says the friendly nurse, who then suggests we stay vigilant at every step. 'It might be a while before her legs are steady. One of you will have to work virtually.'

I avoid my husband's eyes. About her condition, they say, 'She has suffered a series of mini-strokes right here in the hospital. But the first TIA could have occurred as far back as six months ago, or merely six weeks ago or when she fell off her chair.' We leave with more questions than answers.

⧖⧖⧖

My world had shrunk to the size of her room for so long that it was nice to have the house to ourselves for one night. I wanted to shut out work and illness and use these precious hours to decompress with a bottle of wine and maybe some pizza.

Adi spent the next couple of hours calling his sisters.

He updated them on the latest developments and passed the phone to me before I could protest. I made my voice small and tired. Once they expressed concern about their mother, they moved on to their own lives. The work, the night shifts, the occasional concerts, the few good eating establishments and the inept and annoying behavior of spouses. Succumbing to a nameless wretchedness, I let them drone on.

Ma

On the way to the hospital, the wall between the real world and the world of my ancestors disappeared like a barrier of smoke. I cannot explain it. At first, I was sailing backwards in a sea of foam, and then jerking and rumbling forward in a public bus. A red-faced conductor rang his bell at every stop. *Do you want to get off? Where do you get off?* Onlookers gawked at me at each stop. There was something not quite right about them, something missing in each one of them – a limb, an eye, an ear. My heart contracted. Was I in hell?

At the final stop, at last, a face I knew as well as my own. My beautiful mother.

I am told I slipped out of her birth canal just a couple of hours after her water broke, with more ease than an earthworm in the rainy month of June.

But no, it was not she. Alas! It is never she. And there was Father with a garland and a smile. I looked up at him from my makeshift bed and raised my arms in longing. He bit my finger off. I could not move or scream. My legs were bound.

I was struck dumb with terror. In heaven, there is no fear. Only softness. And light. Not dark things knocking behind one's eyes, clawing their way out to cluster in the air like gnats. *Oh God, I was going to hell.*

Then I was clattering down the ambulance on a stretcher. All the familiar monsters disappeared. Instead, I was now surrounded by white, bloodless faces, with a serious air about them. The hospital itself was as comforting as cold soup on a wintry day! The steely- eyed nurse with fingers like instruments, the narrow bed, the white walls and low voices, never quite clear, but always within earshot. Afraid I would want to talk, no attendant ever made eye contact, and no nurse came to my bedside unless it was to poke and pry.

Night followed days, and between the taking and passing of fluids, only the ghosts in my head to keep me company. There were moments I was invisible. My body rose above my bed like an eagle on a hill. Perched on a rafter, above the door, I saw, in the passageway, my son. Around him, men in blue dusters clutching at tubes, clinging to final breaths, as if these wet intakes were the most important ones and all the breaths, they had taken thus far were merely preparation. He came for me, as he always does. My son. God bless him.

I am home. Dozing on my chair with my pashmina dusting the floor, recording its own story of mothballs and food droppings. It will be six weeks before I can use my left hand. I am more dependent on *her* than ever before. I own nothing. Prodded, washed, wiped and clothed by her hands, my real body observes my doll body. I touch my face.

A woman's face should be soft and pleasing as the moon. Everybody knows that!

I recite the 108 names of God. At every pause, I ask Him to either help me back on my feet or help me into the pyre. At other times, I beg my son to take me to my father, the one who told me stories and kept me safe.

I want to sit on his lap and hear the tale of the mighty Ram and the beautiful Sita, exiled into the forest. About the evil Ravana and the giant bird Jatayu and the Monkey king … about a world made up of magical creatures living and suffering with dignity. He tells me I am 91 years old, and my father is dead. My son may be smart, but he is as subtle as a brick hurled through a window. His wife looks at me as if old age is contagious.

Malavika

Far be it for me to intrude on her family, but I am considering calling her. I do not know if she will recognize my voice at once. Will she address me as Malavika? Or *didi*? Or not at all? These are the things I obsess about.

After we lost Mother - *how could I not see she was the love of my life?* - I returned home to help out. It took me a day or two to realize our father did not wish to speak to me. At first, I thought it was a temporary meanness, the by-product of her sudden death, and would soon pass. But he was committed. Committed to treating me like a criminal. Through his eyes, through his gestures and through the measures he took to keep me out of his business, I understood I was and always would be the same old Malavika for him — an ugly, untouchable thing. But I stayed on. Excessive and repetitive abuse had made me hard and slick as a rock, oblivious to the vagaries of the tide. So, the more he punished me, that sick, odious, silent specter, the more I egged him on! It was an odious game we played, and there was no way I was going to let him win.

But Ana-banana. Why did she have to go all mute on me? Why did she mimic his gestures and scuttle away each time she saw me, like a mouse terrorized by a cat? I shuttled between my home and Father's, up until Samir was three, ironing her school uniform, and braiding her hair, even though she was old enough to do it herself, trying to be a sensible influence, through the yawn of routine.

Still, in those close quarters, where we could hear each other's breath, neither of them spoke one direct word to me. Until one day, he picked on Samir. Called him a bastard child of a no-good w*----.

Choking as much from his damning word, as from the damned silence, it was, suddenly more than I could handle. He'd won. I did not want to play anymore.

I told him, I was not a glutton for punishment and was leaving, and this time, I had no intention of ever coming back. Only then did the child look at me directly and with something resembling triumph, screamed, 'Good! Good! And GOOD!' to my retreating back.

Samir

My grandfather was a source of pain for my mother. The thought always gave me a vicious sense of satisfaction. Until, one day, he called me a *bastard*, a word I knew was never to be said out loud, simply by the way he said it. She drew me close, screamed she would never darken his doors again and hurried me out of his home. It was quite terrifying, like seeing a really vivid dream when you know you are still asleep, and you know it cannot be happening, but there are enough elements of realism to scare the shit out of you.

But mostly, I was confused. If she hated me, why would she care what he called me? If she loved me, why was she never around?

My feelings towards my father, on the other hand, were quite clear. His was the voice of reason. The real deal. A bit of an absent- minded moron, but never absent at the table, at bedtime or at a school meeting.

'Who's that with your mother?' Jai asked. He and I were once kicking a ball around in a half-arsed way. I tolerated him because he was willing to do my homework and had a colorful vocabulary, thanks to his older brother, who was in the army. I knew this because he started practically every conversation with, 'My brother who is in the army ...'

There was no point in starting a new game. It was Parents' Day, and we had to head to the cafeteria in about five minutes and watch the adults fawn over Principal Spencer and make long speeches interspersed with really lame jokes.

'It's my father. Who else, arsehole?'

'I thought he might be your grandpop,' he shrugged.

'You are a shit arsehole.' I aimed the hard ball to his shins, enjoying the way the newly acquired curse words made me feel – tougher, more athletic, and more in sync with the school culture.

'Owww! What the fuck are you so pissed about?'

I shrugged and walked away like a pro with long easy strides, repeating the words *fuck* and *pissed* to myself so that they would zing out of my mouth, smooth and poised, with just the right degree of disdain, the next chance I got.

My parents were already at the meet. Father smiled and tried to muss my hair. I backed off. Mother wiggled two manicured fingers in greeting. We were not a demonstrative family.

It was the first time I looked closely at my pop. His shirt, shrunk with too many washes, did not quite make it to his tight belt. One button was missing or possibly burst open, exposing a wiry mess of belly hair. His glasses, round, with black frames, made him look a little owlish. His hair was scant, parted neatly on the side. As I drew nearer, I noticed how he tripped on a jagged flagstone, leaned heavily on my mother for support and straightened. She shrugged off her arm and rubbed it, as if trying to erase his imprint. So acutely did I feel his shame, I felt my face burn.

Was Jai right? Was my father too old? And if so, was it cool to despise him just a little?

4

Annika

The visit to the hospital has traumatized her greatly. Her face, leached of blood, is a ghastly shade of gray. She is so skeletal. She tries to raise a hand in greeting. It trembles like a paper boat in the wind. The bones popping out of her thin skin look like dead branches. However, they are tough and dense, as if cast from an unbreakable mold. She is plagued with dreams. They light up her sleep like small fires, rousing her with a jerk, leaving her shaken and disoriented. Often, she does not know night from day. We can hear her through the Baby Monitor, 'I need a bath. Now!'

I know that tone and give in. Somehow, she unclothes herself.

The skin unpeeling like paint, baring the chipped china of bones; the toothless gums; the sagging reminders of her female parts.

Suddenly she is hallucinating. The hand shower is a snake. The soapbox is a rodent. She points to them, her eyes enormous and the soap slipping from her fingers.

'It's all right. Let me show you.' I pick up the soap, adjust the water temperature and move the shower from shoulder to back, from chest to stomach. I put the soap back into her hands. She looks at me, not comprehending, almost in tears. I mime the act of rubbing, as I hum softly.

This is the way we wash our face, wash our face, wash our face. This is the way we wash our face, so early in the morning. Understanding dawns and she beams, delighted. 'Thank you.' She soaps herself. I am immoderately moved.

She needs to use the toilet again. She seems steady, so I

merely stand guard.

Ninety years of living reduced to this. The slow counting of breaths, followed by the Himalayan trek from bed to bidet to dimly observe the color of pee. The lethargic, reluctant movement of bowels, the hasty swipe with a baby wipe.

She's too weak to raise or clean herself.

I try to help. She pushes me with her elbow and covers her face in shame. Then, defeated, she allows me to help. A stray thought surfaces each time I see her shaking body. How easy it would be to nudge her over, make her topple like a glass of water wobbling on the edge of a table. Nobody would think to investigate. I shake my head hard and recite a repentant mantra. But guilt is a stern warden. My heart is heavy the rest of the day.

Her eyes look past me and beyond the room window, leaping across time and space, perhaps to that patch of dewy grass where she roamed once upon a time, in her farm. Did she play barefoot on the grass with a little girl just like herself? Did the two friends spin like tops, letting the boughs of trees bend to tickle their upturned faces? Did they quench their thirst in the newly emptied milk floating whitely in her bucket, like a pool of sky?

My cold hand on her shoulders makes her blink.

In bed, she needs her son. 'Where is he?' she is anxious. 'He is watching TV. Do you need another blanket? Do you want the nightlight? Do you want some milk?' I exhaust her with options. Let her believe that she *has* options.

She sighs and nods off. I leave the room.

Adi returns and, as always, goes directly to her room. I follow him; tell him about her tremors and her trance-like confusion. He says he will throw out all unnecessary meds. He is convinced one gets sicker after a hospital stay. 'She is having side effects! Her body cannot take these anti-anxiety, mood-altering prescriptions … they need to customize medications based on age and weight and metabolism,' he shouts.

Don't they already do that? I leave him to his ranting. Months later, I read a news article about older, over medicated adults suffering from conditions that mirror dementia – confusion, falls and dangerously high BP, resulting in more medicine and more falls, in a vicious, dangerous, downward spiral.

I need to go food shopping, but the thought of getting dressed just to push a cart around like an orderly in a hospital seems even more depressing than staying in. I give him a shopping list. 'Why don't you go? You could use some fresh air,' he says.

'Wow. You make even food shopping sound like a vacation,' I goad him, kicking a laundry bag out of my way.

Without a word, he drives to the store. Still, I envy the ease with which he can leave. Does his smile get wider with every yard he puts between his living and *her* dying? Or does he too die a little as his mother slowly disappears?

To create my own distance, I sit on the deck, facing the chair towards her room with a basket of veggies. The days are long. The evening sun seeps into my pores. A light breeze ruffles my hair. A rabbit plays peek-a-boo in the bushes. In the distance, I hear the laughter of children swell. I place a hand on my stomach. Flat as a washboard. I wait for the familiar twinge of anguish. It comes. And goes.

I shell peas. I shave Brussels sprouts. I cut half a head of cauliflower into florets and save the rest in foil. I sniff the evening air scented with roses dancing profusely in the neighbors' yard.

Not willing to go in yet, I check my Facebook page after what seems like months. You can't ignore social media. It is like having a public parking lot for a backyard – the din is constant.

I browse and browse pouring over fake news and cute baby videos, tsk-tsking at the modern-day activism and manufactured outrage as if no other action was required other than a "like", and both cause and protest irrelevant with each posting. At long last, I do something I swore I never would — I type *her* name in the search area and watch with bated breath as a few dozen Malavikas pop up. But not *my* Malavika. I scroll down and stop at one. A blurry silhouette and no last name. It has to be my sister.

Music videos. Videos empowering women. Shared recipes. A few paintings by an artist she seems to admire - mostly mountains and cascading streams. The mosaic of her life covered in a few minutes. And finally, a selfie. The same Malavika, really. Wraith like, in an oversized bohemian batik dress, eyes lined with kohl, a wet tongue curled lustily upward to lick a crumb off her gleaming upper lip in that inimitable, *sans souci* Malavika style and a caption- Happy Birthday to Me!

Happy Birthday, *didi*, I whisper. I open my arms. Empty.

Then I notice she has 302 friends. What use could she possibly have for friend number 303? I slam my iPad shut.

Ma

Why do they talk in a different language? Is it to taunt me? Maybe she wants me to believe I'm losing my mind. I won't let her. I, who have lost three sons, can survive her bullying. She is in my face, saying something over and over. It is nothing that I want to hear. She is attentive only to my needs. Of my wants, she cares nothing. I am not a cow tied to a barn and never let out, appeased with an occasional mound of grass. Yet, my son sees, in her eyes, the milk of human kindness. I shut my eyes and drift away like a balloon.

In the photograph, he, the children's father, was bending over, what looked like a table of moss, positioned to strike tiny little balls into pockets of net. A foreign-looking woman with bobbed hair, one arm skimming his shirt, is smiling at him, as if she knows him and all the secret, hidden parts of him.

'It was only a game,' he told me.' Why do you care about the past?' But he saved the photograph for all time. I found it after he died, tore it up, and set fire to the fragments.

To this day, it is I who burn.

What are we if not our memories? The wind blows, the memories scatter and soon we are dead leaves.

My daughter-in-law is saying something again. Soup? Potatoes? I try to form a response. My words are trapped in net pockets, and my fingers cannot reach them. I turn my face to the wall.

She slides something onto the tray table. Tea or soup, perhaps.

From the other room comes the pleasing sound of Vedic chanting. The verse starts out tentatively, a puddle in a wood clearing that turns into a steady stream. It fills my ears and washes over my body. I rub the spot in the middle of my forehead where the third eye is located. A lull. Then quiet, thoughtful conversation and the soothing ping of dishes. Now they are talking about me. I can tell by the tone – curt, on the borderline of disrespect.

'Doesn't *she* want to join us?'

'I've asked her a few times. I guess not.'

'Do you want to take in some tea for her?'

'No. She's had her tea.'

As a matter of fact, I wouldn't mind some tea. It would be nice to sit amongst them, touch fabric other than cotton, hear thoughts other than my own and admire them like little butterflies in a Japanese garden. But adrift in a sea of faces, I sometimes lose my footing. So, I stay where I am. The laughter stops, and soon the chanting blooms with renewed energy. From the pretty patchwork of sounds, I pick out, clear as a bell, my daughter-in-law's soft, self-conscious voice. I am lulled back to sleep, the singsong recitations swelling in my ears.

This happened last month. Or perhaps in a last life:

The old woman, my mother-in-law went into the kitchen, tried her hand at making coffee, scalded herself, and was so upset she grabbed all the prayer books in the house and scattered them like bird food out of the window. According to her, I spent too much time praying and not enough time caring for the family. I happened to be on the balcony at the time, hanging out laundry.

Like a cat on fire, I ran down the stairs, without my slippers. I collected the sacred books and dusted them on my tunic. Then, touching the cover of each book first to my forehead and to my heart, I appealed to the Goddess Durga for forgiveness. Somehow, that evening, I found the courage to declare to the family I would go on a hunger strike until such time that they held a *jagrata* (all night devotional singing) to placate the Goddess.

My mother-in-law tried to interfere; of course, she did. 'The walls here are so thin, you can hear the next-door neighbor gargle, and you want a *jagrata*! And who will bear the cost of musicians, singers and neighbors who come in to bow their heads for a few minutes and gobble half a pound of sweets?' She went on and on. But I persisted. I told her if I went on a fast I would no longer have the energy to cook or clean for her. So, in the end, I had my way. I don't know if the gods ever forgave her, but I did dream about the Goddess that night. There was a flower in her hand that she placed on my night stand and left, a finger to her lips.

At some point, I hear their voices again. I wonder who they are gossiping about:

'Where is she these days?'

'She died two years ago!'

'Oh, is that right? I thought it was the husband who passed away…'

What a talent they have, these young people, to reduce both the living and the dead to ashes, in one swift stroke.

I turn my face to the wall. I hear a grunt. The mattress dips and adjusts to someone making himself comfortable on my bed. I am outraged. What is the meaning of this? Who would dare sit on my bed without my permission? I do not have my false teeth on and cannot scold my unwanted guest, but I will certainly try. Imagine my delight, when I find, it is my husband sitting by my side. 'Where were you? Why did you go away? How could you leave me in a foreign country, in a cold house, where I can call nothing my own?'

My complaints spill out like acid reflux, bitter and uncontrolled. He has no answer, and is looking instead at the clock, the calendar, the weak sunlight filtering through the blinds. I raise myself up, twisting my wrist in the process, and pull at his sleeve. He shrugs away my hand. I am furious. I am screaming now, beating him with my fists. 'Look at me! Answer me!' Then, just like that, he is gone, and it is my son who is shaking my shoulders with his heavy hands, asking me to calm down. Later, I show him my swollen wrist. He massages it gently, tenderly. His eyes are misty.

Malavika

I was never more beautiful as when I was with Captain. Like a froth of spring, I colored his life. Aware of his attention, my posture improved, my hair shone, my limbs untangled and I felt strong, lean and as smooth as a flute. We studied mathematics of course, or rather, he taught, and I studied. I became rather good at it as well. Years later, I taught geometry to ninth graders, for a while. By then the glow, along with Captain, had long since disappeared.

He sat across from me in the living room, his legs knocking against the little coffee table that served as a desk. The dining table had more room for books, but it was occupied by our father, who watched us with his unsettling eyes like a bird of prey. Looking back, I wonder why a man who saw sinister motives everywhere did not subject Captain to his usual grueling interview, even if the tuition was free. Had he done so, I imagine things might have turned out differently. *She might have lived.*

My mother brought in a plate of replenishments, usually in the middle of our lesson. Little round saltines topped with scrambled eggs and dotted with ketchup; or boiled potatoes and peas mashed and fried to make cutlets. I can hear her nervous cough, the rustle of her sari, even sense the blush accompanying the tray. Captain, who drove down to our lesson directly from work, his shirt front damp, accepted the snacks and ignored me completely as he ate, as if he had a "Do Not Disturb" sign plastered on his forehead. I noticed that he did not think to save some for me. At the end of the session, she served tea. His in chipped china, and my milky version in a stainless-steel tumbler.

It was a year later, and I was already in tenth grade, when he plucked up the nerve to ask me if I'd like to join him for lunch elsewhere, in a restaurant. 'To celebrate how well you are doing,' he said sweetly. Little Anika was hovering in the vicinity when he invited me. *At last!* Glaring at her to go away, I told him I'd think about it. She scuttled off. I agreed after about a minute. As once before, he tried to suppress a smile.

Samir

When my parents were out, the ayah would ask me to turn the TV on. She sat straight-backed and cross-legged, like a devotee before her guru, and watched the daytime serials for three straight hours. As far as I could tell, they were all family dramas involving a bunch of women who dressed differently from my mother and plotted endlessly and tediously towards some unknowable end. The men in the dramas looked beaten and dressed like fags. One day, the ayah asked me to join her on the floor. She had me sit on her lap. I squirmed a little, but her hold was firm, so I settled down with my finger in my mouth. She smelled of sweat and dish soap. Her breath was stale, like an old, old bottle of masala. At some point, she drew the finger out of my mouth, settled my head in her breasts and showed me how to explore and nuzzle.

Later she made me French fries and asked me to keep our afternoon "rest time" a secret.

I missed our TV time when I was sent away to school. Years later, I told my mother about the ayah. She grew pale and said she was sorry she was not more vigilant. I told her it was all right. I told her it was the only tenderness I'd ever received from a woman and quite enjoyed it. She looked as if she'd been slapped in the face.

5

Annika

I rose at dawn and took my cup of coffee to the deck. The coffee is long gone, but it is some time before I can muster the energy to lift my head. The air, so pleasant and playful just moments ago, seems to have stilled. The sun stretches its arms in the copse behind my yard and spills the first golden tendrils of light before hiding behind a passing cloud. I need to make breakfast but cannot make myself go back indoors, where the air is just as heavy, if not dead.

I wonder why she chose to use my onion skin letterhead for her note. Did she think I would be tickled? Nostalgic about my "creative" phase, perhaps? Was her choice of paper even significant? Maybe, she merely ran out of notepaper and scrounging around, came upon the pad? Yes, that must be it. My sister had no use for nuance. She fast tracked out of my life when I was not quite fourteen and has no idea whether I even finished high school, leave alone design my own letterhead.

I fold and refold the single scrap of paper until it resembles one of those fortune-teller games we used to play, with questions on the flap and a horoscope in screaming capital letters and many exclamation points on the scrap beneath, proclaiming you will be rich, or you will be famous, or you will have four sons or marry a bald man and so on and so forth. I wish we could sit on a mat on the floor, my sister and I, and peek behind questions and giggle helplessly at the same set of answers like we used to every single time! Advertently or not her letter has opened a door I once slammed shut. I want to let my sister in. I do. But I am deathly afraid that this surfacing, like an unfamiliar lump in the breast, may not bode well for either of us.

That night I dream I am in my mother's home, more accurately, I'm in her womb. The whole family, including my father and my grandparents, is hunched around a big old-fashioned radio set on the dining table. The commentator is spewing out statistics. 300, 500, NO … 800. The panic in his voice mounts as he charts the number of people trampled to death at the Kumbh Mela as they surged through the barriers for a "purification" bath. My mother has stopped listening and, instead, cups her hands over her belly to share a quiet moment with me.

The radio turned off, the air is thick with fear, and a heated discussion around the table ensues. My mother, except it's not Gone-Mother, it's Malavika, applies a little more pressure above her groin, kneads with the padded part of her fingers, and whispers, 'Are you okay?' I nestle in the radius of her warmth and knock five times against the walls of my cushy shell: I *am if you are*.

I carry the heaviness all day, next day, scarcely accomplishing anything but the simplest of tasks. I enter and steal out of Ma's room on padded feet so I won't have to make conversation.

Ma's vision is no worse than it was, a couple of years ago, but she cannot seem to organize visual information. Aphasia, according to the Google gods. She wants to drink out of a food saver. Eat out of an ashtray. The brain recognizes a shape as a "square" or a "rectangle" but does not draw upon past experiences to differentiate between two square objects. Hence, she mistakes the TV monitor for a front door, and the TV Presenter as a guest in her home – who must be entertained. She folds her hands in greeting and simpers, 'How are you Mr. Bacchan? Why did you not visit yesterday?'

The visitor smiles. For one bizarre moment, I believe they make eye contact. A small part of me understands the eye-brain mis- communication. Her face is so close to the screen her breath clouds the monitor. *Good grief, she is actually blushing.* I am choking with mirth. The look on her face when she sees me, as if I've crawled into her bed, unasked!

Chastised, I leave her to her fantasies.

Then there are times she sits in the dark, a barely there thing.

When the rage grows too large, she uncoils and spits gibberish at the wall.

On other days, she is able to grab the words while they are still shining in her mind's eye and present them with a triumphant smile. While she is somewhat coherent, we set up the laptop on the coffee table. Her daughter visits her via Skype. Ma recognizes her at once but greets her like a visitor.

'Why won't you get my daughter a tray of biscuits? Some fruit?' she asks and glares at me, querulously.

'She is not here. She is in Paris. This is her image,' I try to explain, drawing a box in the air.

She turns to her daughter on the screen.

'See? She thinks I'm a fool. Don't go away, darling. Your brother will be home soon. He will make us both a snack.'

'I ...'

She lowers her head and tries to block the screen from me in her passive aggressive way. My sister-in-law mouths an apology. I leave the room. Her complaints follow me like the stink of her piss dribbled all over the bathroom floor.

'Why won't they send me to you? I feel so alone.'

She feels alone! After *everything* we've been through together, everything we've done for her! I wipe my tears, letting self-pity, followed by resentment, frustration and vestigial flickers of anger against her son, wash over me like waves of salt.

My cell phone pings a reminder. It is Wednesday, and the physical therapist, (we are allotted one for five sessions,) should be here within the hour. Putting aside the checklist of wrongdoings, I go in to make certain her room is clean.

I have to go past the kitchen to get to her room. The smell of curry pervades the air, a noticeable patina, despite the vanilla and sandalwood candles melting in every room. Oh well.

I go to her bathroom. I flush the toilet, find some Lysol and spray it vigorously. The decorative cotton rug between the toilet and the shower stall is slightly unaligned. I straighten it so it falls in the dead center. I make a note to self to get baking soda and vinegar and keep under her sink. I close the bathroom door and survey the room one more time. It will have to do.

God! I'm turning into Gone-Mother.

The therapist is here.

'Ma, this is Eva. She is here to help us.'

'Hello, Ma'am.'

Ma looks past me. Past the therapist. The lack of curiosity or any other emotion on her face is typical. 'I have to rinse my mouth,' she mutters randomly.

'Hold on. Let me get your cane.' I grab it from the partially open closet behind her. She looks offended. A frown clouds her forehead. Using the wall for support, she walks past me and gets herself to the bathroom. After she has sloshed and swished about, she makes her way back to the room, shrugging off my hand on her shoulder. The front of her tunic is creased. The therapist uses her initiative and goes to the bathroom for a hand towel. She places it gently on her shoulder. Ma eyes the towel, uses it to wipe her mouth and smiles gratefully. In her eyes, there is a flicker of recognition. Or relief. I guess that's all the introduction she needs.

'I will be in the other room. Eva will help you, if you need something,' I tell her. But she has drifted off again, now transfixed by the sunspots flecking the curtains. Her hands, though, are in constant motion, flicking imaginary irritants from her skin. I decide to let her be and leave the room with a gesture to Eva, letting her know she's all hers.

Ma

I give myself a bath and iron my own clothes. I dress myself, taking care to cinch my pants the right way around at the waist. And my scarf falls around my neck, symmetrically. My socks match; my hair is neat, tied in a knot with pins I was able to find in the bottom- most drawer. All that is left is that I need some cold cream, but it is back there, in the bathroom, and I'm not sure my feet will cooperate. The floor moves, and I press upon my heels in an effort to grasp it. Needless to say, she has not yet bought me a skid-free pair of slippers. Three times I fell this week. She was right there in the room when it happened. She did not help break the fall. 'Tsk…tsk!' was all she said and made as if to help me to my bed. I will show my son the bruises. Outside, the sun is smiling. Soon, it will hurt my eyes.

Hopefully, I will get breakfast soon. She races past my room, a self-important look on her face, talking into that cell phone of hers. Always the cell phone. Women who do not bear children have all the time in the world for fruitless action, I suppose. Her stories race with her.

In my opinion, there are two kinds of people. Those who share way too much and those who greedily withhold information as if every inane fact of their life may be misappropriated or used against them. She shares too much. Although with me, she shares nothing. Furtive as a thief!

When she came into our home, married to my son, her hair was longer. She was attractive in a rumpled, sort of way. I looked into her eyes. They were not the eyes of a child, but they held a child's willingness to learn. Now, she acts as if she knows it all. It is I who feel whittled down from mother to child. A child that no one, least of all my son, takes seriously.

She just brought in porridge, buttered toast and sweet tea. God bless her. She is a good woman. Perhaps you think I am overly interested in meals. But it is not so. Mealtimes slice the endless hours into manageable portions, like one of those long hard breads that cut against my dentures. Yes, I am well cared for and so grateful. I ask her to sit. Talk. Share something of her life. And although she did forget to place a napkin on my tray, I decide I will convey my thanks the old-fashioned way, with a written note.

Malavika

Samir is visiting, with his flavor-of-the-month. Her skirt is hiked up to her thighs, and a simple crucifix, probably white gold, hanging from a black thread, nestles in the V of her bosom. I talk easily with my son as she sits pouting, crossing and uncrossing her legs. This compulsive need to find ways to shock and offend the older generation usually grates on my nerves. But today, I have other things on my mind. A known publisher has evinced some interest in my haiku. She wants to see more of my work!

I heap some gram-flour *barfi* onto a plate and go back to the kitchen to attend to the tea boiling on the gas stove when I hear raised voices. I hurry back to the living room, my hands on my waist.

'Yes. Everything your *mummy* makes is best in the world,' the girl is saying, her, eyes flashing with disdain.

Before I can process this incredible display of rudeness, a hand raises itself and smacks her across her cheek!

'F*** you!' she screams, jumping up, letting the plate of barfi fall to the floor where – thank goodness – it lands on the carpet and does not chip. Then, she runs out of the house, almost knocking me down in her hurry. Her left cheek, where he has struck her, carries his imprint. I glare at him, my chest heaving, until he gets up and follows her out, slamming the door behind him. I listen to their fading footsteps, shuddering in disbelief.

A day wasted! Haiku needs the quiet of a pond, the delicacy of a butterfly as it flits from flower to flower, sipping nectar, without disturbing a stem.

Instead, I have to suffer the irascible son of an absent father and his wayward girlfriend. I touch the soft spot near my left breast and rummage in my medicine cabinet for some aspirin. *Just in case.*

⧖⧖⧖

Captain had no real family to speak of. His mother had long since passed away, and he had no siblings. His father, a proud and private man, forgave Captain *the repugnant, cowardly act of eloping* (his words in a letter to his son) and did visit us at last, when I was heavy with Samir.

I was wary of him at first, as I was of all fathers. Their only function, it seemed to me, was to strut about and roar like lions, in a den of hapless kittens. *Be a man! Pick on someone your size!* I once challenged my father. He smacked my mouth with a fist. That night he also threw himself on my mother with abnormal zeal, possibly to prove he was one. I know because I heard her squealing.

In any case, I told myself, it was a temporary situation. I was not so thin-skinned that I could not handle a few loaded innuendos and cruel insults, from the likes of Captain senior. To my surprise, the old gentleman proved thoroughly polite, quite entertaining, and only rarely censorious. What's more, he gave me a present, every day, for the fifteen days he stayed with us. At the time, I simply assumed he was either loaded or did not have much use for money. It became a sort of ritual for us. I would bring him his aspirin with a glass of warm milk, and he would thrust a few notes into my hand. 'Just in case, you know…for a rainy day,' he'd say, with a twinkle in his eyes.

'But you already gave me some money, yesterday!' I would protest, weakly.

He'd shrug and keep his hands held out until there was not much I could do but take his money. It was only a couple of days before I learned to accept his generosity graciously. 'Well, we do have a heavy monsoon,' I grinned facetiously.

I bought a few pairs of shoes and deposited the remaining cash in a personal account *just in case you know… for a rainy day* and promptly forgot all about it.

Years later, I found my old checkbook. Captain was away on business and called to remind me it was our son's birthday. I withdrew the cash and used it on a Polaroid camera as a gift from both of us.

Samir

I found in my junk pile this old Polaroid camera, a chunky relic of my dubious past. My parents gave it to me as a birthday gift when I was nine or ten.

I suppose I held on to the camera to remind me, although they despised each other, they could be counted on to bend over backwards when it came to gift ideas for their only son.

I was fed up with Principal Spencer and her humiliating enemas. I knew, by the shady way she pushed us towards the bathroom, when there was not a soul in the vicinity, that she did not want the rest of the faculty to know about the bathroom tortures. Jai, who could be surprisingly astute when no one was looking, observed that the punishments seem to take place only after the teaching staff and clerks left for the day.

I asked him if he would help me bring the hag to her knees. He agreed at once.

The next time I saw Old Spencer trudge across the field, shielding the saggy balloons she tried to pass off as tits, with a bulky file, I threw a ball at Jai, shouting at the top of my lungs, 'Take that, dumb faggot!' It was exciting to try a new curse word and witness the effect. Principal Spencer flinched as if I had struck her physically. Hooking her middle finger, she ordered me to come closer. 'See me at 6.00 p.m., obnoxious boy!' The bitch was positively drooling at the thought of my exposed buttocks! Without missing a beat, she walked, with renewed vigor, to the library.

We took the opportunity and raced in the opposite direction to her office. It was 1 p.m. Lunchtime for the staff. Satisfied that no one lurked in adjoining offices, we went to the back of the building. I identified the bathroom window. It was the fixed kind – wouldn't open or close. So, Jai shattered it with his hard ball. 'Make sure the hole is large enough for a head to fit through,' I reminded him. He did so, perfectly. We then ran back to the office, pushed open the bathroom door and looked for stray fragments of glass, glistening around the toilet. I pulled the flimsy curtain across the hole just in case she caught sight of it when she went in to empty her bladder.

That evening, as Spencer got ready to plug my anus with her bloody instrument, Jai climbed to the window on a garden stool we stole from the shed. Conscientious to a fault, he took not one, but three pics with my Polaroid and waited for them to self-develop. I found him kneeling on the grass, peering at the photographs laid neatly in a row. He looked like the man-eater of Chowgarh, salivating over his kill. Still, while it was obvious what was going on in the photographs, he was unable to get Spencer's face in the frame. Apparently, she was angled away from the window. But, I pointed, the expensive Swiss wristwatch on her hand poised above my arse was clearly recognizable, and proof enough.

It had to be.

The following weekend, we were sent home for winter break.

I made sure both my parents were in. Then I put the photographs between the pages of my father's A Passage to India. He was a predictable man, and invariably placed the book he was reading under the table lamp by his desk. Then all I had to do was busy myself on the sofa and wait for him to settle down with Mr. Forster.

'What the hell is this?'

His bug eyes fairly popped out of his head. One of the photographs slid to the floor, by mother's feet.

She looked up from the skirt she was trying to shorten or tighten.

It isn't often that my father raised his voice.

'We took those with the camera you got me,' I muttered.

Mother put aside her mending and bent forward to pick up the photograph. She took one look at the graphic image and turned completely white.

'Explain, Sammy!' Father looked ready to pull his hair out of his scalp.

I told them about old Spencer and our weekly humiliations and how I thought we needed evidence so that our parents would believe us.

'Who's the *we* in this plot?' my father asked.

'Jai and I.'

I was told to leave the room. I stood behind the door, listening to them argue, exclaim, quarrel strenuously over whose fault it was and finally arrive at a plan. Calls were made, other families brought into the picture.

I felt light, floating in space like an astral object. My parents. Concerned citizens. Joining forces! For a few hours, I was both an actor, the lead part in a TV drama, as well as a member of the audience watching and waiting and rooting for a family.

My heart ready to burst, I decided, then and there, to create situations, the more bizarre the better, just so they would consult each other like pukka parents to secure my position in the fold.

Mrs. Spencer was forced to resign, although allowed to stay until the end of the year.

We had a great deal of fun, drawing charcoal bums and puckered lips on the wall outside her office with lewd captions: Kiss my butt, Spencer! Or, who loves arse? Spencer does! She kept mum. What was she going to do, plead abuse? Even the staff treated her like a leper. Her replacement, Father Manning, had the walls repainted. He also appointed a couple of nuns as abuse counselors who basically taught us that our arse was sacred and should stay unfucked.

Jai and I, in an inspired moment, started a rule book titled - How to Survive in Boarding School -

Rule number one: Your arse is private property.

Rule number two: You decide when you need a dump.

Rule number three: Don't pull down your pants for anyone (unless you really want to, hehehe).

Then we got bored.

6

Annika

Eva has barely left and I am clearing away the dishes when the phone rings.

'Mrs. Sharma?'

'Yes, this is she.'

'Just wanted to know if you are still coming?' the strung-out voice at the other end put me on alert.

I realized I had answered an ad in the local newspaper for a wheelchair, a raised toilet seat, and other items designed to make Ma more comfortable. We had an appointment for 2.00 p.m. The grandfather clock in the hallway chimed twice just then, like a "Hear ye, hear ye".

'I'll be there in a couple of minutes, I'm so sorry!'

'I will wait for 30 minutes. Then, the caregiver will be taking over for my father, and I have an appointment with my realtor,' said the strung-out voice, simmering down to an even, matter-of-fact tone.

'Yes. Yes. Sorry! You are just around the corner from us. I will be right there.'

The Grahams, as per the name that was on the nameplate, lived in a large, once white Colonial, on a cul-de-sac. In the front yard, a "For Sale by Owner" sign in corrugated plastic wobbled on one metallic leg. Most of the window shutters upstairs seemed to have blown away during Hurricane Sandy. The lawn itself showed signs of alopecia, and weeds sprouted out of the cobblestone path leading up to the front door. *Money troubles?* I wondered. Maybe not. After all, the woman who called did seem to have her hands full.

I rang the doorbell. The door opened at once. She was obviously waiting for me.

'Mrs. Graham?'

'Mrs. Burke, actually. Anne, to you,' she said and extended her hand. A plain gold band glinted on her ring finger.

'Mrs. Graham was my mother. Do come in.'

She was tall and skinny, wore sensible khaki pants, a full-sleeved shirt and a quiet smile on a plain face. She spoke in short, breathy sentences. Her eyes were puffy. I nodded.

I followed her down a long narrow hallway, slightly claustrophobic in the semi-darkness. *She is so tense!* Her back was taut, her fists clenched at her side, as if expecting combat.

The hallway widened again, like a funnel.

'A few years ago, my parents had this extension built,' she gestured, adding, 'So they wouldn't have to climb stairs.'

She stopped abruptly before a door.

'He sleeps deeply, but we are still careful what we say in his presence,' she said. I nodded and paused briefly before following her in.

Mr. Graham lay, as if staged, in the dead center of a round, king-size bed.

His room was sparsely furnished and so quiet that even the walls held their breath, but it had good energy and did not reek of sadness.

I took a soft step closer to the bed. His skin glowed under his furrowed face, and his scalp shone under his fine silver hair. His lips, partly opened, looked pink and smoothened with Chap Stick. A beloved human being, unafraid and accepting, who was willing himself a good end.

'Isn't he wonderful?' I gave a little start. I'd tuned out Anne standing right beside me. It was as if love had transformed her homely face and made it beautiful.

'Yes. He is.'

Almost immediately, her expression changed, like she had the wind knocked out of her and her hands dropped listlessly, to her side. Whatever it was that made her beautiful disappeared and left in its place a somewhat abject version of herself. With a sigh, she leaned against a chair but did not sit down, as if the act would be construed as a sign of weakness.

'The raised toilet seat is in that closet, behind you. It is still in its wrapping.' I moved aside to let her pass. She found the toilet seat and held it out to me.

'Let me open the garage door. The wheelchair is in there along with other stuff you might find useful. He won't need them anymore,' she said quietly. I followed her to the garage. The wheelchair was light, functional and simple to operate. Still, she handed me the instructional booklet that came with it.

She wanted to show me some of the other stuff she planned to sell or give away. I took a cursory look at the board games, food planners and other assorted objects, but now I wanted to get as far away as possible from the house and the certainty of death clouding the air around it. I had heaviness of my own to contend with. Perhaps she sensed my reluctance to linger, because she put them aside quickly, nodded and followed me to my car. We loaded the toilet seat and chair in the trunk and I opened my purse. I gave her the $25.00 we had agreed on and said,

'I have something else for you, as well.'

She looked startled. I handed her a CD sticking out of an unzipped pocket of my purse.

'This is some music I picked up at a Buddhist temple, a while ago. It's very soothing. There is no chanting, just music,' I clarified, adding, 'Maybe it will help your dad as he sleeps, even though…' I colored.

She stared at the cover. 'Thank you,' she took it gingerly and turned abruptly, brushing her cheeks with the back of her hand.

I got into the car hastily. Now, as much as I wanted to leave, I also wanted to stay. I wanted to pull a smile out of Anne's overwrought face, like a rabbit out of thin air! To power wash her house, to weed her yard, to bring her a roasted chicken and arugula sandwich and to shove an envelope under her door with tickets to a show. To do any number of things that would light her heart with firefly moments of joy despite the looming darkness. Instead, I stayed, clutching the steering for a bit, and then drove myself home.

Soon, within the margins of domestic walls, busy with the business at hand, aligning the new toilet seat so that it sat high and unmoving on the old, my disproportionate affection for the now plain, now beautiful Anne fizzled as suddenly as it had sparked.

We were two ships that passed each other amid the wailing foghorns.

⏳⏳⏳

'Sit. Talk. Say something, it's too quiet around here,' Ma patted the seat beside her on the couch.

The first time I met her, I was childishly disappointed. She did not resemble Gone-Mother at all, with her eyes hidden behind glasses and her fair coloring. Still, I thought I saw wisdom in the gray hair pinned behind her head in a neat little snail-bun, and kindness inscribed on her face.

So, I sat with her as requested and began talking. I told her how my mother, when I was little, had this compulsive need to fatten me up, 'Just as you do,' I said and smiled at her.

It worked. She took my hand, urged me to go on.

'Very early in the morning,' I tell her, 'probably at first light, the milkman would tap the door once, and then leave a couple of bottles of milk at our doorstep. My mother rose at the sound, picked up the milk and set it to boil on a low flame even before she'd brushed her teeth. As the milk warmed, she made herself a cup of tea. I like to think she was at peace then, in this half-awake state, as she bowed a couple of times before an old kitchen calendar stuck forever in January, from which the goddess Lakshmi, in gaudy greens and oranges and with a slight smirk on her rosy face, held up her hand in blessing.'

'Her first cup of tea was a special, very strong blend of

three types of tealeaves hand-picked and boxed by day laborers in Darjeeling, Ceylon and Assam. I know this because each box carried an illustration of cheerful-looking women in native costume. By the time she was done with her tea, the milk was probably bubbling and boiling. It was time to lower the heat and then turn it off.'

A layer of cream settled on the milk as it evaporated. Gently, without disturbing the milk, she skimmed the surface and folded this cream in a bowl. Every morning she boiled, skimmed and added to the bowl, so that by the middle of the week, she had a dense, healthy heap collected and stored way back in the refrigerator, where no servant hand could reach. And every Wednesday and Thursday morning, she was able to dish out a banana sliced thin, swimming in a sea of cream. And that big, beautiful bowl was my breakfast!' I said, spreading my hands, in a show of extravagance.

What I do not tell her:

I found Gone-Mother wedged between the kitchen and the hallway. Behind her head, a thin trail of milk splotched the floor like afternoon light. I followed the trail to the stove, with my eyes. My first thought was, it will be hard to scrape the scalded residue off that pan. My second thought, she is dead, and my sister no longer lives with us. I will have to be the one to clear this mess. My throat was a Sahara. I tried wetting my lips, but I was all out of spit. The taste of fear is metallic.

Ma smiled in a befuddled sort of way. Somewhere along the line, she'd lost interest and looked as if she was about to nod off. I realized it was all the reaction I was about to get and stood up, feeling cheated.

Then she looked up shyly and said what was probably all along, on her mind, 'I want to write you a letter. Is it possible to get me some paper and a pen?'

Mystified, I bring her a notepad and a pen. 'You want to write me a letter? Why not just tell me what's on your mind?' I laugh.

But she is in a fog again. One advantage, albeit a dubious one, of being that old is you can wear or shed your senility at will. She bends over her work. I watch her scribble, and despite the wispy gray hair and the back hunched over with osteoporosis, she looks, at the moment, very young.

Much later, I go down to check on her again. She holds up her note shyly, like an apple for the teacher. A smile plays on her lips but the corners of her eyes radiate nervousness. I take the note out of her hands eagerly. She is studiously avoiding my eyes. I flatten the sheet and begin reading. Not only are the words jumbled – like alphabet blocks pulled hastily out of a toy box –but she has inverted the letters so that the p is confused with b, the w with m and so on. I strain to make sense of it and give up at last.

'I don't understand,' I say as gently as I can. The language she learned when she was four is now a complicated assembly of dots and dashes, an advanced programming code neither she nor anyone else can decipher.

She stares at her own handiwork. Her eyes are filled with frustrated rage. She presses her lips in a grim line.

By the end of the day, her sad scrawls appear on every conceivable surface - Toilet tissue, paper towels, napkins and notepads. The words travel up and down, hither and thither, an army of black ants that have nowhere to go.

Surrounded by the mounting evidence of her unruly mind, she beats her impotent chest. Her face is screwed up like a child's, but because she makes no tears, the anguish looks almost incongruous. I am torn between sympathy and impatience.

'Get some rest,' I urge. 'You are overreacting. Why not try again, tomorrow? I will help you.' She shakes her head and sobs again. I leave the room.

Ma

She gave me a pen and paper at last after going on and on about some story about her past that made no sense.

How could I have forgotten the alphabet? When I was five, my father put me on his lap after dinner and read to me. Perhaps there was something he saw in my eyes, as he read, the way I hung on to the words, as they rose from the page, like a tail at the end of a kite, drifting slowly above the clouds to explore other lands. Or, perhaps, he saw the naked longing on my face, licking my lips as the stories unfolded. Whatever it was, it impelled him to read to me every night, that is, until he remarried.

I remember my father's smell. The starch on his *kurta*, like boiled rice mingling with sweat and tobacco. I remember burying my nose in the worm-eaten pages of the book, the black and white illustrations looming large as I crept close and closer until he had to push my head back in order to turn the page. For thirty minutes every night, I disappeared inside the pages. Then he got busy with New Ma.

A month and a day after she settled like a permanent pile of dirty dishes in the kitchen sink, I crawled out from under his desk and tugged at his tunic. 'What are you doing here?' He asked sternly. I held up a book.

'No. It is time *you* learned to read.'

'I have read this book. Can you get me another?' I asked holding my breath.

'Maybe you can write your own book,' he said. Behind his

glasses, his eyes twinkled.

When I was nine, I wrote a story based on my dream.

The God of Death asked me to pick the parent I loved best. I could have only one. The other, he would take. I could not decide; so, the God of Death took them both. In my dream, I cried and cried and made a sea with tears. Then God, in a moment of compassion, sent me a boat. He told me if I crossed the sea, I would find my parents. But I was afraid I might drown. So, I swallowed my tears and lived by myself. The end.

Without words, the world is a suggestion, an inexplicable motif. Without words, you are a singer without a song, an alphabet without vowels, a creature of sounds –without words, you have no history.

I make three columns on a sheet of paper. I ask her to label each column with a name. I will practice until I get the names of my son and my daughter's children right. Then I will move on to sentences and then I will move on to stories. I will save all my stories under my bed in a box. I will label it "My life".

Malavika

Was I ever in love with Captain? Perhaps not in the traditional sense. I was fifteen and a half and thought I understood my heart. He was thirty-five and took to me like a fly to sugarcane. I enjoyed him. Enjoyed stretching out in his beautiful black Chevrolet, pretending I owned the car. I absolutely loved going to the pool club with him. That moment when I managed to stay afloat, and later, with long eager strokes, crossed the pool from end to end, still makes my eyes shine with happiness.

I loved pouring tea for his friends, my hair tied in a top-knot like a model, my first-ever sari draped around my body like a second skin. I watched their eyes on my nail bitten fingers, as I poured, and I was ashamed I could not afford a manicure but also knew, without putting my thoughts in words, that it really did not matter, and perhaps even stoked their middle-aged fantasies. I laughed with abandon, sang for them as a dare and wondered if people at the next table were as envious of me as I used to feel peeking at the glitzy women in fancy cars as I bumped along in a rickshaw. It was a heady time, and he couldn't keep his hands off me.

On school days, I met him at lunch break. We had just enough time to make it to the cinema two afternoons a week at the tail end of the morning show, hands clammy and eyes steamy with desire. There, in relative privacy on the last row, in the balcony seats, I sat on his lap and let him unhook my bra with one hand and pull the elastic of my pants with the other. Then he had to run back to his office, the smell of semen on his fingers, his kerchief binned in the trash can nearest the cinema.

She knew. My mother knew something was off. 'Where did you get the perfume, the skirt and the silver anklets?' she whispered fearfully. She laid out the gifts I received, brought them out, one by one, like exhibits in a courtroom trial, leading up to the damning proof of my sordid, sinful relationship. It made me angry. I was rude and dismissive. Her blood pressure shot up. A doctor was called in. The medication, at first, made her better, and then affected her in unhealthy ways. She was chronically depressed. I couldn't wait to get away from her dreary advice, her pointless melancholy. I stayed out as much as possible.

And little Anika? She stayed home and tended to our parents. Let me in, in the middle of the night, a finger pressed to her lips. 'Shhh! They are asleep,' she warned, as I stood in the doorway, blinking and swaying to the music in my head. She was eight years old, and I had begun to rely on her as if she were the *didi*, and I, the erring child.

Samir

Twice, when I was a child, someone called me a dog, within earshot.

I was shuttled between our home and Grandfather's at least three times a week. In Grandfather's home, where my mother now resides, I was usually deposited on a mat in the living room or on the balcony with my favorite toys. Sometimes, however, if I really got underfoot, my mother would let me go downstairs and kick a ball around in the parking area under the apartment building.

I was weaving in and out, playing football with imaginary friends, when a car drew up. Out came the Jolly family in two by twos. Mrs. Jolly, always dressed like a slut, had on a sheer tunic with no under slip. Her nipples poked through the pink fabric like autumn berries. Mr. Jolly, walking beside her, saw me and grunted hello. His older son made as if to muss my hair. I drew back shyly. His younger son reared his head at me and went Waaaaa. I stuck out my tongue. His daughter had her nose buried in a comic book and walked past me like I was invisible.

When the last of the Jollys cleared out of my way, I went to retrieve my ball. That's when I heard Mr. Jolly ask his wife, 'Who is that kid, again?'

'That's Malavika's boy. A *dhobi ka kutta*. A pariah dog that belongs neither here nor there.'

The second time someone called me a dog was when my parents separated. The divorce was not yet finalized, and I was shunted off to boarding school. Quite inconveniently, for my mother, we had two months off in the summer as well as a short spring and winter break.

It was early March, so it must have been spring break, when she picked me up from school and told me, as we drove along, that we were housing temporarily at a friend's place, since there was a water issue in Father's home. 'None of the toilets work,' she said, her eyebrows dancing comically. Like most kids, toilet humor always made me smile, but then she warned me to behave myself and make sure I was extra polite to her friend throughout my stay.

I could tell by her tone that she was anxious, a bit too willing to please this "friend", and her anxiety made me scared and resentful.

The first thing her friend, a ganja-smelling arsehole with facial hair and no smile of greeting on his face, said, 'So, his father won't keep the mongrel, ha?'

Something must have snapped inside. Not given to analysis, I do not know what it was. All I can say is, I got out of the car, a child, and bounded into his home, a dog off his leash.

I am proud to admit that those were the ten worst days of my mother's life.

I wouldn't bathe. I wouldn't sit at the table. I wouldn't speak like a human. What I would do was pee on the bed, lick food off the floor, crawl on all fours and growl ferociously each time I saw his stinking feet. When they broke off their relationship, soon after, I howled at the moon.

The trouble was, I quite enjoyed being a dog and saw no reason why I had to drop the act just because I was back in school. For a few months, I got away without brushing my teeth, or bathing or throwing my clothes into the wash. I looked and smelled like a genuine pariah dog and even bit like one.

Calls were made to my parents. My father came in, sat silently by my side until the Principal left, and then made an effort to talk to me. I barked him out of the room. My mother did not show up for the meeting.

I was feared by students and staff alike and left alone. That was just fine by me.

Then the unexpected happened. Valerie Pinto, an Anglo-Indian with long silky hair and the wide blue eyes of a made-in-china doll, joined in the middle of the school year. When she stood at the head of the class, a look of studied indifference on her Germanic face, a jolt of electricity shot through my heart. Then I caught a glimpse of my dog-face in a glass-framed picture of the original school building and headed for the shower stalls.

7

Annika

She sat hunched over her handiwork over eight hours each day, for twelve straight days, stopping only to eat and pee.

So great was my relief to see her safe and docile on her chair that I risked stepping out of the house for a few bracing minutes each day, when the sun was at its highest, and every tree wagged its branches in delight. Like a parolee greeting the open skies, I held my face up to the light. And when I returned, giddy with joy, shaking leaves out of my hair, I found her the way I left her, the pencil shifting like a finger on the Ouija board, her shoulders round and tense, her tongue peeking out from between pressed lips.

Perhaps, I thought, I will survive her dementia after all.

She lifted her head and held up her work. I smiled and nodded encouragement from afar. On day six, I picked up the sheet and exclaimed in wonderment, 'PERFECT!' Then she took back her work with both hands, as if accepting an award, and climbed gratefully into bed. I watched her face with the focus of a chiromancer – life, heart and brain lines rushing and colliding, adding new fissures to old in the papery skin. Soon she turned to her side, her cheek resting on her homework and her breath curling the ends of the paper so that they tickled her chin like blades of grass.

On day seven, she lost momentum, the letters no longer stood in formation, proud of their identity. They flecked the paper like bird droppings. She took one look at my dismay and started afresh.

⧗⧗⧗

Adi held my coat in his arms. The plastic wrap from the Laundromat was still on it. I took it from him wordlessly. I patted the top and bottom. It felt empty.

Then he fished out something from his pocket.

'Oh, the Laundromat found this in your coat. It is addressed to you.'

'Hmm. I was wondering where my letter disappeared,' I said, smiling weakly.

'Who is it from?'

'My sister.'

He stared at me quietly for a few seconds. 'Have you responded?'

'No.'

'Why don't you just call her? Isn't it easier?'

'No!' I snapped and stuffed the envelope into my bra. *What did he know!* Then I went in to start dinner.

I feel compelled to read my sister's letter over and over, as if it were scripture, divining new meaning in the same verse every day. Then I stare at her profile on her Facebook page. *Who is this stranger I once knew like the taste of my own blood?*

That moment when she first eloped with Captain, I felt as if I had been struck in the chest with a hammer; my lungs seemed to collapse, and I could not breathe. In fact, my breathing difficulties followed me into adulthood and disappeared only after I met Adi.

I never did like her Mr. Captain. No one did. Father tolerated him because the tuition was free. Mother was hospitable because that's who she was. But ever since I heard him ask Malavika out to lunch, I had this icky feeling I could not put my finger on, a sense of wrongdoing. Of secrets and lies. But I was only eight at the time and had other priorities - school, play and staying in Father's good graces.

I do not know when or why my sister decided it had to be *him*. The one who would rescue her. Then one day, I saw the flush on her face as she groomed herself before her evening walk, the way her hands fumbled as she tried on new earrings and her zipper stuck as she writhed into her dress. And I felt a tearing and repositioning in my heart, as if adjusting for an absence.

Desperately, I held her skirt. She tugged it free. 'Don't be a baby,' she said, crossly. I followed her down the hallway. She walked faster, not turning once to wave. I went back in to wait for her return. When the last rays of the sun sank in the ocean, and the streetlights came on as far as the eye could see, I knew she was not coming home.

☒☒☒

I dream I am in my parents' home, on the balcony. Hands wrapped around a mug of tea, I am staring blissfully at a roseate dawn, when a gusher rises out of the ocean and darkens the sky. Only it is not a gusher. It is a battalion of crows so persistently harsh with their cawing that I wake myself up with a start. It takes many deep breaths before I can convince myself a congregation of crows, in a dream, is still just a dream, and has no bearing on reality.

Ma

There are ways to trick the brain; I learned that a long time ago. When my vision became cloudy, I spent weeks memorizing important phone numbers. I have twenty-one numbers circulating in my head, so I do not need *her* help to call my family. When I lost the ability to form words with one language, I found myself using the language of my childhood. Amazingly, it has stayed, untouched by senility. I now communicate through this alternate route! How I wish I had learned to write in two languages, as well. For, however hard I try, the letters come out crooked, misshapen, wrong side up.

I have been up all night, forming a plan. I will write as I always do. Let the words fall like leaves, I will give them new shape. What does it matter that my *b* looks like a *p*? One must adapt to the new alphabet.

My plan gives me great hope. I will soon attempt a story.

I lie on my side, facing the wall, but a few inches from me, I feel the mattress give a little, as if she is sitting behind me. I am filled with fear. The pull-out drawer under my bed is partially open. What did she take from in there? More importantly, is she tampering with my medication? That would explain the dizziness. That would also explain the confusion, the forgetfulness, the loss of words. Like an ill wind, each time *she's* been in the room, she brings in a new illness. Even through all the medication muddling my brain, I sense her thief-like movements.

I call my daughter. She lives on the other side of the ocean, I think. I use the speed dial although I've memorized her number. I whisper my fears into the phone. 'That girl, Ani, is killing me,' I tell her. She sounds annoyed. She says it is 2 a.m. I need to keep the time difference in mind. I look out of my window. It's broad daylight. I am convinced now that they are cooking a plot. My daughter has joined forces with *her*.

I'm more afraid than ever. Each minute that passes is one less left. Each breath I draw is one breath diminished. In the gutters outside my childhood home were the discarded remains of water balloons. Shape and purpose lost, they drifted in the grimy stream until they disappeared or stuck inside a crevice, and we lost interest in them and returned to our games. I will be lost like that.

I balloon my cheeks and hold my breath as long as I can. But then I have to exhale. In the next room, seated on a yoga mat, I hear her draw breath after powerful breath. She is stealing all my air! I will not name her in my will. Ha! I will give everything I own to my son. I will tell him so, right now. Where is he? It is bright sunshine outside. I will explain to him how she steals all my medication. And all my breath. How I cannot trust her.

I see my son. I will go to him now. From the hallway, as I slip my feet into my slippers, I see them on the deck. They are murmuring, their heads close together. With thumb and index finger he pulls something out of her hair. A leaf maybe. Then he tweaks her nose. She makes a face. He throws his head back and laughs into the sun. He looks like Lord Krishna, blissful in the company of Radha. I avert my head, slide my feet out of my slippers and go back to bed.

Malavika

When my father, with customary malice, told me one day I was wasting my time on books and should not get my hopes up because there was no college in my future, I knew it was time. I had no reason to believe life would be any different for me than it was for Mother. Worse. She, at least, had chosen her fate!

I went to meet Captain. Perhaps he did not see the storm in my eyes because he blurted out the moment we met that he was being transferred to Singapore, and would I wait for him for two years?

Two years! He may as well have said twenty. 'No!' I told him. I would most certainly not wait. I suggested he marry me at once, or I would tell Father that my tutor had his way with me, and I would run off with the next boy who so much as looked at me. He saw I wasn't making sense but I guess he got the gist. He agreed that we elope.

In all these years, I never once thought how my absence would affect Ana-banana. Despite her spirited older sister, or perhaps because of her, she was a quiet, undemanding, sensitive child. I see now, my mother's petrified silence, my father, with his rage spattering the walls and, in their midst, the ten-year-old, sitting on tenterhooks with her rag dolls and her homework. It could not have been an easy time.

But children are resilient, and time is merciful. It allows you to forget, to blur the lines between reality and imagination. Still. How much has Anika forgotten? More importantly, how much has she forgiven? And, how will her forgiveness factor in my future?

Samir

I gave Mother a tongue-lashing and then watched her pale. It was a talent perfected over time and gave me even more pleasure than the first time I hurt her. She did not show fear and did not play the victim, but her body went slack. The little lines under her eyes, which she concealed so well, cracked through the polished patina of her face and radiated outwards. Her skin looked thinner, exposing a crisscross of blue veins. She became, instantly, old.

One day, fueled by meanness, I said something undoubtedly cruel. She closed her eyes, shook her head hard as if she had a spirit attached to her scalp and muttered, 'I should have known you'd come back to haunt me.'

A framed portrait of my grandfather stood on the wall facing the front door. I jumped back in disbelief as she rammed a clenched fist into his face. It crackled like microwave popcorn and spat mouthfuls of glass all over the floor. I thought *it's me she really wants to hit.*

I tried to make an effort from that day on. When the heat was too intense or when I was caught up in yet another ball crushing relationship or my last deal did not close and my fingers itched for a fight and I felt as if I would die from lack of oxygen, I would look at Grandfather, still trapped in his original frame, his face marked with three distinctive Zorro-like strokes, and then look at my mother's hand, the knuckles still marred with the memory of crushed glass, and simply head for the nearest bar to beat the shit out of some unfortunate dunderhead out for a beer.

I was on a roll, venting my rage in a bottle, when this

uncomfortable thought, slithering below the surface, reared its ugly head: my mother did not speak to Grandfather for most of her life, and judging by the crack in his portrait, I'm not sure she forgave him, even in death.

Could I, her unemployed, undereducated son, therefore, afford to stoke her anger?

Realistically, where would I go and who would I turn to if she threw me out? Not my father. Behind his deceptively kind face was a cold-hearted bastard who did not think twice before he flew the coop, picking up a pudgy new wife along the way and leaving me here to rot.

So, perhaps, I figured, it would be wise to cool it for a while and not punish her for a failure that was not entirely hers. After all, when all was said and done, I had to admit, it was she who stayed.

Motes of anxiety still disturb the air. My grandfather's face, marked with a Z, still stares out of the glass-framed photograph, an eternal reminder of the way we were. But these days we do breathe a little easier in each other's presence, Mother and I.

8

Annika

I know paranoia is a symptom of her condition. But since when has logic ever made one feel better, especially when you are in the moment? Prone to self-doubt, I count and re-count the number of pills I give her, even taste-test the meals to make sure I haven't poisoned her in a Fu Manchu fugue. Who knows, maybe one day, her mind will reshape itself, and she will trust me again. *And the moon is made of green cheese, and there is such a thing as happily ever after.* But for now, I will cook both dinner and breakfast oatmeal – in case she is confused about the time.

For the third time in as many hours, she refuses her pills with a peremptory wave. I suppose she will take them from Adi. She has no problem accepting the meal trays though. I ask her to slow down, she is eating too fast. She huffs and pushes away the plate, insulted. I move the plate closer and leave the room. When I glance back, she is stuffing her face with fistfuls of *dal*, like a recalcitrant child.

Naturally, she throws up. I mop up after her, wrapping the lower half of my face with a scarf so I wouldn't retch as her undigested lunch swirls down the drain. I think I hear her moan. I drop the rag onto the floor and go back inside. I know she must be mortified, and probably wants to draw attention away from the stink, her damp tunic and the extra work she's now created.

'I want to die, oh, let me die,' she is wailing, her hands raised to an unmerciful god, located somewhere on the rafters, and watching me from with the corner of her eyes.

I glare at her, afraid of my own anger and what I might say.

'I wish it was over. I wish I could die,' she repeats like a mantra. Now, on a roll, she switches to a new theme. 'How restful it must be to escape from this life.'

'You will be fine,' I tell her. *I have watched you lay your hands on your heart and worry over its rhythms with the attention of a piano tuner!*

'Maybe I need to go to the doctor,' she says, as if to prove my point.

'Or, maybe, you need to watch what you eat,' I retort. Just as I feared, the words fly out, unrestrained. Now, I *am* ashamed. She is silent. Particulates of pain float in the air. Her nose is red. Soon, she falls asleep.

The phone rings once, and then again, after a brief interval. I stare at the number on the Caller ID. *Malavika.* My skin prickles. I ignore the call. I spray the bathroom with disinfectant. A moist smell settles in the air, like cheap perfume, not quite covering the stench of vomit. It's no use. I feel my sister standing right beside me, waiting her turn, the fingers of both hands interlaced in front of her, as if preparing for a recital. I pick up the mop again. I can feel her cool breath on my damp neck. The hair on my arms stands on end. I ward off her ghost, as I always do, first thing in the morning and last thing at night, the haunting hours, with a trick of my own. I engage in a mental activity that allows me to disappear into the characters I am developing for some future screenplay:

Naila (Protagonist) is bathing the baby. The warm water makes his cheeks rosy. She is crooning a tune as old as time…

Come with a whoop, come with a call,

Come with a good will or not at all …

The baby pees in his tub, unimpressed. She giggles and kisses the wet hair curling over his ears. She picks him up, dries and powders him and rubs the powder in. He giggles in response, his chin dimpling. After he is dressed, gleefully chewing the string of his bib, she holds him in her arms and reads "Goodnight Moon". He stares intently at the sliver of moon on the fairytale sky. The thumb and index finger of one chubby hand mangle the corners of the page. His sweet baby mouth is wide open; his baby eyes are round with wonder.

Her breath catches.

Vera (Friend) is wearing her good blue suit. Her back is appropriately stiff. She presses a crease on her skirt with the palms of both hands. This is her one hundred and forty-fifth closing. She is aware the two lawyers are eyeing her legs. Some may consider their wisecracks injudicious. But soon she can close her fingers on a well- earned commission check. She ignores the invitations in their eyes, nods and smiles at her client and wonders if she has time to stop for red pears on her way home.

A homeless woman (Secondary character) comes out of one of the stalls. She is dressed in several reeking layers and looks sodden, as if she's been washing herself in the toilet bowl.

An attendant wags a finger at her and asks her to leave at once. The woman, hair like dried vegetation sticking out of her scalp, waddles out, scratching, itching and releasing curses like fart rings.

The phone rings again.

M fumbles with her keys, pretending to rub sleep out of her eyes. She is still in a bit of a fog and not sure she can lie with a straight face. Her mother is wide awake. She opens the front door, turning on the hallway light, just as she finds her keys.

The phone rings again. With a start I realize, I am no longer developing a new character. I am remembering Malavika. One M leads to another.

"Sorry, I'm late. Umm, I had this thing…" Malavika says.

Mother lifts her chin with thumb and index finger to make her look into her eyes.

'You were always a good girl. I hope, I have taught you well.'

She pats her daughter's cheek, lets the tip of her fingers rest lightly on her bitten and bruised lips. Slowly, she pushes down her daughter's lower lip and in the dim hallway, inspects it like a dentist for signs of gum disease. Then she drops her hand listlessly and shuffles off to the bedroom, her slippers thwacking the floor.

⧗⧗⧗

In the gray light, her gray face. Small puffs of breath escape from her mouth and send out signals of life. I stick the mop in the pail. The floor is gleaming; the Lysol seems to have done its job. I flip on the exhaust to suck out any residual moisture. It sounds loud in the small bathroom.

At the sink, her dentures lie in place of the hand soap. How often have I asked her to place them out of sight? I smack shut the maw and place the horrid thing in a drawer. Evidence of exertion beads my neck. My sleeves are flecked with the remnants of her lunch. There is a sample-sized toothpaste with its cap off, also not in its place, in the medicine cabinet. I squeeze a little paste on my finger, hoping to rid my mouth of an overall bad taste with its refreshing, minty flavor. *Goddammit!* It's hemorrhoid cream! I gag. My blood pressure hits a new high.

I drop everything and go into the kitchen. The answering machine is blinking urgently. I listen to the administrative assistant's message, a little tinny, a little too upbeat and floating through the machine:

Hey, there! Haven't seen you in a couple of days. Jack was asking. By the way, do look at your work emails, at your earliest and pay close attention to the one marked "early retirement". Take care, now!

I open it at once, mull over the underlined header, crafted with judicial care, <u>Your benefits should you decide to take the package by said date.</u> Links to HR, Your Health, Your Finances and Legal Advice, preemptively provided.

Ah! Great, Annika. Why be miserable when you can be both miserable and unemployed? I snort. Almost immediately, I'm filled with a sense of gloom, of being unmoored, my body no longer on solid ground, drifting slowly toward sea. Not being a drinking girl, I make myself a cup of tea with a double dose of ginger.

Ma

I cannot tell what time it is, but a playful light works its way through the blinds. The pear tree outside my window blooms. A mishmash of smells, sweet and fetid, gusts through my body, making me reel. My longing has nowhere to settle. It hovers like a bee over dead flowers. It buzzes in agony. I want. I want. I want. High above my head, a solitary spider hangs from the rafters, advancing his silken territory. I curl and flex, curl and flex my fingers.

'What are you up to?' the girl, Anika, wants to know. I open my mouth to say something, but she has already disappeared. Piff! I go back to my task. What was it? I have lost the bookmark positioning my thoughts. I stare at my hands. The Y shaped veins disappearing into my wrist look blue and puffy, so close to the surface of my thinning skin. *Are these really my hands or did she replace them?* I lean forward and thrust them under my hips. I will have to sort this out later.

I find my glasses. They are right on my chair, squeezed between the cushion and my right thigh. The minute hand crawls across the clock, as it always does.

The afternoon spreads before me, lonesome as an echo. Time does not fly. The mind does. It drifts from place to place and person to person.

I pull out my writing pad to begin a story. Yesterday and today, childhood and old age, stand side by side like an ancient writing tablet with two hinged leaves.

I am beginning to remember:

I was in the courtyard of the house where I once wore frocks. The long tunics and pants came later, at age ten, to hide my new curves. That was when I first learned that I owned nothing. Even my body was not my own. Every decision regarding its maintenance was made by someone else. My tongue was as useless as an unplugged phone and swabbed daily of opinion. I knew there was nothing required of me, except helpfulness. *Education makes a woman dull.* Everybody knows that. Desire was a bad word, to be aborted at the first sign. I did not fear the future. I was told it was exactly like the past.

I put away my pencil, a little tired. But memories, like forbidden foods, tempt and tease, and make my head spin:

The heads of children sitting cross-legged on the floor, playing a complicated game that involves eight round pebbles and much snapping of fingers.

Mothers, gathered like bees over jam, exchanging tales of the British Raj, of flinging foreign clothes into the fire, in a show of support for the cause, a small part of them mourning the loss of all that pretty lace and silk gone to waste.

Housemaids bartering - pickles for potatoes, table cloths for headscarves and dresses for dishpans!

I wander back to this moment. My sheet of paper is a muddy field of dots and dashes. *Who did that? What does it all mean?* Someday I will understand.

It is 2 p.m., and I haven't seen my son at all. Where can he be? It is Saturday, so I know he is not at work. The house is so still I can hear the wood expand and settle. From upstairs, the sound of her laughter.

Perhaps she is only on the phone. Yes, surely, she is alone and conversing on the phone *–A woman must not laugh too loud. Or shut the bedroom door, by day.* Everybody knows that.

How easily she discards the rules of civility, like an uncomfortable inner garment. Although I must admit, it is not just her. It is this generation. Their open intimacies make my face burn.

I too was married once. Ah! Those happy days! Like white invitation cards lined with silver!

He was my sun, and I was his axis, tilting the earth towards him. He would come home and fling his clothes from his body, with reckless abandon. He was always warm, hungry. The outside world clung to his pores, and I sniffed and sniffed, trying to recognize the smells.

I made six children for my husband.

But with each new bundle, I became more frantically immersed in motherhood. Content with the daily grind of changing diapers, packing school bags and lengthening the hems of my daughters' dresses, in time he became no longer my lover and a friend, but a sometimes visitor, an onlooker at the mother-child drama forever unfolding.

It was I who pulled their ears, held them by their collars and yelled holy murder at their bad behavior. He was gone for days, weeks, who had time to keep count? I had a family to raise, and I raised my family well. Then one day, when I looked up, I was old and he was not.

No, my son will not let his mother lie alone, facing the wall and talking to shadows. Still. The air around me is stale, my hair is scant and my toothless mouth gapes like a dried-up well. I wonder if he is repelled by my sight.

I reach under the bed and pull out my sheet. I write: I am not this body. I am not this mind. I am not this illness. I am breath. Love. Memory.

He comes down at last. His face is aglow and he is humming to himself. Like a broken hand drum, my son is tone deaf.

My brother used to play a hand drum at affairs held at the temple. He once hit it so hard with the heel of his hand that he tore the drum. It sounded flat and hollow after that, like a weak imitation of its former self. My father did not replace the drum when he learned it was made from cowhide. 'You cannot kill a sacred animal and hope to produce a sacred sound,' he said.

Later, after *she* emerged from bed, they told me they were going out for a movie and would be home in three hours. I asked him, 'What if I needed a snack?' He did not say anything but brought in a tray laden with popcorn, cookies, nuts, and a flask of tea.

'Don't go near the stove,' he said and left.

Outside, white flowers drop silently to the green grass. Spring. I stare at the veins on my hands. I imagine splitting them open. I imagine picking the phone and calling them at the cinema. 'I am bleeding,' I will say in a voice fading fast. They will rush home and minister to my hand. I can feel the soft pressure of the bandage he will apply to my wound. I imagine Anika's face flushed with anger, her eyes looking everywhere but at me. But what if I angered him as well? I decide not to look for the knife.

They did not return in three hours. More like three and a half! I called him on his cell phone but it was *she* who answered! I put the receiver down at once, throttling her voice. A giggle escaped my throat.

Malavika

The actress, now jaded, walks solo along the shore, communing with the sun god. She is dressed in tennis whites, her dark, dry lips glossed with the blood of roses, her face, like a study in contrast, drained of all color.

Does one wear makeup to hide or to reveal oneself? I have often wondered. I used to rise at 6 a.m. even on weekends, to follow her at a safe distance because she would not suffer her fans, too close, and not once did she speak to us! I had taken to dressing all in white just like her, and from afar, one reporter wrote, we looked like little ducklings, all in a row, following mama duckling wherever she may end up. Usually, she ended up in the church on the hill and stared in stony silence at an abject Mother Mary, for what seemed like hours, perhaps seeking answers, perhaps not sure of the question.

⧗⧗⧗

With all that Captain had to offer, I was still a little out of my element. I could order the servants, drive to the shops, dress as I pleased. But that was the problem. The servants, as old as the apartment, operated like a well-oiled machine and did not need ordering. To be honest, they were also quite intimidating. They guarded their territory with shut down faces and politely took the ladle, the dust rag, the sewing out of my hands. *Madam should get some rest. What are we here for?*

And driving around in a luxurious car can lose its attraction pretty quickly in the congested traffic and smoldering Mumbai heat. Besides, nobody really looks inside your car, unless you are an actress or a celebrity.

I was sixteen, self-centered and with more time on my hands than ever before.

Naturally, I made up my mind, I needed a fabulous, new persona. It would have to be a cross between elegance – after all I was an engineer's wife -and mystery, I thought, dreamily. Staring at the sunrise from my kitchen window, or rather, the slow whitening of the buildings, touched by the sun's glow, a fond image of the actress and her morning strolls along the shore of my childhood home grew in my mind.

How unforgettable she was, persisting in memory like a Vermeer painting! I stood in front of my mirror and, on impulse, decided, I too would paint my lips in a cupid's bow, and gloss them in liquid mahogany, pull my hair in a chignon to show my swan neck and finally, drape myself in shades of white from neck to toe.

Little did I realize, in so doing, that my marriage was already off to an inauspicious start. When neighbors and vendors sniggered or pinched their noses as if I was a bad smell, I thought that perhaps rumors of the elopement had drifted down our street. Captain, bending down to bite my cherry lips, assured me it was all in my mind or that people were merely jealous. The fact that a new bride should not dress in widow-whites did not once occur to me, nor did anyone think to enlighten me.

Samir

I could brush my teeth till I tasted blood, take three showers a day and slick back my hair with a wet comb so that it shone like boot polish and stayed smooth as black tar, but Valerie Pinto, with a girl's nose for sniffing out losers, had me pegged for one, long before our eyes met across the chalk dusted classroom. Still, she cured me of my barking and I guess, that was a good thing.

Every woman I've ever met is like one of those sick, twisted Rubik's Cube puzzles. You try till you are ready to blow your brains out and still cannot get them straight.

There was this girl, Rita, who hinted she'd let any guy who owned a motorbike, go "all the way" with her. Back in the day, showing your tits meant going all the way. Obviously, we were too young to ride motorbikes, but the cops in that sleepy little hill station, no larger than a hamlet, usually looked the other way when it came to motor scooters. I figured if I bought myself one of those babies, I'd still be the only kid in school who could have a girl ride pillion. So, I chipped and chipped until I wore down Mother's resistance, and she bought me a Lambretta.

Rita, the fickle cow, chose to go out with the chess nerd, after everything I did for her. By the end of the term, they were diving in every available bush in the schoolyard to smooch until their lips turned purple.

Rita and Rubin

Sitting on a tree

K-I-S-S-I-N-G

It became a sort of class cheer that speared my dreams and ruined my waking hours.

Still. The scootie came in handy for beer runs for the older chaps, who high-fived me in full view of my classmates, and suddenly I went from "that crazy dog Samir" to Scooter Guy. No longer treated like a pariah, I could now insinuate myself into any group and choose the way I wanted to spend my free time.

Mostly, we did what adolescent boys do, everywhere in the world. We clumped together, feet dangling from the high wall separating school from the civilized world, our eyes glued on the voluptuous tribal women, who, untethered by convention, clad in skirts the size of dish towels cinched at the waists, swung their naked breasts every which way, setting us to groan and fumble in our shorts.

I loved reading literature, but it was a well-kept secret hidden between pornographic books to maintain a "cool" reputation. I suppose, at some level, I was trying to be my father's son. The one other hobby that got me some positive attention was my talent for doodling. Head bent studiously over a notebook, I let my teachers assume I was taking diligent notes. I even perfected the con, lifting my head and nodding intelligently from time to time, as they droned on and on about the phases of the moon, Pythagoras or colonial India. My ruse worked. Where others got picked to go up to the board or answer questions, I was left alone, with my notes, and, ostensibly, my ponderings.

By mid-afternoon each day, I had almost filled an entire notebook with my drawings. Over the years, the random characters I created turned into real comic book heroes with caped crusaders, pirates and ace detectives, their clipped speech and wild exclamations, "Whoa! Yippee! Gotcha!" borrowed heavily from old Westerns (washing over into my country a decade after they were first published) yelping out of speech balloons.

And for a few incredible minutes at the end of the school day, I was surrounded by fans clamoring for my comic books.

Once, after a particularly thrilling climax in "Meet me at Sundown," in which everyone in the story died in a shootout, hats, guns and body parts strewn graphically across the pages, except for the hero, of course, who, battered, scarcely alive (but still muscular and sexy) clawed his way toward the desert sun, the entire class showed its appreciation, lifting me spontaneously in the air, cheering, "Hero! Hero! Hero!"

Years later, I was doodling on a napkin as I waited for a distributor, I hoped to impress with my T-shirt samples, when a waitress sidled up to me, saw my artwork and asked, 'Is that a bird?'

I looked at her blouse, stretched at the chest, and thought how easily I could pop a button, with just one flick. 'Yes.' I said, crushing Captain Hook-nose, and dropping him into a bin. She smiled and bit her lower lip.

We dated for two years, Rama Jain and me.

She liked to play the delicate maiden, swooning at the slightest provocation, like one of those heroines in the Victorian era, with the tight corsets designed to cut off circulation. At first, I thought she was genuinely frail and did not mind. In fact, I enjoyed playing the chivalrous knight, carrying her to a taxi, surrounded by mobs, babbling *what happened here what happened here*, laying her on a couch and rubbing cologne on her forehead, waiting until she felt better.

But then her dramatics got expensive. It occurred to me her fainting spells came on whenever she was the least bit uncomfortable. Like when we were waiting for a bus. Or grabbing a meal in a restaurant without air-conditioning. Or when I got stall–instead of balcony tickets—for a movie.

As a woman living on the wrong side of the tracks, working as a waitress, surely, she ought to be made of sterner stuff? I found myself thinking resentfully.

Not only did Rama love playing the damsel in distress, the only time she was ever really turned on was when I was called to protect her precious virtue.

'There's this guy who's always following me,' she'd say with round, petrified eyes, or 'You will not believe what that toad said to me,' or 'That oaf just touched my arse. Aren't you going to do something?'

Then she would plant herself under the shade of a magnolia

tree and pretend I was a freaking gladiator in an arena of wolves and watch and applaud as I swore and spit and kicked the unsuspecting fool in the groin.

Of course, there were times when I got as good as I gave, and frisky though she was after the dog fight, a cracked rib and a black eye can put a real damper on one's sex life. Still, she did put out at least once a week, and it was the most action I'd ever had on the street, and in the bedroom.

In the two years that we went out together, Rama Jain made me give up cigarettes. My red T-shirt. My neon Nike sneakers and my silver bracelet. She said she hated my whistling. My obsession with chocolate. My taste in music. The way I parted my hair. Then, one day, she told me to stop doodling in public, as it was making her teeth itch. Unfortunately, she caught me at a bad time. Thanks to her, I was still reeling from the broken nose and cracked rib earned in a skirmish. Turning rabid, I told the mouth breathing bitch she could do you know what with her itching teeth. We were *finito*. Over. Done. No more, us! She pretended to swoon. I downed my drink, threw my share of the bill onto the table and left. It was a good eighteen months, maybe more, before I felt the urge to ask another woman out, making dead sure first that she was not living inside her own head playing Hema Malini or Raquel Welch or whoever.

9

Annika

After he returned from his father's funeral, a distracted Jack told us, over a working lunch, that he was not quite three when he was lifted out of his sleeping bag in the dead of night, by a man he'd never seen before, who told him he was his father, then clamped a hand over his mouth, and drove him to Mississippi, six hundred miles from home.

'I remember stretching out in the backseat of his clunker, using a spare sweatshirt for a blanket. He warned me not to raise my head, and as we barreled through the highway like we were being chased by the devil, the song blaring on the radio was "Hit the road, Jack, and don't you come back no more...." Bleary-eyed, snot running down my nose, I thought the song was a message for me.' He shook his head from side to side, struggling with emotion.

'Man! Ray Charles may be a god to some, but for me, he will always be a motherless hood – aiming a gun—you can't go home no more, no more, no more.' His voice died at the last mo.

Apparently, (in part two of the story, narrated at a subsequent lunch) Jack was left to stew in a trailer as hot as hell until a white lady with three kids playing in the dirt around the trailer park, spooked by a pair of burning eyes staring out of the barred windows, stood under his window and under the guise of casual chatter, learned little Jack was left to his own devices for eleven hours each day with a box of cheerios, a carton of milk and a bottle to pee in, while his father went out "to make us some money". She made an anonymous call, tipping off the cops.

The story, shocking and sad though it was, did not endear

Jack to his team. He was a paranoid, small-minded man who thought he rose in his own estimation each time he knocked us down, both privately and in public.

When I learned they are doing away with flex time and work- at-home, I decided to take the retirement package. It was generous and, as a bonus, I would never again have to see, hear or receive any written communication from *hit-the-road-Jack* again.

Besides, I had been teetering on a rope bridge for far too long. At any given moment, anything could happen to Ma. Despite my ambivalence, I knew, from a rational standpoint, she could not be left alone.

After the initial knee-jerk reaction, when I received the voice message from my administrator asking me to look into my benefits, any residual sadness I felt I attributed more to the breaking of a habit, an executive routine, than to breaking ties with former colleagues and proximal friends.

Of course, one cannot box up a good part of one's life and leave it on the dresser like a souvenir. There were moments, plenty of them, when you wouldn't want to peek inside my heart. On most days, I felt just fine. I could even look with affection at my laptop - no longer ticking like a bomb redlined with messages. In time, it became my friend, helpfully converting incoherent thought processes into cogent, publishable essays, screenplays and a book. But there were also days, I felt as if a piece of myself had gone missing; then, frustration turned to rage and bubbled like lava just below the surface. And the very traits that I reviled in others I found myself adopting.

⧗⧗⧗

'Listen to this poem,' I tell her, and read aloud:

When you are old

When you are old and grey and full of sleep,
And nodding by the fire, take down this book, And
slowly read, and dream of the soft look, Your eyes
had once, and of their shadows deep;

How many loved your moments of glad grace, And
loved your beauty with love false or true, But one

*man loved the pilgrim soul in you, And loved the
sorrows of your changing face*

*And bending down beside the glowing bars, Mur-
mur, a little sadly, how Love fled,
And paced upon the mountains overhead, And hid
his face amid a crowd of stars.*

- William Butler Yeats.

I sit back, my hands folded under my chin, hers clasped as if in prayer. Maybe her hearing is getting worse, I think. I draw closer. Her cheeks are wet. I brush the tears lightly with my finger even though she is skittish about being touched. But she allows the touch and with a rare dart of tenderness, takes my hand, presses it against her cheek and kisses my wrist. The silence is absolute. It is a moment I will carry like a candle to guide me through the impending storm.

Ma

A sudden downpour that cleared just as suddenly. Clouds pillowed across the sky, split at the seams, and feathered off. Soon, it was as if they never were.

When my first son died, still a child really, at the age of 27, my eyes dried up. I huddled in corners, afraid of the light.

In the darkness, I could pretend I did not exist. There was no difference between my body and my shadow. But one day, he stood before me, in the doorway, between my room and his. His child was nestled in his arms. *Look at us! Just look at us! He said.* He was exuberant. So, I rose and went to her room.

She was sitting on their bed, staring without expression at a photograph, harkening back to a time when he was alive and she undead. I picked up a brush and dragged it through her hair, braided it and secured the ends with a rubber band. I took her child and set her on her lap. I looked into her abandoned eyes, and she looked into mine. We made a pact then, to raise each other, his wife and I. No words were ever spoken. In the face of what had occurred, what are words? More salt in an ocean of salt.

Where are they now? Does she braid her own hair? Does she let her infant suckle at her breast? Why won't they let me see her? The pillow won't muffle my sobs.

My son, the living one, (God bless) is in the room. He is cradling my head and whispering, 'There... there...' I feel better. I tell him, I am fine now. I think I need to sleep.

Between the desire to sleep and the desire to rise, I barely get any rest at all. My tired eyes travel through the years, sliced into days, slivered into moments-the nausea of pregnancy, the unending school lunches, the daily drama of black eyes, torn shirts, broken ankles, the terror of malaria, the taunting of neighbors, the unfolding of travel plans and all the dying, the dying and the dying.

At last, my eyes alight on the bedside clock, which does not seem to have moved at all. But of course, like the earth, it too sticks to its cycle. Eventually the dark shapes on the windows will bloom into curtains flirting shyly with the breeze and dawn will part the shadows and brush stroke each corner of the room with timid gladness. And my living son will come to my room once again to wish me good morning, and say in his joking way, 'Another day, another dollar.'

He does not come. I'm told he had an early meeting. My daughter-in-law is in a chirpy mood. I try to show, by my silence, I'm not in the mood, but she wants to talk.

'Tell me a little about your early life. You know, when the kids were little. How did you manage with a full house? Six children plus mother-in-law!' she asks, her eyes wide with interest. But she could be faking.

My oldest daughter. What a piece of work she was. The sound of her voice blasting your eardrums! Embarrassing me daily with her intelligence and ready wit, and the way she carried on with the local boys even when she was older! She knew it was not seemly to get into tug-of-wars and wrestling matches and run around in short dresses, but she wore them, despite all my threats, ignoring the winks and wolf whistles, interested only in competing with her brothers, their friends and even the neighbors who invited her over for card games and Coca-Cola and pretended concern about me, 'Why is your father always away?' and covered their mouths, laughing at her, laughing at me.

In the front seat of the bicycle, almost in his lap, she rode home from school with a boy! Disappeared for hours, as if I did not know. I waited at the door, and when she came in, I smacked her face. She merely stood with that look in her eyes, bold and calm. The whiff of his smoke-filled breath on her hair followed her to her bedroom, and I knew he was inside her head, and inside her skin, and she was reckless. And that she would pay.

'We managed. I had a good maid. A good cook,' I said, adding, 'Her specialty was eggplant. She split the baby eggplants in the center, but still attached at the bottom, stuffed them with seasonings and ground peanuts and cooked them in a cast-iron skillet. Then she made saffron rice. She layered the rice with eggplants and served it on festivals.'

'Very nice! Did your daughters cook too?'

She, the older one, stole food. I always thought it was the washerwoman and fired more than one. Then I caught her red-handed. My own daughter, stealing food for him! Her lover! Perhaps it was romantic in a way, but I did not think so, then. I told her brothers. They wanted to whip her, but she was strong. 'I'll whip your backside from here to town,' she challenged them. Her father, too, did nothing. He said that raising the girls was my job. In the end, we had to marry her off to that boy, for better or for worse.

'No. They had to study. They did well in school,' I said.

'But my cook was good. She also made stuffed okra. Goatmeat...' 'You ate meat?' my daughter-in-law shrieked.

He loved goat meat. My fifth one. All those red, blood-soaked body parts. He liked it rare. Sometimes I think it was the meat that corrupted him. The hot blood of animals, running through his veins, is it any wonder he was always angry, always violent? Then he moved abroad and married and beat his wife. When I found out, I knew I would suffer. A woman who raises wife beater meets a bad death! Everybody knows that.

'Don't be ridiculous! Only the children ate meat,' I said sharply. The memories were beginning to pelt like rain on windows. My head ached. I wish she'd leave.

'And Adi's dad. What was he like?'

He was a decent man. A clever man. Settled firmly in his station, like a giant poplar, striving always for something higher, unchanged by circumstance and weather. I spent much of my life trying to make him proud. But our marriage is not a TV drama to be retold for her entertainment. I will take it to my grave.

I pretended not to hear her. How I felt, feel, about my husband is a private matter.

We were silent after that, each absorbed in her own thoughts.

You cannot revisit the people who dwell in your past.

They are like the soft scuttling sounds you hear in the attic. Or like footprints in spaces that were once favored haunts. They are elusive, and illusive. You have to let them be. Occasionally, they rise like dust in an unexpected storm. I tamp them down, so they cannot upset a hard-won balance.

On occasion, someone, your son, your daughter, brings them up, in conversation.

You speak of them for a while, and then, even the remembrance becomes parrotlike. Like the mantras you recite the moment you wake up or just before you go to bed in another language. To an unknowable God.

I turned my head to the window and worried the itch in my scalp. She left at last.

Malavika

This morning, one of the little monsters had the temerity to send a ball crashing through my kitchen window, and now I've cut my hand, collecting all the sharp little shards, some gleaming like diamonds, some hiding in the pattern of my floor. Just when I think I've got them all, I find one more, treacherously close to my big toe, or poking out like a tooth behind the door or stuck in the strainer in the sink! Of course, I won't make a scene. As I recall, Mr. Jolly's favorite punishment, perfected on his children from wife number one, was to strip his kids down to their skivvies and have them sit in the parking area to be humiliated by neighbors and passersby. Not surprisingly, his parenting style, with family number two, has not evolved. And like their half brothers and sisters, they are turning into vicious little creatures, disobedient and perverse.

One daughter, for whom the second Mrs. Jolly has a bit of a soft spot, has been sent off to a boarding school in the hope that she will return to them transformed – an elegant, marketable version of the crude template.

But who am I to mock? I was never a good mother. I carried my pregnancy like excess weight I would have to shed. Samir, sensing my reluctance even as an infant, writhed in discomfort and finally found reassurance in Captain's solid arms. When he was older, it did not get easier.

I came from a family of girls. Little boys, with their penchant for scraped knees, rowdy tumbling and grimy shoes, leaving trails of dirt on the living room floor, require patience, tolerance, a sense of humor. Qualities sadly absent from my DNA. Captain, I suppose, made up for my deficiencies. He was a sly, cautious man who made sure to hide his deviance from his son and showed him only the side that was tolerant, paternal and responsible.

When our trial separation got ugly, then uglier, we bundled Samir off to boarding school. He seemed to be doing so well, I thought it might be best to let him stay on after the divorce came through. Captain did not disagree. Most children single out one parent to blame. There cannot be two villains in one plot. My son chose me, and tiresome though his relentless blaming and shaming is, I've never faulted him for that. Next to his father, I was a veritable troll –ineffectual and unavailable. But little does he know, for I haven't told him, that his old man has eaten him out of his inheritance and is, right this moment, swatting flies on a deck chair in *Pulau Ubin,* with his chubby new wife and two bratty boys, with rhyming names and matching fat pants.

Just to be clear, we never did get to Singapore, after we eloped. A misunderstanding about the terms, according to Captain. He thought he had negotiated a full-time job with a signing bonus and benefits until he read the small print in the contract. He did not find the terms favorable and kept his old job while we were married.

I moved into Captain's apartment in a seedy gray building above a row of grocery stores. Every apartment faced an identical twin within shouting distance. But all the curious eyes in the world did not deter the many nimble thieves in the vicinity from clambering up the water pipes and into our homes through this open access. As a security measure, the residents had the balcony enclosed with wrought iron bars as well as wooden shutters that locked from the inside. Entering the living room, therefore, was pretty much like entering a walk-in coffin, and had it not been for the bright tube lights left on from dawn to dusk, many a housewife would've thrown herself out of the window in sheer despair.

Glancing up from the sidewalk, after these dreary renovations, one got the eerie feeling that all the residents had vanished, barricaded out of their homes by the very thieves they tried so tenaciously to keep out.

The bedrooms, too, suffered a lackluster fate, since curtains were never drawn, for privacy reasons. Outside the windows, buses, rickshaws, cars, milk and produce trucks groaned and shuddered, the cacophony of sounds making it impossible to have a phone conversation.

I had to turn off the television, unplug the stereo system and order the servant girl to operate through gestures. My ears needed rest and could not take even her mild patter. Suffice it to say, that noise was my enemy. Followed by a dismal lack of ventilation and little natural light.

'But I thought we were rich! Why are we living in this grubby old place?' I stamped my feet.

'This is Mumbai. Every street is narrow, and every apartment building is dark and grubby, unless you are lucky enough to live on oceanfront property, like your dear daddy,' Captain taunted. Then he sought to cheer me up and twinkled, 'Put up with it for a while. We will soon be moving to a posh new location in town with two sets of elevators and a rooftop pool and where not just vehicles but even human sounds and smells require ...'

I missed the tail end of his speech as a juggernaut truck shook the building with its farts.

'When?' I begged. 'I really do not relish giving out this address to my snooty relatives.'

'In the near future,' he said, letting his eyebrows bob with mystery, 'Meanwhile, not every man is able to afford the City Club and a lovely car, my dear, so count your blessings.'

I suppose he was right. I drove around in the Chevrolet, never having to worry about the price of gas, we could order meat and pie any day of the week, and we did have lifetime membership at the best club in town. Not too many people I knew could say that. So, for a while, it was enough. It was acceptable.

Samir

I had long since outgrown the acne-and-adenoids stage and even filled out a little. My parents' divorce came through, but the settlement, not for a while. When it finally did, my mother found herself quite comfortably off, if not wholly comfortable with her new status. She went through phases, as far as I could tell, either living like a nun cloistered in her apartment or screwing every dubious character on the street that checked out her arse and invited her over for a drink. It couldn't have been easy for her, I suppose. But it was not her change of circumstances that I obsessed about.

When they split up, I felt as if I were slowly being leached of blood, or a giant hand was pressing upon my chest, squeezing out life, one breath at a time. I did not know there was a name for what I had. Grief is not a word that came up often in my Cowboys and Indians universe.

What I found was that there was no way to circumvent the pain. But at some point, I did find a way to camouflage it. Rage, I discovered, was a powerful weapon. Focus on the criminal, not the crime, and suddenly, a whole other world opens up, a world where you are the perpetrator, not the victim, and you can, as the song says, be the hammer, not the nail.

It was years before I stopped dwelling on my mother's sins against the family and paid attention instead to my own fevered longings. By the time I met Sherri-with-the-legs, I was reasonably well groomed, well dressed and well over the waitress who disliked everything about me, especially my doodling.

Sherri-with-the-legs. Millions of youth will forever be indebted to the Art of Living courses popping up all over Mumbai like toddy shacks for the spirit. Gullible, wealthy women, bored with luxury, intent on being seen at the trendiest joints attended them in droves, and naturally, we chased the scent.

She was sitting cross-legged on the floor mat that first time I spotted her, her mini skirt skimming her thighs. All male eyes riveted to her knees; her own eyes fixated on the speaker. So, of course, I dropped the tepid glass of mango *lassi* that I was really not supposed to bring inside the meeting hall, I was sipping thirstily, and licked my lips instead, imagining her long creamy legs wrapped languorously around my neck in the backseat of my car, some steamy afternoon.

'What do you think?' I asked her without preamble, pointing my chin toward the raised platform. I'd scoped the joint out and finally found a spot outside the third exit in the back of the hall, closest to the ladies' room, where, judging by the coffee flask warming her hands, I assumed correctly she would pay a visit at some point during the break.

'Oh, fantastic of course! I learn so much every single time, don't you?' she said, underscoring every other word for emphasis, then lifting her chest and exhaling an overflow of positive energy into the universe.

I smiled quietly, going for the sage effect, and keeping my eyes anywhere except the rise and fall of her perky breasts. And that's how we connected on the earthly plane.

I am not a good man. I am the first to admit that. But with Sherri, I really did make an effort. She was young, but not naïve, smart, but not pretentious, and had this way of cutting through the bull shit that made an exciting contrast to her polka-dotted girlishness.

'Let's go for a beer. How are you for cash, today?' she'd ask, in her forthright manner, and there was no way a man could hem and haw. By the second or third week after we began dating, the desire to get between her legs, although always there like an itch that needed to be scratched, was surpassed by my longing to know her better.

To keep up with her, I began making forays to bookstores

and libraries, devouring literature like a repentant philanderer returning to his first love. *"Is my son a dunce, Principal Spencer?"* My mother's voice still burned through my brain.

Sherri would never have to wonder, I swore to myself.

And when I was with her, I delved into her life the way one delves into a puzzle, piecing it together with questions: Did you wear braids in school, or pigtails? Do you like chocolate or caramel? Jane Austen or J.D. Salinger? Cricket or tennis? Chinese or Mughlai? Europe or the United States?

And no matter how she replied, I was enthralled.

In spite of my unsophisticated ways, I began making some headway.

She confided to me one day, her eyes wide with remembered pain, that she once overheard a particularly lascivious friend of the family say about her, *'The kid's a plain-Jane, but those legs, woof!'*

'And look at you, now!' I said, touching her face. I think she fell a little in love with me, then.

Sherri became my temple and my mosque. My Everest and my Ganga. When she was not by my side, I was restless. I couldn't sleep, traversing city streets at night to walk off my insomnia. During the day, when she was not by my side, I stalked her. This happened slowly, over a period of time, and it was not what I thought I was doing. I just wanted to get close to her. Sherri had a huge network of friends, male and female, and often made plans on the spur of the moment. When she was "out" two consecutive weekends, I started getting antsy. And so, it began.

I knew all the best places, the trees, the walls, the ledges where I could crawl behind, over, or on and spy undisturbed, with a pair of binoculars I had received, years ago, as a gift from Mother.

From the moment she hit the alarm radio, pushed one lock out of her dream laden eyes, filled her mouth with toothpaste, rinsed and towel-dried the droplets glistening in her hair, wiped the misty bathroom mirror to check her face, first one side, then the other, until she slipped into her frilly white panties, her little blue dress with the hem raised to the legally allowed limit, I devoured her with my eyes.

I followed her into restaurants, wearing her sunglasses pushed high up like a headband, sipping on cola, nibbling on a cauliflower fritter, balanced exquisitely between thumb and index finger.

I followed her goofing about with her friends hiking up their skirts, extending one leg forward like tramps to thumb a ride and then cheering in triumph as bikers swerved and motor cars screeched to a halt. And I thought she was magnificent.

I followed her once to the university and saw a white sports car slow down, and then come to a hard stop, right before Sherri entered the school gates. And this moment, one might say, is where my romance took a bit of a turn.

The man who swung out of the car, debonair as Sean Connery, greeted her with far more enthusiasm than seemed warranted. Sherri, too, hugged him like a long lost relative and no longer seemed in a hurry to get to class.

He had on a pair of loafers, black jeans and a dark tee shirt that I could tell from a few hundred yards made my entire wardrobe look like *raddi* from factory outlets.

It was not his sartorial sense, however, but the way he threw his head in the air, the casual way he offered to light her cigarette, and even the way he stood, exuding self-assurance with a wide ship captain's stance, oblivious of the gawking crowds (not too many sports cars were seen in those days) that rendered me speechless. Any girl would smilingly give up her weekends, cancel on her girlfriends and even sacrifice the needs of her family for a man with such poise, I thought, bristling with envy. Suddenly, I was convinced that if I were to make Sherri mine, in any meaningful kind of way, I had to get inside this man's skin.

It was hard, neglecting her, but I told myself that it was imperative that I do so. Now, it was the man I stalked. I followed him to his club and watched him drink, (whiskey sour). I hid in a booth way back, in the discotheque and watched him dance – like a marionette but smiling; followed him with my binoculars, to the beach and to the park, where he sauntered easily as a tiger in his natural habitat, and once more, I was filled with awe. Then I went home and practiced my *Bond, James Bond*, in the mirror.

It was a few weeks before I was satisfied with my transformation.

I called Sherri at last. She was excited to hear from me, scolded me for having been aloof and said she wanted to see me soon, the very next day if possible.

It did not go well. Sherri was a sharp girl, and not one to spare your feelings when she felt strongly enough about something.

'What's with you?' she asked.

'What?'

'The weird laugh. The stiff posture. The *whiskey sour, please!*' she said, with an exaggerated smirk. 'It's corny. Snap out of it.'

'I thought you like your men a little classy...'

'My men! What men? Have you been following me?'

'Of course not! What do you take me for?'

She stopped giving me the third degree, but the fact that she seemed so spooked made me wonder, if at some level, she was aware of my sorry arse lurking in the shadows. In any case, I abandoned my post behind the magnolia tree, the bush, and the statuary. For a while.

Sherri was the fire. I was a lost creature, a moth, drawn bit by bit to her all-consuming flame. I couldn't help myself. A week later, I picked up where I left off, following her right to her doorstep. From behind her magnolia tree, I watched her ring the doorbell, hand her bag to a maid and disappear in the cool confines of her villa. Then, I slipped behind some marble statuary, and caught her in the dining room, setting the table, knives to the right, forks to the left, napkins folded precisely, the tip of her tongue sticking out with the effort. Eyes peeled, I imagined sitting beside her, awash in wonder as she ate with appetite, talked with gusto and raised a loving glass to her parents. At some point, during the meal, her eyes looked deep into mine, and she touched my thigh under the table. I sought her little hand and held it tightly. We were a unit unto ourselves, self- sufficient, indivisible. Or so I imagined.

I was spying on her one day and was spotted. The watchman, who could pass for King Kong, and familiar with trespassers, beat me black and blue before prodding me like an animal with a thick stick, toward the front gate, where Sherri's father stood waiting, clothed in judicial robes! I thought I'd died and ended up in a

Western comic of my own making. I had no idea he was "the law".

I told the old sod I knew his daughter, and she had no problem with my "looking". In retrospect, I guess it was the wrong thing to say, to make it sound as if she were somehow complicit in my sordid little fantasy. He let me go, seeing as I was already beaten to a pulp, but not before rounding up the staff and telling them to keep a lookout for this pervert and to call the police if I so much as glanced at his house. Then with the air of one who, despite his line of work, preferred to rise above the fray, he went indoors.

The next day, Sherri told me her parents were sending her abroad to live with a cousin.

I asked her if she would ever forgive me. I told her I meant no harm, that I was merely trying to create a photo album and… and… gift it to her. I improvised, frantically. She pretended to be convinced. 'Perhaps someday,' she said, sadly. But something was broken; I could tell by the look in her eyes. In place of affection, I now saw fear, interlaced with a feeling akin to revulsion. I knew Sherri-with- the-legs was yet another chapter in my pitiful book that I would have to tear out.

10

Annika

'*Music,*' Father would declare, in a tone that established in no uncertain terms, he was Judge and Jury, '*is a form of worship. But dancers belong in harems!*'

Naturally, we did not argue, however outrageous his pronouncements. For one thing, arguing with adults was considered a punishable offence. For another, having said his piece, he usually strode out of the room, nostrils flaring and shoulders drawn back combatively, thereby slamming the door on any reasonable discussion.

Needless to say, we were denied dance lessons.

I shake my head in a conscious effort to dispel the sorry memories and allow myself to be seduced by Mr. Manna Dey. His voice is like oak leaves shaking off the rain. I feel a twinge. Surely it must be joy! For yes, there was a time I still found happiness in ordinary things – a glass marble with a white eye winking in the light; the way the sunlight filtered through my window grille, making half- moon shapes on the floor; a myna bird, rocking insouciantly on the branch of a tree, poking its yellow beak at the squirrels. Manna Dey draws a last note and sighs into silence. The past, I think pensively, intrudes, sometimes like a lullaby to help you sleep. At other times, it is a vulture, pulling at red meat.

In my dreams, I am lean and strong. History is not yet written in the corner of my eyes.

On impulse, I press restart and sing along with Mr. Dey, and for the length of the song, I am hopeful again.

Rain drumbeats on the roof, susurrates in the trees, snakes

down the window panes, and fills my heart with sweet contentment. Finally, some relief from the oppressive heat of the past few days.

It falls continually, effortlessly, hour after hour until the sheets of rain begin to feel as normal as nightfall, and a clear sky becomes the anomaly. I listen to the rhythm for a while, and then get restless.

My pink boots beckon. I pull them out of the utility closet and check anxiously for leaks, putting my hand right inside the leg of each boot and poking around for holes. Thankfully, they are just fine. With everything going on with Ma, I have not had time to shop for galoshes. Briefly, I remember, she's been hinting for a new pair of slippers, but the very thought of driving her to the store, finding parking and wheeling her across the graveled path to the shoe outlets makes me shudder. She will wince, hold the lower half of her face, rock in silent pain – her trigeminal nerve set off by the bumps –and then complain of the noise, the crowds and the air conditioning –*No thanks!*

We have tried it before you see. She gets increasingly anxious, asks me to make a choice for her and when I do, I can see the skepticism written all over her face. Once home, she will examine the slippers carefully for color, the stitching and the heel, as if, in truth, it was I who was being re-examined, and of course, I and the slippers come up short. She will not wear them. Ever! I remember how frustrating it felt, this waste of time, this pursuit of perfection, be it in a mitten or a hairpin or a shoe, her ungracious rejection of my many gifts tucked under her bed, still in their original wrapping.

At last, overburdened with the demands of work, I learned to ignore the rebuffs and, except for a preemptive twinge at the subject of shopping, moved on.

I take advantage of the fact that Adi is working from home and decide to give myself a couple of hours off. Whistling optimistically, I hasten to the kitchen and literally throw an apple, a jar of peanut butter, a granola bar, and a tub of Greek yogurt into an insulated lunch bag.

With a guilty wave to Old Coot staring fixedly from his window seat like a seasoned voyeur, I leave for the park.

In the parking lot, there is just one other car. Judging from the way they are steaming the windows, I gather they are kids from the high school across the field. I park, facing my car away from the lovers, and let myself out silently. With every squishy step, as far from the tennis court and noisy playground as possible, I shrink in age, and soon I'm stomping on leaves, worms and other rot in a guilty, gleeful, six-year-old way. The fact that my boots are getting streaked with mud only adds to the illusion of being a child when dirt was synonymous with play.

I find my pine tree, settle on the park bench with a happy sigh and dream about those childhood years when I ate and slept and played, secure in the knowledge of my sister's knobby arms. We did everything together, Malavika and I - free as the birds cutting across an ever-changing sky, brown as berries from chasing chickens, feral cats, rubber balls, and each other. Hand in hand, we went inside when the sun sank tiredly to the ocean floor, and streetlights made monsters bloom under our feet. Of course, once she was fourteen all that changed.

I was no longer sure that she loved me most.

From under the wobbly canopy of trees, I notice the downpour has eased a little. It tapers off to an unenthusiastic trickle and soon stops completely. I eat my hastily packed lunch.

My thoughts soon turn to the present when I get that eerie feeling of being watched. Perhaps it's a doe, and not a perv gazing at me with lustful eyes, lurking behind a bush. I sit as still as possible. I hear a rustle, but no doe. The eerie feeling won't go away. Then I see her.

Gone-Mother, staring out of a ridged and puzzled red pine tree, dark holes for eyes, following me. Every leaf on the tree is trembling. Every hair on my body is a pin prick. I have been seeing her, for many years, but lately, she seems everywhere, at once, impelling me towards someone or some end. *But what?*

I jump up, shake the excess rainwater off, and start running clumsily, pushing my fingers through my ponytail and unclamping the sticky, ropey mass without slowing my pace. I don't stop until I'm within touching distance of my car. It's solid, cave-like exterior calms me down, almost at once. I use my scarf to towel dry my hair. My hands and feet have turned to ice. I must get home. Blocking out all disturbing images, I turn on the engine. It purrs reassuringly. I warm myself with visions of hot cocoa.

⧗ ⧗ ⧗

Inexplicably, my mind turns to Ma. How does Adi's mother handle boredom? Does she even get bored, or is she so focused on making it from one end of the room to the other, without incident that there is no space for boredom in her psyche? In a fit of magnanimity, I stop at a crafts store and get a few things I'd read in some blog that helped stimulate and excite the Memory Impaired.

Weighed down with a tub of magnetic upper-case alphabet letters, a jewelry-sized box full of nickel-sized buttons, coloring books with a pack of washable crayons (so that they don't roll off a lapboard or table) and a pack of cards, I can scarcely make it to the cashier.

I forego the doll, the set of Dominoes and some jigsaw puzzles for the moment. I don't think she is ready for the puzzles, and she hasn't regressed to the point where she might enjoy playing with a doll. At the last second, and because they are right on the cashier's aisle, I get a few balls of yarn in different colors and a new activity pad that turns any flat surface into a non-sticky place for food, books, etc.

I stand in the driveway still reluctant to go in. The clean brick exterior of my house looks inviting. Daffodils and azaleas, all spiffed up by the rain, burgeon in the front yard. Still. I know there is something wrong. Homes, like people, exude an aura. Tension, like a tremor, ruffles the curtains of her window. I decide to leave the activity bag in the backseat, for now. It feels wrong to enter a crisis situation with a cheery bag of shopping. In any case, there is no hurry. One has to assess the situation and wait for low-ripple calm before bringing up the topic of structured playtime.

'Come in, come in, I am with Ma. She's not doing…'

Aiieeeeeeeeeeee! A shriek lacerates the air, followed by a paroxysm of expletives. I feel my skin prickle for the second time this day.

… very well,' Adi finished. I nod, pull off my sodden boots as fast as possible, and leave them on the front steps to dry. They flop on their sides, muddy water trickling through the insoles like tears streaked with mascara.

Then I go to her room bracing myself for whatever is in store for me.

Adi is a big man, I remember thinking. Or perhaps it is his oversized sweatshirt and sweatpants that make him look as if he is looming over his mother, who, pinned to her bed, hugging her knees drawn tightly to her chest, her eyes squeezed shut, is rocking fiercely in a steady cradle-and-child motion, as if it is all that is needed, this constant, metronome movement, to get through the hours. Two more things jump out at me. One, Adi was holding, with a defeated look on his face, his mother's pants. And two, the fact that she wasn't wearing any.

'I couldn't get them on. She kept kicking me. She's never done that. She's wet herself!' he shouted. Adi always shouts when he is frustrated. She seemed to shrivel before my eyes.

'I told you, you need to let *me* help her with those. It is embarrassing to dress her. You could have waited a few minutes.'

'I help her every day! I am NOT embarrassed.'

'Not you. She is! And you needn't shout the fact ... that she wet herself... it's humiliating for her.'

'I think I know my mother better than you,' he says frostily. I pick up her pants. They are soft, silky.

'I'll take care of this. Please leave.'

He walks out, his back a little hunched, like a scolded child.

The room springs back to its normal size.

What galvanizes some people into action usually slows me down. My mind needs to process the onslaught of information before I can determine what to do with it.

So, twisting the silky fabric between thumb and index finger, I sit on Ma's chair and simply watch her for a bit, thinking things through.

Exhausted from the tug-of-war, the rant, her fear of the hulking presence, she rocks silently, back and forth, back and forth, with a faraway look in her eyes, as if she is rocking back and forth in time. After a while, she loses momentum, comes to a halt and is back to the present with a creak and a sigh. Now, she sees me, and a flicker of fear, then recognition, and then tiredness flits across her face like a slideshow. She shuts her eyes and sighs again.

'Are you cold?' I ask her softly.

She nods, her eyes still shut.

I move forward slowly, not wanting to startle her in this under-ether state.

I lay the pants like a coverlet on her naked legs. Let her feel the warm fabric against her skin.

'I will help you with these now.'

'Aaaah!'

I want to use my hand as a lever to raise her a few inches so I can push the pants up to her waist, but she doesn't get what I am trying to do and turns to face the wall. I shake the pants over her legs to remind her. Something clicks in her mind, and she turns slowly around. Finally, I have her dressed.

As I step away, I feel her touch on my arm. From the box of tissues by her pillow, she picks one. It is folded neatly into a square. She presses the tissue into my hand and balls my fingers to keep her gift safe.

'Is it enough?' she whispers anxiously. 'I have more.'

Carefully, she picks another square, holds it out for me. I realize she thinks she is giving me cash.

'No. You've given me more than enough. Thank you.'

She puts the square back in the tissue box. Smiles sweetly and draws a blanket over her head,

'Get some rest,' she says.

I throw her wet pants, lying in a heap on the bathroom floor, into the wash, and take deep chesty breaths, to regulate my breathing. But it's only after a hot bath and two cups of ginger tea that I feel myself recover from the vagaries of the day.

Ma

My son got me a new pillbox. He sits by my side with a handful of pills. The box is plain and transparent, but it has many slots. It can hold all sorts of nuts and candies, I think dreamily. He puts two little pills in one slot. A large white one in another. Three colored ones in another. The slots are labeled with the days of the week - Mon, Tue, Wed, etc. and also by time – 7 a.m. Noon. 3 p.m. 9 p.m. I memorize the shape, color, and number of pills so that I will know if *she* mixes them up.

Uncle's visit was a highpoint in our lives. Much to New Ma's chagrin, (she thought it was unseemly), his first order of business, after removing his dusty sandals at the threshold, was to throw me in the air, put me down with a thud and ask me to shut my eyes. Then he would, with great ceremony, press a candied nut in my hand. Never once did he arrive empty handed!

He was a tall man and had to bend his head so that his turban did not get caught in the low hanging ceiling fan. He always asked for water and drank thirstily out of a silver tumbler reserved just for him. His breath was stale, and his clothes reeked of foreign lands. His face was red as the desert sun.

Word of his arrival drew in other relatives, and soon there weren't enough chairs to go around. He greeted them all in a loud and excited fashion, then dried up suddenly, like an old camel, and retired to his room, letting us kids sniff and prowl with delicious anticipation, outside his door. Refreshed after his nap and clad in clean, white lounging clothes, he was finally ready to give us our present. At last, he put his bounty before us, smiling with uneven teeth, as New Ma kept up a tirade of *why so much? You always do too much* -dates, cashews, raisins, figs, pistachios, each precious treat in its own paper nest, in a double-decker box with many compartments.

What an abundance of riches, for kids who dined on the same old overcooked vegetables and sweetened milk every day of the week! I'd wrap my figs and dates in a kerchief to share with my friend. On lazy summer afternoons, she'd grab my hand and urge me to climb the tree in her yard. Swinging our legs, from a sturdy branch, we'd spy on the *gori* madam, on the other side of a wall, fanning herself on her porch in her shapeless, flowery dress, her naked legs dotted with angry, red, mosquito bites, her feet resting carelessly on a table meant for tea and lemonade.

Chewing our sweet fruit with loud sucking noises, we would make up stories about the white lady's sad, childless life. One day, we told each other, racked with loneliness, she would knock on our doors, and beg our parents to give her their daughter. I know, my father would not want to give me up, even though he felt sorry for the madam, but stepmother would pretend to wipe her eyes and then happily negotiate her price. In the end, she would sell me for the price of a cow, I stated, with exaggerated melancholy.

We made a pact, my girlfriend and I, that we would not be separated, for we were like real sisters. We would insist the white madam adopt us both. Not to be outdone by New Ma's haggling, she would eventually adopt two girls, for the price of one, we decided. Then we giggled at the happy ending.

With my tea this afternoon, Anika brings me some dried dates. They are seedless, or perhaps she split them open and removed the pit. Even before I've put them in my mouth, I can taste the heavenly sweetness.

Those impossibly delicious moments, like shimmering notes of music, winding through a sunbeam. How then, to ask for death, when somewhere in mouth and memory, and the brain within your heart, such happiness exists? I thank her politely, but keep my voice toneless and my face without expression. *A woman must never show too much emotion.* Everybody knows that.

Malavika

The sun was going down. I fixed my eyes on the horizon, watched the ocean change colors as it drank from his light. A taxi drove up the ramp, distracting me from my reverie. Slowly, painfully, a rotund shape, like a G. K. Chesterton caricature come to life, emerged out of the cab.

It was Shroff. He had a stroke a few months ago and had only just recovered the use of his legs. He stood with the cab door open, managed to navigate his hand to his trouser pocket, and draw out his wallet. The cabbie had his engine running. Shroff held the wallet like a living thing that kept trying to slide out of his recalcitrant hand. I wanted to look away, but my eyes were drawn to his flailing fingers like a magnet. I think I stopped breathing.

The cabbie turned off the engine and stepped out. He did not want to seem impatient, but one could tell he was champing at the bit, from the way he shifted from one foot to the other. My eyes went from the minute hand on my watch to poor Mr. Shroff and his right hand, fluttering on the wallet. It took him full six minutes to withdraw the required amount to pay the cabbie. His index and middle finger stuck together like glue, the remaining fingers trying to maintain their hold on the wallet and remove the bills at the same time. The cabbie checked the bills carefully, fished out the change, and held it out to Shroff.

Taking the money required a few more painstaking maneuvers. Finally, Shroff captured the coins with his left hand and dropped the change inside his wallet with the unruly fingers of his right. At last, the transaction was complete. A couple more minutes were needed to command his brain to turn his legs around and position them toward the stairway to his apartment.

The cabbie slammed his door and drove off. Unfortunately, the engine backfired as he left, startling poor Mr. Shroff out of his wits. He looked ready to pass out.

I leaned over the railing and asked him if he was all right. He looked up. He did not answer. There was no trace of recognition in his cloudy eyes.

Once, he was my healer, my true guide. How fortuitous that the servant was busy and Mother asked me to get a measure of starter yogurt from Mrs. Shroff! How lucky that I agreed instead of rambling off to play with my tomboy friends!

I knocked, but instead of waiting at the door or following Mrs. Shroff to the kitchen, I stood gaping at the shelves and shelves of books lining one wall.

Mr. Shroff wandered in from his bedroom, saw the transfixed look on my face, and gently pulled out a copy of *A Tale of Two Cities*. 'Here, try this one!' he said.

I remember the book well because it was the first of many gifts from his shelves.

With his help, I endured adolescence, Mother's desperate departure, Father's compulsive, goading violence, little Anika's mute longing and, to some extent, the scandal that followed me upon my return, like a cheap perfume.

'*Yes, please don't ever smile. The world is not yet ready for your dimples.*' Or '*Oho, someone is upset. Did the sun not rise in the east, this morning?*' he would tease. His jokes were always the same, familiar and outdated as a weekend sweater, the Sunday comics, the Radio Hour, but his eyes twinkled with such merriment, of course, I had to smile. Then he would cover his face in mock agony and cry out, '*Help! Blinded by a pair of dimples!*'

And steer me toward the bookshelf, my inner sanctum.

Shroff took a deep breath and looked down in order to negotiate the wrist strap of the cane stuck under his left arm, to his hand. That accomplished, he pressed the pronged base to the ground for support and took the stairs, his head bowed.

I sat on the balcony for a long time, lost in melancholy, staring at the space he filled and then emptied, with a wheeze and a shuffle.

Soon, this body too will falter, and its outline blur with the shaky brush of time.

And when the sun goes down, startling the leafy trees with a final spasm of light, and we shut our eyes for what might be the final time, will we remember with a sigh, only our last acts – *I filled the new prescription, I paid the gas bill* or reflect on the most significant one? *I was a true leader, I was a true lover.*

And if we do wake to see another morn, shall we simply press on, like my dear, dear Shroff—one wobbly foot at a time—until we are patted down like divots in the turf? Yes, of course, we shall. What choice do we have?

Meanwhile, a persistent, atonal ringing in my ears sent me scrambling to the bedroom, where the phone and possibly, the caller, was going berserk. Reluctantly, I drew my mind to the here and now.

Samir

I ran into my father, quite literally, in the lobby of the Sheraton where I stood waiting for yet another distributor to change the course of my life. I had an appointment for 3 p.m. and arrived thirty minutes early. By 4.15 p.m., even I had to admit, he was a no- show. Lighting a smoke and dragging my fat hold-all behind me, like a passed out drunk, I was heading for the men's room and missed seeing the old man until he nearly tripped over my bag and sidestepped with a jig.

'Oy, watch it, son!' he said.

'You watch it, old …' I stopped in my tracks. That soft professorial voice, that owlish stare behind round metal framed Ray- Bans. It was him.

'It's you,' I swallowed.

His eyes widened, and then actually filled once doubt changed to certainty. He extended his right hand, changed his mind and tried to go for a hug. Repelled, I backed off a little.

'Samir, how fortuitous!' he said. *I bet the old fart uses vocabulary words just to compensate for his non-existent penis.*

'Ha!'

'What are you doing here?'

'I had a meeting.'

'A meeting!' he repeated in a bewildered sort of way. I wondered if he was going senile.

'And what are you doing here?' I mimed his tone.

'I have a dinner app …' he looked past me. A girl, young, in a black leather mini skirt and a satiny green blouse, pale under her smile, was tottering towards us. A small, round Band-Aid just below her right knee, where she'd probably cut herself shaving, looked as if it was coming unstuck. Her legs, despite the full display of thighs, seemed disproportionately short. Her heels looked worn. Both her lips and her nails were painted hooker red.

"Well, enjoy the appetizer," I said, leering and blowing a smoke ring in her face, watching with malice as she turned crimson. My father took a step forward, then backed off, defeated.

I snorted and headed for the washroom where I turned on the faucet full force and splashed cold water on my face. I stared at the shock of black hair, the hastily trimmed beard and the raging- bull eyes. *I look like a freakin' mass murderer.*

When I came out, they were walking furtively toward the elevators, his hand on the small of her back, in the direction I needed to go. There was a very real possibility I would catch up with him and do something seriously damaging, like breaking the hold-all full of swatches, on his dumb, fucking head. Instead, I turned and almost sprinted down another exit.

11

Annika

She is on her rocking chair, quiet as a mouse. Her eyes stray from the wall to the window and back. It must be no fun, cooped up like that. I wonder why she is sitting in the dark. With a start, I remember her legs have been jittery of late. She's probably too afraid to get up and switch on the light and too proud to ask! I switch on the light. She blinks and swallows.

I must try to be nicer. I will be nicer. Perhaps In time, we will learn to weather her manic rants with equanimity. Maybe even treat them like a distraction during those long, wintry months when the afternoon gloom merges seamlessly with the dusk. And, really, she is so malleable in the aftermath of the storm. Like a pallid house plant, subsisting resignedly on filtered light.

I put an extra spoon of milk into her tea. I slice up a banana plating it so that it retains its shape. A dash of cinnamon sugar cannot hurt, I think, and sprinkle it on. It gleams like velvet dust. I carefully remove the pits and heap the cherries in the curve of the banana. I slather some cream cheese on her lightly browned toast, making sure to cut off the crust and place it on another plate.

I go to her room and turn on the television. I point the remote.

'Any preference?'

She does not answer.

I set the tray in front of her. She looks away in disgust. I walk softly out of the room and slam the tray onto the center island.

I clean off the banana mush with a damp paper towel.

I think perhaps we can go out to lunch but remember the last time we took her out, soon after one of her hospital visits.

Having been confined to a bed for days, floating in a medicated haze, she was frightened by any sudden street noise, harsh light, or even being in the proximity of strangers.

Her son held her hand as we walked to a table, making reassuring sounds along the way, squeezing her dry fingers. But in the restaurant, the screeching of chairs, the clang of dishes, the scurry of waiters, other movements merged and melded into one giant, shapeless threat, and striking her forehead with her fist, she whimpered she had to get away, her head was splitting.

She picks up her knitting half-heartedly. The knitting needles that were once an extension of her hands feel like a weight, now that her eyes are weak, and arthritis cramps her fingers.

When she first came to live with us, I thought knitting was just her way of keeping busy. Years later, I realized, she was more than simply knitting; she was weaving the ones she loved into her fold, through yarn and needle, warmth, and color.

The hours ticked, her needles clicked. Like a child who rushes through vegetables to get to dessert, her knitting fingers flew towards the finale.

Slowly, with the length of the scarf and the width of the sweater, her reward took shape.

The goal was before the temperature hit 40° F, sweaters, throws, bonnets and scarves should wind around the necks, stretch across the chests and yarn forward into the lives of others, knotting them in place.

When, the final row was knitted and released from the needle, and the extra bit of yarn snipped, she'd smooth out and fold the cardigans or turtle necks as compactly as possible and have us parcel it out to relatives. *I have a present for your child, your brother, your husband, your niece...* she would write, with carefully concealed exuberance. Then await their thank-yous with delicious anticipation.

I do not know if they treasure her gifts, but they say they do. And throw her the crumb of an occasional phone call, which is what she expects all along. Which is, in her mind, a largesse.

I have plated her meal again. She is pushing it away with the ball of her hand. I grit my teeth and think of the pesky housefly that just won't leave. You pull the blinds up or down, but it nestles insouciantly between the slats. You pull up the window, but it flits to another room, instead. And when you finally give up with a disgruntled sigh, it settles brazenly on your pie, not on the periphery of the crust, no, that would be too easy, but in the moist, gooey part of the morsel you like to dig your spoon in or squats like a study in contrast on the plate of strawberry ice cream you've been looking forward to all day!

'Have this now, and we will have pizza, for lunch,' I tell her, in a fit of inspiration. Her eyes light up. She inches the tray forward.

Victory is mine.

As a child, although we lived one spam meal away from food stamps, my mother could make even the humblest of meals delicious with a few sprigs of cilantro and home-grown tomatoes. When she did have cash, she would turn our humble kitchen into a gastronome's heaven. Fish in banana leaf, kedgeree, kabobs, paella and *jalfrezi* were as much a part of our food conversation as beans and potatoes, peas and scrambled eggs. I can see her now, picking up produce and condiments like pearls from oysters, infecting me with her excitement, 'Smell these mangoes. Aren't they beautiful! Look. Look at the size of these prawns! Oh my!'

It was a strange feast-or-famine way of life, with the famine starting around the middle of the month. By the end of the month, we were down to runny lentil soup and potato fritters, which she forked into our plates, the whole ruddy lot of them, insisting with pale face and hungry eyes that she'd already eaten. I used to wish I could bottle those start-of-the-month moments, and sip from it at the end of the month when both joy and savings dwindled.

Here's the thing though. We never had any cake unless she baked it herself. It was as if at the last second, before she got to the bakery counter, her courage failed. She remembered we needed dish soap or roach killer or toothbrushes, and any dessert, other than homemade, was a luxury we could not afford.

It was Adi who introduced me to real dessert. The first of many we shared, I think, was a tub of Haagen-Dazs - Macadamia Nut Brittle. It was orgasmic!

⧖⧖⧖

Ma woke up around 3 p.m., a little late for pizza. For about thirty minutes, I bustled about getting her tea and a couple of those eggless, digestive cookies she favored. After that, the inevitable visit to the washroom, where she struggled with her drawstring pants, but pushed out her elbows, when I tried to help. They are not stubborn, the elderly. I can say that now, having had time for reflection. When the world contracts to a 7'x10' space where you reside alone with a disobedient body, and even thoughts slip away like butterflies from between your fingers, one tends to get territorial about pajamas. She did hold on to my arm to get back to her chair though, and I saw that as a good sign.

Once she was settled into her chair, her hands flew in alarm to her hair. The knot had come untied. She was looking for her hairpins. I found them fallen like neat rows of ants leading up to the bathroom. I picked them up and offered to do her hair. She closed her eyes, nodded and let me. There was a hand mirror in her bathroom. I held the mirror behind her to show her the result. She looked startled, then giggled a little, and pushed the mirror away. 'It's vain for an old woman to look in the mirror,' she said. 'Everybody knows that!' I shrugged and continued to hold the mirror. She stared at it, passed one reflective finger at the lines running parenthetically around her mouth and sighed softly.

Ma

On the news, they are going on about an apartment building that caught fire in the early hours of the morning. Fear everywhere. Firemen rescuing babies, holding them to the wall of their chests. A red-faced babe, unused to the curve of a stranger's arm, rounds his lips in preparation of a scream. Sirens and police cars drown out the commentary. At one point, the reporter asks a wild-eyed man watching his home turn to dust before his eyes, *Tell us what you are feeling.*

'I want it all to go back to the way it was,' the wild-eyed man whimpers. Someone covers his shoulders with a blanket. The reporter, dissatisfied, looks for another victim. I wonder what kind of answer she was hoping to get.

Another woman flails her arms, clutches at the reporter's sleeve. The reporter twitches her nose, as if she is being soiled. The camera lingers on the reporter's sleeve, now creased and dampened.

Beyond her, the building is collapsing on itself like a house of cards. Once a solid structure, with protective roof and firm foundation, it housed all sorts of families. Now, all is rubble. The building has lost its address. Its residents have flown like memories. The world is wrapped in smog. I click off the TV.

I touch the wall behind my head. It feels cool and firm. The ceiling looks solid, as if it will hold for a hundred years. But a fire burns in my head. There is tightness in my chest. A cold sensation in the pit of my stomach. I was never one to see nightmares with my open eyes, but now I see ghosts in the scattered light, floating on unused surfaces. In time, they too will leave, like all the elders in the family, like my husband, like my son, like my sister. Then, my bones too will melt, the breath muffle, the eyeballs turn opaque. I can feel it. I go into the bathroom and pour a mug of cold water on my burning head.

Malavika

Samir. With each sullen truce, our uneasy friendship trudges on. What a troublesome child he was! Grating on you, with his spindly arms and legs, his hair over his eyes like a beatnik and his face ridden with acne, and just when we thought he was past the odious adolescent phase, morphed into someone new–ill at ease, angry and possessive to a fault.

Perhaps, Captain, the smart one in the family, ought to have handled him differently. Or was it my indifference, my lack of interest in his kites and marbles and cowboys and Huckleberry Finn that made him lash out, years later, like a wounded animal, intent on drawing blood?

When he was little, I left him alone often enough, with an ayah handpicked by my husband. Within a year, she had fattened him up so that he couldn't shift his weight from the commode to the floor without help. At the time, thanks to his rosy cheeks, I did not feel like a bad mother, which I surely was.

In my defense, I was also studying at the time. Unlike my own father, Captain took pride in my education and did not falter from his stance that it was important, despite the fact that between college and my forays to Father's home, I scarcely had time for my boy, now no longer a troubled child, or even a trouble-maker, but troubling nevertheless.

'I'm sorry, I'm such a burden to you,' he said, one day, out of the blue.

It was that rare glimpse of tenderness, the naïveté that made him believe that tomorrow would be different, that shot through my heart. Which is why I agreed to his latest proposal before I even heard him out.

'You are all I have, Samir,' I replied. Then we escaped to separate rooms, embarrassed.

At this age, especially, I wanted to befriend my son, which is how his idea for a home-based business in partnership with his current girlfriend came to pass.

As he firmed his plans, my initial enthusiasm cooled, and the thought of losing my hard-earned freedom and my privacy, made me toss and turn with anxiety. But he was convincing. Just a few clothes samples to show designers what we can do, one tailor, at best, sharing our flat, for a few hours each day he said, and fool that I am, I gave him my blessing.

He converted my home into a boutique-cum-beauty salon, much to the consternation of neighbors, who complained at every chance that we lived in a prime residential area, until some people chose to defile it.

The transformation did not happen overnight. One day, I saw his girlfriend in my kitchen bending over a huge cauldron of some sort of honey-colored brew. She was stirring the pot with a wooden spoon, sweat pouring down her brows, blisters dotting her palms as the stuff simmered, bubbled and threatened to boil over. Trying to suppress a cruel thought that she looked like the wicked witch in a children's pop-up book, I asked her if I could help.

That is when I discovered it wasn't a soup or stew thank heavens, because it looked as foul as cytoplasm, but hot body wax that she was making for her clientele. Before I could ask, what clientele, the doorbell rang. And rang. And rang again. At all hours of the day and well into the evening, women sprawled about in various stages of undress, caked with honey or clay or rosewater-infused whitening creams, and to add insult to injury, it was my towels, my coffee and my lemonade, they used as they relaxed during treatments! I had to sidestep bodies and clear a space between a box of vials and a pile of sheets just to rest my back in my own home!

Often, despite the afternoon heat, I sought refuge in the

balcony, my eyes on the borderless ocean, and imagine myself floating in solitary splendor as far as the eye could see.

It got worse. In order to create space, Samir had the balcony covered with tarp.

And within that ugly enclosure, sat one tailor, alternately streaming betel leaf juice into a spittoon and grinding away at the world's noisiest sewing machine; one flimsy wire rack, teetering with the weight of women's garments; one laundry bag of samples, swatches, buttons and bits and one other idiot seated like a fly on a pincushion – that would be me.

How could I let it get this far? My home, my space that I hold sacrosanct, turned into a stop-n-shop?

'It is up to you to tell her to take her business out of there,' I was often scolded by friends. I made light of it and regaled them instead with a funny story - how the girl (in a moment of magnanimity) offered to wax my upper lip. There I was, sitting cross-legged on a mat on the floor, my face pushed up, as she leaned close, her cigarette breath making me nauseous, and stuck a strip of cloth slathered with wax on my lip. Before I could react, she pressed the rag lightly then peeled it off in one swift movement, going in the opposite direction. For the rest of the afternoon, I could not stop staring at my upper lip. Now a bald canvas, it drew attention to the distance between my nose and mouth and at how hairy it made the rest of my face look!

The unceasing noise, the sad, filtered light rendering my little haven as unlivable as the house where Captain and I first cohabited - naturally, something had to give. When Samir tried to clear yet another space to make room for a bead maker, I made my displeasure about the encroachment on my property felt in no uncertain terms. Samir bore my attack with a stoic expression. His wrath is not shrill or hysterical; it is like a slow rolling boil, always on the verge, but never quite spilling over in the usual ways. It is complex and vengeful.

Now, when I try to recall those days, all I have is a fragmented memory. His abject eyes, her blistered hands, the tightness in my chest.

And, it occurs to me that maybe this is who we really are.

Not flesh and blood beings but images and smells and sensations attached to consciousness like dreams, swirling in a suspect reality.

Samir

I promised myself a celebratory, air-conditioned cab ride home if the meeting with my distributor went well and I struck a deal. Since there was no deal and no meeting for that matter, I jostled my way past commuters convened at Victoria Terminus, not bothering to apologize each time my hold-all knocked against a shoulder, a jaw or a breast, and hopped on a local train, grabbing hold of a steel rod for support, just as it lurched out of the station. Of course, I hit my elbow against the door handle in the process.

What followed were a shooting numbness and a zinging pain in the funny bone, so intense that I wanted to jump to my death. Then, just like that, it eased. Awareness returned, along with the nauseating cocktail of urine and sweat and the synchronized *helloloser, helloloser* chugging that seemed to emit from the engine and the tires grating on all that metal and steel crap.

Desperate to get as far and as soon as possible from the mocking *ritardando* of the train, I decided, on an impulse, to get off at the station close to Mother's apartment. The day was shot anyway, and perhaps the ocean air and a little food might help mitigate the headache, I now felt coming on, I thought, wading through the crush of bodies. Zigzagging my way through the city, I found my way home at last. She was perched on the balcony, doing her eye exercises, gazing at the sunset, and somehow, just the sight of her, ensconced in a routine as familiar as a nursery rhyme, gave me comfort.

'What's wrong?' she asked, 'You look wretched.'

I shrugged. 'Nothing. Local trains, you know.'

'Ooof!' She shuddered in empathy.

She made a simple meal for the two of us with bread and eggs, leftover potatoes and cucumber salad. We ate in the balcony, seated on low stools, the food on a round, side table she dragged out from the living room. 'I'm out of most things and too lazy to shop,' she said, handing me a glass of soothing buttermilk, smiling complacently. Clouds rolled past a hammock of a moon, and I kneaded my neck muscles and surrendered at last, to its unbiased tranquility.

When we were done with our meal and my headache quite gone, Mother, asked me if there was anything I wanted to watch on TV. She was fiddling with the remote, her back still on me, when I found myself asking,

'Ma, how old were you when you married my father?'

She paused, and then said quietly, 'More or less fifteen, when I met him. We eloped when I touched sixteen. You came two years later.'

'Sixteen. No wonder you made mistakes,' I said, thoughtfully.

She looked a little startled. I guess, she'd never seen my sensitive side before. But then, I had never seen my father with a whore in green satin before.

'Yes. No one should marry for the wrong reasons,' she observed with a small sigh. Her shoulders slumped.

I switched gears.

'Why did you not ask me to come down when Grandfather passed away? I could have helped.'

'You were in design school at the time, remember? I called, and your room-mate said you were quarantined in another part of the building. You had chickenpox.'

'Ah!'

'Why the questions, Samir, after all this time?'

'No reason,' I yawned. Then I asked her if I could visit her again over the weekend.

She opened her mouth to say something but changed her

mind and nodded slowly.

I wanted to give her a hug before I left, this woman who had given me birth and a shelter of sorts. But we don't do these things in our family. Instead, I said, 'Bye then,' and she wiggled her two fingers in customary response.

I stepped out of the building, turning back once to nod and wave. The moon hid behind the clouds, and in the dim street light there was no way to tell whether the woman, standing in the balcony, erect as a sentry, her long hair skimming her waist, oblivious of the housedress billowing at the ankles, was very young or very old.

12

Annika

Adi hands her a pill, one at a time, with an air of seriousness. It's a slow process. She takes it with a sip of water, swallows, and looks at him for approval. Then she takes another, swallows. 'How many left?' she asks, each time with the air of a martyr. I leave them to it.

I know she's perfectly capable of swallowing her pills and is not so inept she cannot do simple subtractions. But it's a ritual, a tender start to an uncertain day. I watch from a distance and can't help thinking how tractable she is with him, like a child who is sure, daddy knows best.

Rites and rituals. They give me no solace.

When my gone-mother keeled over between the kitchen and the hallway and with obvious relief gave up the ghost, someone must have notified my sister. She came on the fourth day, along with other guests, for the *kriya,* the time when a soul is prepared for its final journey. We sat in a semi-circle, sprinkling sandalwood, nutmeg, ghee, and a host of propitious objects into a fire pit, as directed by the priest. As the fire rose, I saw the body of my mother relegated to the pyre and couldn't stop shaking. A kindly aunt put her arms around me. Malavika, head covered with a white scarf to mark the occasion made as if to sit down beside me. My father's head shot up. Stabbing the air with his finger, he directed her to the door. Startled, she hesitated, then rose, and left like a ghost. Meanwhile, I was afraid I was making too much noise but my teeth wouldn't stop chattering. Someone lifted me to my bed and let me sleep off the rest of the ceremony.

For about forty days, we subsisted on the kindness of relatives, friends and neighbors. There were platters of food everywhere. Fruit on the dining table, curries in the refrigerator and packets of wholesome snacks in the pantry.

Silently we ate our meals, Father and I, piled dirty dishes in the sink and saved what was left in smaller, disposable boxes. Anything that looked funky, we binned.

After forty days, people moved on to tragedies closer to home, and I suppose, through silent consensus, decided that our situation was no longer dire. The nutritious, well-planned dishes that came to our door along with warm hellos and heartfelt hugs, slowly dwindled to hastily sliced fruit or leftovers from their table and sent across by a servant. Finally, like Gone-Mother, charity, too, became a thing of the past.

My father delegated the cooking to the cleaning lady, who evidently saw no difference between dishwater and curry. I do believe the steady diet of runny lentils and *sago-khichree*, compounded the loss of my mother, by a thousand-fold.

Reluctantly, Father gave her notice and tried his hand in the kitchen. Together, we sautéed vegetables with a generous, if haphazard, sprinkling of spices. Then we ate our blackened cauliflower or ghee- soaked cabbage or soupy beans and washed it all down with a tub of yogurt. Dishes done, we sat in our respective corners, dully imagining that someday soon, we would be all right.

Over the years, my culinary skills improved. I thought we managed breakfast and lunch quite effortlessly. By dinner time, we were both so hungry and fatigued – I had homework, laundry, other menial chores that took precedence, he had lectures to prepare – that I put together what was quickest and topped the meal with a glass of hot, sweetened, cardamom-flavored milk. Incredibly, he did not criticize my cooking.

Every once in a while, he asked me if I was doing well in school. I shrugged a yes. One day he noticed my bangs.

'How can you study with all that hair in your eyes?' he snapped.

I thought it was a rhetorical question and didn't think to answer. Then he asked me to come to the other room.

Carefully, he placed me on a chair, put a towel on my shoulders, and taking a heap of hair between thumb and forefinger, I could feel his phlegmy breath on the tip of my nose, began snipping with a kitchen knife, until I felt the jagged ends hover just above my brows. Then, he set to work on the rest of my hair. Finally, he brought a hand mirror to show me the result. Divested of my locks, I noticed with horror how my ears stuck out, the dark circles under my eyes deepened, my shoulder blades protruded, and my neck looked like a bruised carrot. An expert at blinking back tears, I nodded my thanks and went in to shower. For the rest of the evening, I escaped to my seat in the window, facing the ocean and the snaking street, to dream my favorite dream:

When Malavika returns, I will be the first to see her. She will start out as a speck in the distance, and then solidify into a shape as she draws nearer and nearer, and finally, I will see all of her. She will be home. Then things will be as before.

I waited until the fine hair on my arms prickled with cold. But Malavika did not come. And by the time she did, I was a different person.

At school, my haircut earned me the nickname – Orphan Ani. Personally, I thought I looked more like the children in one of those Missing Children photos staring out of the classified section of the newspaper, and wished fervently, that I was, in fact missing. Father obviously thought he did a fine job, because it became our ritual, every couple of months or so, always with the same awful result.

As I grew older, I was assigned more tasks. Often, the faucets dried up without warning, leaving us with semi-washed clothes or soap in our eyes. I had to fill every bucket in the house as a backup plan. Then I had to light a lamp and recite a short mantra before Gone-Mother. The flame reflected between her eyes in the portrait. She heard me out without comment. Then I made us breakfast, filled the ink in all his pens and finally set out for school.

There was no show of resistance on my part. I did as I was told, the alternative too frightening to imagine.

⧗⧗⧗

The pills helped stabilize her heart, blood pressure, trigeminal nerve pain and irritable bowels, but they also affected Ma's behavior in inexplicable ways, so that every day was an adventure. On a good day, she might walk the few steps to the bathroom, bathe and dress herself and ask for her oatmeal. She would swallow her tabletsand make four or five perfectly coherent calls on her private line.

On a bad day, she might talk to the shadows.

Because she went nowhere and saw no one, it was easy to see how she would become a rest stop for weary relatives. Glowing with the certainty that they were doing her a service simply by accepting her call, they broke down the slow progression of their days into aches and pains, the excessive heat, the price of fava beans and the sullen son or the dour daughter-in-law.

Deaf in one ear, but attuned still to pitch and pith, she heard them out, and when their speech slowed down or trailed off, she cunningly extended the conversation reminiscing about marriages and births, their lovely spouses, their beautiful homes that she had heard so much about, allowing each person to sigh with satisfaction, and confide with affection how much she meant to them -their guiding star, their spiritual mother.

Then, like a faithful emissary, she deposited the succulent eggs of gossip, speckled with adlibs and annotations, into the grubby hands of her brother, her sister-in-law, her distant cousins and other old crones, hungry for connection.

But there were days when pyrogens coursed through her bloodstream, her forehead burned and the past clawed its way into the present. Then, through the milky scrim of her weak and defiant eyes, she fought with phantoms, her tongue clenched into a fist, her speech unintelligible. And when her feet gave, she skulked in corners like our family dog, a few weeks before he heaved his last sigh and shed his beautiful silky fur in fistfuls, the foul smell of liver disease forcing us to leave the room in guilty disgust.

She would not take any phone calls then, and in the body of the living, invoked the ones that were no longer present: '*Oh, there you are, my sister ... where have you been?*'

She would hug the bewildered maid. Or call excitedly out to the jogger outside her window.

'*Wait for me! Let us gift roses to the English madam in the bungalow across the fence. Maybe she will let us sit with her on her porticos and share her sweetened iced tea! Teehee!'*

And coward that I am, I would escape to the kitchen, fingers in my ears, and rattle the pots and pans.

Clarity, when it came to her, was awesome to behold. During one of her zoned-out moments, my nerves were so frazzled I managed to drop a tray of tea things to the floor. Through the onslaught of tears, I saw her in her frayed brown pajamas, her legs like saplings outlined against the flimsy material. Then she grunted, shook her head, as if clearing away voices, tiptoed through the fine china and stood in front of me. She pulled a piece of glass out of my hair and brushed my sleeve with her fingers.

'Help me find the broom and dustpan,' she said softly.

'And mind your feet.' Silently, methodically, she cleared the debris. Then she washed her hands, dried them with a kitchen towel, patted me on my shoulder and went back in to rest.

Ma

I draw my chair closer to the shards of light drifting through the kitchen transom. I am so happy I want to purr. At dinner, we sit in a circle – my brother, my son and my sister-in-law. I sniff my fingers from time to time, still redolent of the smell of home cooking. Why can I not live out the rest of my days here, where I am treated as a respected member of the family, not one evading death? I plead with my son. But he needs to hurry back to his wife. I beg and I beg. He finally relents. I can stay for a couple of weeks. Then he will come back for me.

Every morning, my brother's wife massages my hair with coconut oil. She measures my foot and knits warm socks that fit me just right. I tell her without fear of reprisal - I like my orange juice cold and my soup warm, not the other way around. She knows to part the curtains only at my say-so, and just enough to let the light in and keep the sun out. She does not hide my dentures under the sink so that I have to break my back in order to get to them. She does not leave me in my room like an apology whenever she has company. She is considerate of my age and my status as an elder. But most of all, the ground does not sway in this home. My tea does not feel strange. I am no longer plagued with double vision. I show my son the fading bruises. I try to tell him as gently as I can that it is *his wife* who has caused the bruises. How is it I never fall in my brother's home? I ask him. How is it I never get sick here? It was *Anika* who was making me sick!

He turns a dangerous shade of red, mutters something about paranoia and blood thinners and leaves the next day to be with her. Well, at least I have bought myself some time.

Malavika

O sleep it is a gentle thing
Beloved from pole to pole
To Mary Queen the praise be given
She sent the gentle sleep from heaven
That slid into my soul ...

- Coleridge

Samir's home-based business was not as lucrative as he would have his friends believe. At first, he blamed the long summer afternoons: 'Who wants to be out in this humidity! People are too lazy, too indolent to leave their homes to be out shopping.'

Then, he blamed the savage monsoon for an order for some dresses that he couldn't fulfill. 'No one works in this rain,' he shrugged.

'If people were as mercurial as the weather, life as we know it would come to a standstill, wouldn't it?' I said, in a tactless moment.

When he was not cursing the weather, he was bemoaning his karma. Because nothing *he* did was ever wrong. Perhaps my show of displeasure was the final straw. In any event, he agreed to leave, for all oursakes.

Oh, he did see me once or twice before he left town. By then, thankfully, the cat and mouse tension that defined our relationship seemed to have eased, and then settled into a more digestible irritability. He came alone, so I guess, Miss Amazon no longer figured in his plans.

We shared an omelet, made promises to stay in touch and I slipped some money in his wallet when he wasn't looking.

Soon after that, he simply folded his tents like the Arabs and was gone.

Gone! That perpetual state of anxiety that hounded my dreams and made life impossible. I slept like a baby for eight hours each night and wakened to the call of the muezzin, and welcomed the rosy light of dawn.

Call me selfish, but I felt no guilt. The first thing I did was to raise the piece of tarp caging the balcony and simply draw breath. Then I took in the ocean, the sunshine, the seagulls winging across the blue skies and yes, I thought it was worthwhile having my son disappear into the maw of any country that welcomed cheap, semi- skilled labor so that I could have my peace restored.

In just a few days, I had my living space rearranged, with the few sticks of furniture that I cherished. Wiped clean of the fingerprints of strangers, vacated of tailors spitting into their bowls, and emptied of waxes and creams and undisciplined clutter, (which included *the girlfriend du jour*) I luxuriated in the arms of my house like a reunited lover.

I spent my days frivolously. Discipline disappeared from my life. I ate sporadically; elaborate party-style meals or bread dipped in milk, whatever my heart desired, exulting in the fact that there was no one around to snort and complain. I took my evening walks, but instead of rushing home at sunset like a child, I stopped to talk with the neighbors, reveling in their now open smiles. How wonderful it is to be surrounded by goodwill. What a blessing to sample the joys of an ordinary day.

Before I turned in for the night, I stood once more in my freed space and gazed at the ocean, admiring the slowly changing colors of sky and water and welcoming the deepening hush, like an ode to peace, disturbed only with an occasional plash of the fisherman's oar.

Samir

After Sherri came a string of women as memorable as yesterday's newspaper. There was one I introduced my mother to, only because we needed her apartment for business. When that relationship (and business) went belly up, I was able to leave home and try my luck in Kuwait, thanks, in part, to a sudden windfall from Father.

After our chance meeting at the Sheraton, the old man started messaging me, saying he was in town every couple of months and would like to reconnect.

I decided it wouldn't hurt to meet him, and when the time was right, touch him for some dough. What else are fathers for, anyway? I sent him a note, saying yes, that would be okay.

We decided on the hotel lobby, around 8 p.m., after he wound up the day's business. I could see he was in a swivel, although he had his back to me. He stood up, then sat down and then was up again, passing his hands hurriedly through his scant hair and shuffling his briefcase from floor to chair.

'Samir!' He stood up and mussed my hair. The receptionist, a flat-chested girl, bent her head to hide a smile. Even so, that one simple gesture took me back to the years before I was shipped off to boarding school, to the drawing room sofa, where I sat enthralled, with my comic books, and he with his accounts and the only sound is that above our heads of an old- fashioned clock counting the hours between his solid presence and Mother's unspoken absence.

I would look up in mild irritation each time he rose from his desk to get a cup of coffee or use the bathroom and ruffle my hair in passing.

His nod of approval, whenever I asked for permission to play cricket, the gruff way he had of shoving a bill in my pocket, the occasional hair ruffle and the glass of orange juice on the side table when I returned home from my adventures on the street, shirt sticking to my back and throat parched, were the moments that lulled me into believing he cared.

For some women, motherhood is a calling. For others it is a date, marked with a circle, an obligatory celebration. My mother was always rushing away from us, her high heels on the stairs, evincing excitement with each click. And when she returned, her head was in a cloud, her clothes reeked of sweat mingled with something I did not recognize, and even before I knew the meaning of the word, I thought, SLUT.

We were chatting over drinks, beer for him, scotch and soda for me, when he told me about his new life with the Bengali woman, he married about eight years ago. He had twin boys, he said with a nervous smile, and they now lived in Malaysia. Their names were …

'So, you come into town for what, a little side dish?' I lashed out crudely, any trace of nostalgia quite vanished with the mention of his encore life and the last drop of scotch.

He winced. 'Samir, can I do something for you, anything?' he asked, obviously eager to change the subject. I debated whether to continue in the same vein, punish him for dumping me like so much excess baggage but decided against it. I had a better idea.

'I need some capital to start a business; Mother cannot help me, as she is dying,' I blurted. I told him, on the fly, that all our savings were depleted after her last surgery, that she had cancer, hadn't worked for over a year and was completely bald under her hairpiece. Then I shut up. What use is a prestigious boarding school education if you don't know exactly when to stop embellishing your story so you are completely credible?

Of course, he fell for it. All of it. Trembling with emotion, he coughed up a check, big enough to give me the start I needed. I suppressed a pang of guilt, smiled, passed a hand over my eyes and piled on some more bullshit about being sorry for my rudeness, and how it was great seeing him. His glasses fogged.

'Uh! Take care of yourself. Take care of your mother,' he muttered.

'Uh! I will.' I almost snorted.

I left before the fog cleared, determined to cash that check before the old fart got over his fit of conscience and closed his account.

13

Annika

To celebrate my temporary freedom, I decide to meet up with a girl friend at a diner in the business district. I am early and spend the time eavesdropping shamelessly on a group of corporate executives on their break. They order quickly, heap forkfuls into their mouths and ingest every morsel with the absorption of greedy children and animals, looking up every once in a while, to exchange perfunctory remarks.

A slim, prepossessing young girl, almost halved by an oversized Michael Kors tote and black-rimmed Gucci glasses, joins them at some point during the meal. The air crackles. The men sit up straighter. The one older woman in the group slumps, as if trying to make herself vanish.

My girlfriend arrives and props her Lord & Taylor bag on a chair with a flourish.

'See what you are missing?' she says, taking in the suits with a single side-glance, doubtless putting her own spin on the situation.

'Lunch on the company account?' I grin.

'More like you scratch my ass, I scratch yours,' she laughs. One of the reasons we hit it off so well is she can swear with aplomb.

'Oh, you don't know shit until you've walked in someone else's shoes,' I snap at her.

She laughs again and says something, probably irreverent. But I've stopped listening.

⧗⧗⧗

Father was unwell. The maid absconded, and I was at the end of my wits. I remembered the aunt who'd wrapped her arms around me in a half hug, through gone-mother's funeral. I called her and burst into tears. And three days later, there was my sister, a little curvier, a little more polished, hair in a knot, hoops in her ears, but otherwise the same Miss Know-it-all. Father was too weak to throw her out of the house. In any event, she simply stepped around his thick, tree-trunk body and marched to her old room like a homing pigeon. She arranged her stuff on and around the bed and looked with warring eyes at anyone who dared disturb the cozy little nest she'd made for herself.

There was no excited chatter. No hugs, no presents, no I missed you, my how you've grown. She simply found another maid, set to work in the kitchen and separated clothes for washing, ironing, mending, etc. She asked me if I'd done my homework and if I could please fetch father's plate when he was done eating. I did as I was told. Tension spread over the house like a silent virus. It made my palms sweat and my stomach hurt. It took away my ability to grasp simple requests. I scratched my hair and cleared my throat as a nervous response to everything.

Father never looked at her or talked to her directly. I thought perhaps I ought to take his cue and do the same. It was a way of keeping myself safe. It drove her crazy. 'Why are you punishing me? You don't know shit until you've walked in someone else's shoes,' she screamed at me.

I walked out of the room and left her alone.

⧗⧗⧗

Once home, it hits me again that Adi's ma is away.

Her room is empty. Sterile. I imagine her in her usual position, propped against the wall, feet resting on the cushion, heels like grey moons, limbs as weathered as trees that have logged hurricanes, fires and diseases long since eradicated.

All at once, I feel bereft. I can count on one hand the number of times she had a kind word for me. Still. Her absence fills the house.

It is she who lends shape to the objects around us. *Her* couch, *her* bed, *her* chair. Without her, they are simply space fillers.

Perhaps, too, she lends a structure to my day that has since been disturbed, and this lack of urgency to wake up at a certain time, prepare a meal, plan a nap, a tea-time snack or even a bathroom break is a little disorienting.

Perhaps I'm no different from Old Coot.

You would think that a pet would escape through an unlocked door, in a heartbeat, run like the wind toward freedom, wouldn't you? But he won't. And not because he is unintelligent. I do believe there is a certain amount of happiness, or at the very least, relief, from knowing where you belong, having a curriculum, a daily bone.

I am inclined to think all that barking and pushing against the fence, all the prancing and jumping as you put your sneakers on is not so much because Old Coot wants to escape but a simple assertion of his rights -*I can be free. I'm just not sure I want things to change.*

Adi's ma usually calls in the evenings. Her exchanges with me are formal: You are doing well, I hope? All is fine here, thank you. Like a salesperson on a cold call, saving her spiel for the "real" head of the household. Nonplussed, I yell for Adi to answer the phone. I hold on to the receiver for a few seconds as they speak. There are no missed beats between them. The pauses feel warm, the exchanges tender. I place the phone back on the charger, feeling resentful and undeserving.

Ma

My brother does not want me to make long distance phone calls. This morning, he told me he will not throw good money on gossip. I paled at the meanness but said nothing.

The only fruit they ever bring home is a banana! Yesterday, I asked her for cold cream, and she said there wasn't any. She gave me olive oil to rub on my skin. Ha! Am I a piece of meat she intends to skewer? Perhaps I will ask the beautiful white woman, her daughter-in-law, for help.

There are so many people in this house it makes me quite dizzy. My brother and his wife, their son and daughter-in-law. How tall she is! Taller than a man. Her hair hangs loose and borrows color from the sunlight, warm and golden. Her clothes are shapeless, yet I see her shape, strong and lean. Her expression is changeable, now a Madonna, now cold and impersonal as a hospital nurse. Sometimes she places her child on my lap and gestures, 'I will be back in a few minutes.'

I hold her little infant with his marble blue eyes, to my bosom, slumping a little with the weight of him, and stroke his fat cheeks gently with the back of my hands. Then I lay him flat on my lap, view his plump body, satisfied on mother's milk. I turn him over and rub his back to make him burp. He spits out his supper in a thin trickle. I wipe off his vomit with a wet wipe.

He pulls at my ears and holds me rapt. His beauty glows like a carriage light in the pitch of night. My senses fill.

How does she adjust to the sounds and smells of this foreign household? My brother says I must not stare at her as if she is artwork in a museum. And I must not spoil her – watching her baby while she enjoys a long shower or basks in the sunshine planting unnecessary flowers. He says she pulls at her nose when I oil my hair or at the smell of my cooking bubbling on the stove and whispers furiously into the ears of her husband, *I did not sign up for this. I do not want my child exposed to these village people.*

How does my brother know what she whispers? He says I have always been partial to white skin. But who isn't?

A woman's skin must be light as the surface of polished gold. Everybody knows that! A pity my son chose a woman with a sallow complexion and no hips.

Still, I miss Anika. His wife.

She lets me wind and unwind her yarn into a ball. She is a good girl. Family.

Why does my son not call? Five days after I gave him birth, I left him snug in his cot. There was work to be done. I lugged a sack of wheat from the grocer, his two older brothers dragging their feet behind me. When I returned, we did not hear the baby, and I was relieved. He's asleep, I thought. What was it that made me go to his room before I knelt in the kitchen sifting chaff from the grain? I will never know. He was on his stomach, a small bump smothering under a heavy blanket. I tugged at it gently. The corners had caught under the mattress. But that was not all. The string of his bib was constricting his throat. Raising his head with one hand, I used the other to loosen the knot. His face was blue and his tiny little throat circled with angry red marks. How valiantly he tried to suck in air, his little fists clenched, his tears puddled between neck and shoulder. Gathering him up, rubbing his little chest, getting him to snort and gurgle, I cursed myself for having left him in the care of his grandmother.

The musky scent of incense and the solemn rhythmic rise and fall of her devotional chanting served to enrage me further. For the first time in my life, I strode up to her, shook her by the shoulder and made certain she got a good look at her grandson, his face still blue, his life barely flooded back. Of course, she wasn't repentant. Without any sense of wrongdoing, the 108 names of god turned into curses in that wicked mouth.

Never since have I felt such anger. I wanted to squeeze her neck with my bare hands as she breathed her last Om to a god unknown.

I wonder what became of her? Did she die? I have no memory of that. Every one of my babies was greeted with a lament. Her cries rose higher and higher and blistered the air like acid, and soon my joy turned to ashes as my husband left my side to be with the one who gave him birth and would let him love no other.

I gave him birth ... I saved his life... why does my son not call? Is he afraid of his wife? *A man must perform any deed, great or small, with the spirit of a lion.* Everybody knows that!

Malavika

Perhaps I should ask Samir to reach out to Anika. I am sure she will thaw when she hears the appeal in her nephew's voice:

'Mom really misses you. She has something to say. Won't you speak with her, *Auntie?*'

But to ask Samir for a favor is like asking a bank for a loan.

Too many questions and, at the end, a brusque, unapologetic NO.

When we eloped, Captain did send a message through his houseboy to let my family know we were not missing or dead, but away on our honeymoon. Unfortunately, the messenger was lax and did not convey the note to my mother for four days. Naturally, it must have been a terrifying time for my parents. To make it worse, rumors, like a bad smell, were already beginning to spread far and wide. *She was* raped. *She's run off with a married man. She was seen carousing with a strange man in a hotel.* Afraid my glaring absence might mar my little sister's chances and the family's reputation forever, no police report was ever filed. Instead, my father claimed, I had tuberculosis (better a life-threatening disease than the threat of disgrace) and was sent away for a cure.

I returned from my trip, radiant as a warrior princess, naively expecting to be greeted with warmth and regard for my new status. Instead, Mother came to the door, like a matchstick with burning eyes and pushed me out, hissing, 'Go away and never come back if you value your life.'

Father reviled Captain openly, thunderously. Later, after

Mother's death, he took to reviling me. I was a slut, a whore, a bitch and once, in a moment of inspiration, monkey in a red dress. This, *after* having devoured the three-course dinner I put before him.

'You are welcome,' I snarled and left him, hoping he would choke on his own bile.

When Samir came along, I took him a few times to visit his aunt and his grandfather. Ana-banana, still a little girl herself, eyed him with curiosity and then opened her arms to receive the little boy until she saw the flint in Father's eyes and, petrified, averted her face and kept it averted for the rest of our stay.

It could have been worse. To give credit where credit is due, Captain was rather easy going those first few years. He had a high tolerance for clutter and was unfazed by my many disappearances – *I was out shopping…. I was at my father's home…I went to the movies.* He'd come home, shower, change into comfortable loungewear, give Samir a pat on the head and pour himself a drink. We still fornicated almost daily, with me on top (he was lazy, that way), but, like most married couples, we rarely had anything to say to each other. Perhaps, we knew, we could never outdo what we had already done, and with our biggest adventure behind us, we were saddened, and at a bit of a loss, but not quite so sad or quite so lost that we tried to change anything.

In college, though, I soon discovered that boys found me attractive. Marriage had smoothed away the irritating childish qualities most girls carry into their teens; I did not smile too readily or blush too easily. I did not wrap my arms around my breasts self-consciously, sauntering instead, with my head held high. I made eye contact and spoke easily to my teachers. My self-possession made the boys nervous. All I had to do was ask something, however mundane, what time do you have… how was the lecture… are you going in this direction…and watch them squirm or laugh like hyenas. It was fun. During breaks, I hung about with the South African students drifting through college and strumming on their battered guitars.

I was two years married when the hippie culture exploded in my city, and I decided I no longer cared to play the-lady-in-white. I reinvented myself one more time – with embroidered tunics, peace pendants, leather headbands and a pocket full of tiny hash pills, like some delicious secret I shared with my newfound friends.

Dressed for the part, I was naïve enough to believe I could pull off any number of identities as long as I did not let one part of my life bleed into another. So, for a while, when I was with Captain, I was with Captain. When I was with my little joy pills, I dwelled … elsewhere. And during those foggy uninhibited moments/hours/days, I paid attention only to the music in my head.

It was only in my father's home that I lost my composure. I regressed once again to a little girl stretching out her hand for approval, only to find that my hands were not long enough to reach his heart. When his aversion became too overt and the silence rife with violence, I ran out the door and over to the Shroffs' residence, occasionally with Samir clutching my skirt. Mr. Shroff had lost his wife by then, but her absence did not deter me from knocking on his door.

'Do you have anything to read?' was my standard greeting. He pointed to his library. I made a half-hearted attempt, perusing the biographies, cookbooks, general fiction, poetry and children's books stacked in alphabetical order on various shelves, by author. Randomly I picked a book, generally a Hardy or Austen and then stood about until he said, 'Sit down. Make yourself at home.'

Over tea and sandwiches, Shroff asked me all sorts of questions about my studies, my interest in haiku and whether I liked biographies or general fiction. He lifted me out of the mire of self-effacement and showed me a world that was larger than the walls I had shackled myself within. All I had to do was open my eyes. In time, I believed him.

One day I asked him about his wife. I had spoken to her very briefly, as a girl, and scarcely paid attention, when she passed away.

'Did you love her?'

He looked taken aback and then smiled.

'Hmm! We were married a long time, you know.'

He could see I was disappointed. It wasn't a real reply, was it?

'We were not in love in the way, youngsters imagine, I think. But she was a lovable woman. And we tried very hard to make each other happy.'

A *lovable woman*, I thought, squelching the unexpected dart of loneliness. Timorously, I confided to him that I had made many mistakes. He did not comfort me with stories of his own transgressions or minimize my pain with a flippant "who hasn't?" Instead, he was quiet for a while, took the book out of my hand, slid it neatly back in place and said, without turning around, 'Mend whatever you can and let go of that which you cannot. It always works for me.'

I decided I would take his advice to heart. Perhaps I would never be a *lovable* woman, but if I could add up to a little more than the sum of my mistakes, who knows, I might still be all right.

Samir

Dispirited by the run of bad luck, even the surge of malicious pleasure from having conned my father out of his cash soon abated. I realized his donation was not so much a victory as a gust of pleasure, an adrenaline rush that eventually lowered my self-esteem.

When the girl I was dating at the time also shoved off to parts unknown, I decided, on the advice of a friend, to put Father's money to good use. I renewed my passport and bought a ticket for Kuwait, and a few weeks later, there I was.

The city, blinding you with purple opulence, filled me with awe. At night, I cowered in my lodging, anxiety, sitting on my chest like a forty-pound weight set. Maybe the concrete skyscrapers would spring to life, and in a stampede, crush me like Godzilla under their pillared feet. I covered my head like an ostrich. I tried to talk myself out of my fears. *The skyscrapers in Mumbai are no different. What is the matter with you?*

Day time was just as bad. I knew no one. The Arabs looked hostile, the Egyptians self-absorbed and the Indians like rats, intent on saving every crumb they foraged from the mouth of another. I took a bus to Al Kaut beach and found some rest watching the rush and regress of waves or gazing upward at the cloudless sky without expectation.

No one approached me. Loneliness, like the proverbial perv in a raincoat, sends out a bad smell and must be avoided at all cost.

⧖⧖⧖

I filled out the initial paperwork and waited my turn to speak to the counselors as they called themselves. They gave me a number and asked me to take a seat. Two television sets hung on either side of the room. On one channel aired an enthusiastic game of football. The lack of sound (Both TVs were set on mute) took away from the game and almost forced you to focus on the players. Eyes wild, teeth gnashed and posturing like bulls, they lunged into their opponents, like a scene out of a Martin Scorsese movie, except it was silent.

The closed captions were more like a suggestion, the bottom halves of words sliced off the screen. On the other set, two women in headscarves, one matronly, one young, appeared to be nagging each other to death.

I angled myself towards the football, probably giving the wrong idea to the mouth breather on the next seat. Reaching between my legs he tried to pick up the ticket sticking out from the House of Mirrors brochure I held in my lap, for no apparent reason.

'What's your number?' he asked.

'Thirty-five,' I snapped, slapping his slippery fingers away from my crotch. He put both hands up as if capitulating, and smirked, 'I am 9. Good luck Bro. You're going to be here all day.' Hatred shot up from my shoes all the way up the trachea. What I would give to castrate every freakin' stranger who assumed he could cop a feel while calling you a bro!

At least there was air conditioning.

Eventually, 35 flashed on the ticker tape. I brushed baklava crumbs off my beard and found the interview booth. Uzma Habib was my counselor.

'Fill out these forms, please,' she pointed crisply.

I took them from her and filled them as best as I could.

We sat in silence as she bit her lip, trying to appear impressed by my meager resume. High school, two years of design school, self- employed, broke.

Weeks after we began dating, she told me that the only reason she'd passed my resume onto D&D Construction was she did not like ending the day on a negative note.

She took down my cell number. 'You left it blank,' she said, accusingly, and then, sticking a bunch of papers into her tote, stood up before I could ask irrelevant questions. I pushed back my chair, careful not to look at her as she smoothed down her skirt, suggesting she wasn't that pretty anyway, when, 'Good Luck. Someone will be in touch,' she said and stepped out of her office.

Five days later, she called me, telling me to show up at Dawood & Dawood Construction in a white shirt if I was still interested in the warehouse manager job. She tended to end declarative sentences with a question in her voice.

I said I very much was.

'You might also improve your chances if you lose the Bin Laden look, no offence,' she chirped and rang off. And there it was, the full-frontal directness that worked like a shot of vodka on my frozen heart.

14

Annika

My inertia did not last long. For one thing, I started rising at 5 a.m. to practice meditation. I tied myself to my desk and did not come up for air until I had logged a few hundred words every day. It did not matter that I had to delete ninety out of every hundred.

Glowing with satisfaction and a deep-rooted contentment simply from establishing a new routine and the added bonus of gorgeous weather, we took to spending leisurely evenings at the boardwalk, Adi and I, followed by coffee or ice cream at our new favorite place – The Cake Walk. I let him stride ahead of me, his digital fit-o-meter wrapped determinedly around his wrist.

The air was tinged with sea salt and smoky sausage from a nearby bistro. The sun moved ponderously down from his abode and changed the horizon from pallid to fuchsia with one lingering kiss. A host of exotic paper kites danced in the wind like winged creatures, and on the sand, shirtless men and tank-topped women jumped higher than cheetahs, for the ball, bouncing like a prize between them.

To be able to look past the geriatric bed and beyond the mullioned windows, to be able to witness this exuberance first hand, instead of your Twitter feed, was exhilarating. I found myself laughing without reason and chatting non-stop.

Driving home from the boardwalk one afternoon, I received a call from a familiar sounding name, Anne Burke. She said she was calling to say her father had passed on. I mumbled my condolences. 'Thank you. We are reconciled to it. I just wanted you to know I did play the Buddhist music you had so kindly given me, and I'm certain it helped. He went peacefully.' Again, I murmured unintelligibly.

'I have been meaning to ask you if you'd like to go out for a walk or coffee, sometime, whenever you are available, of course.'

'Oh, for sure! Maybe you can bring your husband as well, we'll do a couples' night,' I said, enthusiastically.

There was an uncomfortable pause.

'Umm. I did introduce myself as Mrs. Burke, but, uh… I will be dropping the name soon.'

'I'm sorry! I didn't…'

'It's all right.'

I said I was sorry again, now wishing she hadn't called.

'No worries,' she said graciously, and went on, 'By the way, The First Baptist Church in Long Branch has a meetup, for caregivers of people with dementia. In case you are interested.'

'A meetup?'

'Uh, it's a sort of support group. I don't mean to interfere, but I think you might find it helpful.'

'You are not interfering at all. That's very helpful, Anne. I'll look into it,' I said, and promised to call her soon, making sure to say, *for a girls' night out* this time.

I put Anne out of my mind and focused instead on a future alive with possibilities, friends I hadn't seen in months, over mulled wine and fondue or sliders and wings.

Absorbed in my private daydream, I did not realize Adi too was on his cell phone and had been for a while. I raised my brows, *who is it?* A minute pause, a soft escape of breath, an abrupt, 'I'll be there'

Then he turned to me, 'She fell down. We have to bring her home.'

Of course, of course.

It would be a long time before I broached the subject of parties or meetups again.

Ma

My son did not answer my greeting when he came for me. What I mean is that there was no answering warmth in his greeting. He merely helped pack my bag, asked me if I had my dentures on and did a final check in the bathroom where my hair oil, face cream and hairpins were on the sink. I told him I needed those things packed. He shoved them into a baggie and stuck the lot in the zippered pocket of my suitcase. I wanted to hug him but patted his back instead. It is what we do. My brother dragged my bag down the driveway. His wife dabbed her eyes with a crocheted kerchief and held me with a gentle smile.

Suddenly, I didn't want to leave. In that little house, under my own rhombus of light, I was treated like an elder. With respect. At mealtimes, we all moved to the den, with our lunches on a tray table. My brother cut the bread into bite-size pieces and gave me the softest bits.

I wanted to thank him for his love, but he said, 'Hurry up, the engine is running.' I wanted to stay on. I was afraid to let go of the chair. They carried me off without so much as a smile or a promise to have me back soon. Meanwhile, their daughter-in-law busied herself with her cell phone, her baby nowhere in sight. They do that, don't they, hide in their devices so they do not have to deal with people?

He had no questions for me. Did I take my pain medication? Did I feel less sore today? My brother had filled him in about my fall the moment he entered his home. He ignored me as I sat like a potted plant, and they shook hands. 'Yes, I know she doesn't listen,' and, 'Yes, I agree, it wouldn't have happened if she wasn't so stubborn,' he was saying, following up on a phone conversation, no doubt. It was hurtful. Maybe that is why I did what I did next.

Malavika

I pottered about, helping Father with household chores, long after my pep talk with Shroff. It was with Anika that I hoped to reconnect. She was my baby sister, and I made it my business to remind her of happier times, doing whatever I could, even bribing her with chocolate and *gulab jamuns*.

It was futile. Terrified of Father, she spurned my treats and responded to my direct questions with gestures, as if we were playing dumb charades. I became increasingly frustrated and petulant. I started bringing Samir along, confident his puppy dog eyes and shaggy hair would surely melt her little heart – Anika was always a sucker for strays. But just as she was about to let down her defenses, father wandered in, saw Samir and muttered under his breath "a little bastard from a little…w****". It was the final insult.

Anika, too little to understand the devastating words, heard only the pejorative tone and instinctively backed off from the boy.

'That's it! I'm leaving!' I screamed. 'Never. Never will I return to this hell-hole again!'

He looked startled, then with a malevolent smile, pointed to the door, said, 'Go right ahead,' and walked away.

I shouted at the bewildered Samir to pick up his artwork strewn all over the floor, grabbed my bag and keys in one swift movement and hastened out the door, looking back once at a red-faced Anika, striking the air with her fists.

'Good!' I heard her tremulous shout as I rushed out. 'Good! And good!'

I have often wondered how little Ana-banana was able to manage father. Acerbic, derisive and simmering in self-righteousness, no one came away from his special brand of vitriol unscathed. In the end, I did not have the strength to defend my character. Let's face it…I was on shaky ground there, anyway. I ran away. Anika obviously took the bull by the horns and even fed him nightly.

Years later, I saw her at her wedding reception. She looked luminous, clothed in traditional red. Her forehead sparkled with colorful dots. A fine gold chain stretched from her twinkling nose ring, curved past her right cheek and latched on, cleverly, to the right earring. The groom, one tentative hand on the small of her back, seemed tall and a little uncomfortable in the absurd turban. I stood staring openly. Sensing my stare, she raised her head. By the time the shock faded from her kohl filled eyes, I was nudged aside by a wedding guest, and then another.

I dropped the gift envelope in the designated box, realizing only after it slid out of my hands that I'd scrawled my congratulations to Ana-Banana, instead of the oh-so-dignified Anika.

My father, thankfully, was nowhere in the vicinity. I left without being introduced to her husband.

It has been decades since I've laid eyes on my sister. I see her only in fragments now, and I'm afraid, if we ever crossed paths, I will no longer recognize the little girl I once knew.

But the shock in her eyes. The dampness of her fingers as she clung to me. The glint of her nose ring as she stood under the wedding *mandal*. Her scream in the hallway, at my back

– Good! Good! and Good! Those things, I do not forget.

Samir

I was treated like a peon by my superiors, local Kuwaitis, furious that one of theirs was denied my position, and with coldness bordering on hostility by the workers I supervised. Fortunately, I have a thick hide and didn't give a shit what anyone thought of me as long as they got the job done. At the end of the month, there was no nod or handshake, just a check warming my pocket.

It was a restless time. I tried tiring myself out, setting the timer on my watch for sixty minutes, running with long, even strides, at the end of the day when the Kuwaiti sun was still harsh but no longer enflamed with devilish intent. By the time I staggered to my apartment, gasping for breath, a cold shower and a beer felt infinitely sexier (and far less taxing) than the thought of seven virgins descending from heaven, for my private pleasure.

At this time, Uzma Habib, the only woman I knew in the country, began figuring in my dreams quite prominently. The way she smoothed her skirt, pressing it with her hands, her long, braided hair begging to be unraveled, the three holes in each ear, three hints for seduction, pierced with metallic studs, but most of all, the way she looked me in the eyes, straight as an arrow: take me or leave me.

When she called more than twice "to check about the job", I realized, with amazement that it was not just professional courtesy, and I asked if she'd like to go out for a beer sometime. To thank her, for all her help, I said. We began seeing each other once or twice a week. Soon, that was no longer enough. I adjusted my run to the pre-dawn hour and met her at the end of each day. Mostly, she talked and

I listened. And when I touched her soft cheek with the tips of my fingers, my first thought was, *am I clean enough? Will I cast a shadow on this truthful face?*

I told her she was the most beautiful woman I had ever met. Not entirely convinced, she answered with a smile. But I was not so naïve I would admit to her it was her unsurpassed honesty that turned me on. Women like to be told they are gorgeous, smart, sophisticated, slender and sexy. To compliment them for their goodness would be like withholding the juiciest bites of the fruit, or like leaving a sentence hanging on a *but*.

I used to look at women with the eyes of a carnivore, savoring the succulent, healthy parts, and discarding the bony, brainy bits of them. Had I but treated them as fellow travelers, trying to find a passage home, perhaps I would have met my Uzma sooner.

Was I angry with women? Or did I fear them with a fear so deep it was indistinguishable from anger? I do not know. What I do know is that I no longer need a machete to untangle my path. With Uzma by my side, I'm already home.

15

Annika

Sunlight sneaked in through the window and stroked each one of my body parts until they shook awake. Old Coot stretched his paws languorously, and I could have sworn there was lust in his eyes. It was the kind of day you do not want to ruin with a peek inside the refrigerator. But I did anyway.

Ice forming on the tissues of days-old ham. Pickles floating in a murky jar like dead fish. Peanut butter that had to be scraped off like cement.

Minutes later, I was at The Buttered Biscuit, wiping jam off my mouth, wrapping up leftovers – a tiny piece of crumb cake, half a turkey croissant, and a barely touched mac-n-cheese pie that would do nicely for lunch and possibly even a midnight snack. Mmmmm! Like sex, but without the complications.

Which reminded me that Adi was due back today. Sorrowfully, I nosed my car towards Wegmans. I hate food shopping.

I'd barely stuck the groceries in the refrigerator and sorted the recycling when I heard a car honk on the driveway and thought it very unusual. My husband does not ever honk. He thinks it's rude. I opened the garage door and saw the parked limousine. Their bags were outside, and the limo driver stood waiting, the back door ajar, cell phone to his ear. It appeared my husband was trying to urge his mother out of the car.

'Hi. What's the matter? Does she need help?'

He looked exhausted, white as a sheet, the tip of his nose red, as if he'd been crying. *What has she done to him?*

'She won't get out of the car.'

'What do you mean, she won't get out?'

'I guess you didn't hear me. Just help me get her out, will you?' he said, taciturn as heck.

She remained in the car, stiff as a board, catatonic really, and would neither budge nor respond to anything we said or did.

'You can carry her out,' suggested the limo driver, voice heavy with boredom, picking his nose surreptitiously with his index finger, one hand still to his ear and still pretending he was on a call.

Adi finally managed to get her out by first pulling her forwards by her legs, then folding her to his chest like an infant. I grabbed one slipper as it slid off her foot and walked ahead of them. He carried her, flailing and mewling, the few yards to the house. Suddenly she found her voice and screamed unintelligible curses at my back. He must've lost his footing, because when I turned around to face them, they were in a heap on the utility room floor, surrounded by shoes. She shrieked as if she was being murdered. He picked himself up, got her upright and went on through.

I squeezed past Adi as he urged her into the den and tipped the limo driver who, mercifully for him, did not do an eye roll or show any emotion whatsoever that would force me to divest him off his teeth. He backed out of the driveway with a quick nod, and I braced myself for whatever came next.

Once in her room, she recognized her chair, her TV and her prayer book. She touched the bathroom door, stuck her head in and seemed reassured. When she sat down and looked sufficiently composed, I asked, 'Would you like some tea? Toast?'

Her eyes lit up. I made myself busy as she itched and belched.

'Sound of music,' I muttered.

Later that night, he gave me a blow-by-blow account of his misadventures on the trip home.

'Until last night, we all thought she wanted to come home. I'm really not sure what went through her mind this morning to make her react so ...' he searched for the word and gave up. Everything about him sagged so that he looked smaller, older. His head, as if tired of sustaining weight, listed to one side. His facial hair, ungroomed, gave him a patchy, infirm air. His skin reeked of failure.

'I had the cab waiting. I packed her bag and put it in the trunk. She was in the breakfast room. Her brother said his goodbyes and tried helping her out of the chair. But she wouldn't get up. It was as if she was comatose, although her eyes were open, and she was sitting up. We tried talking, shouting and prodding. Other than shrugging off my hand from her shoulder, she was completely unresponsive. I pulled her up to a standing position. Her body was stiff. She wouldn't move. Her feet dragged behind her like a sack as I urged her into the cab. Finally, I had to carry her. She began screaming. She became heavy. Deadweight. There was no easy way to affix her in the seat – she wouldn't bend! I think she bumped her head on the edge of the window. There was nothing I could do.' He stopped for a moment and covered his mouth.

'At the airport, it was the same story. This time, she wouldn't get out of the cab! I tipped the driver, had him bring me a wheelchair. She simply would not cooperate.'

He tugged at his hair, frustrated and reliving the scene.

'The airport attendant insisted she keep her feet on the footrest. She wouldn't do it. He refused to wheel her until she sat correctly. I asked him to pick up the bags, if he didn't mind, and I wheeled her inside myself, diving every few seconds like a ruddy whale to shove her feet in the footrest.

'She adhered to the pattern -wouldn't get in the plane. And once seated, she continued to play dead. I told the stewardess not to bother, she wasn't hungry. I ate my cold croissants and drank my tea. Then, somewhere along the way, she woke up. She peered at the brunette seated two rows ahead on the aisle seat and took it in her head it was a relative. She regaled her with news and maintained a loud, one-sided conversation for the rest of the trip.'

'What did you do?' I asked, mortified for him and secretly glad I wasn't on that flight.

'I put my headphones on and made myself deaf and invisible. The other passengers glanced at her and averted their heads. The stewardesses were helpful, but I couldn't ask them to take her to the washroom. Thankfully, she didn't soil herself,' he mused.

'When it was time to debark, I half-carried her down the stairs, one arm around her and one hand on the railing. In the baggage area, I made her sit down and threatened to use force if she so much as moved a muscle.' He looked ashamed, miserable and completely whipped.

'And, of course, there's no point rebuking her tomorrow. It's not as if she will remember any of it. It's like complaining about a nightmare.' He held his head in his hands.

A nightmare that's not about to end anytime soon, I thought, for clearly, her dementia had accelerated.

'You should have a drink,' I said.

'No. I have a presentation to work on. Due tomorrow,' he said, taciturn once again, and shuffled off to his study.

She might just outlive him, I caught myself thinking, and then hastened to the prayer room to recite, three times, the only mantra I knew, for universal health.

Ma

*Satyavaan was destined to die just one year after his marriage.
When Yama, the God of Death, appeared on his chariot to take him to
the kingdom of heaven, his wife, Savitri, blocked his path to plead her
case. For three days she pleaded, debated and finally impressed Yama
with her understanding of the laws of dharma. Touched by her deep-
rooted faith and pleased by her learning, Yama granted her a boon. 'You
can have any one thing in the world you desire, except your husband's
life,' he said.*

Then Savitri, a woman as clever as she was desperate, said,

*'I want to bear a hundred sons and give them my husband's
name.' A stumped Yama was forced to acquiesce. Satyavaan rose from
the dead and followed his wife home.*

I have long been haunted by that ancient tale. I could not
bring my husband back from Yama. He thrashed about the bed as if
his body was on fire. I touched his forehead with the back of my
hand and knew it was malaria. Why did he get up from the bed? Did
he need a drink of water? All he had to do was tilt his head in my
direction. Instead, he rose, swayed on his feet, fell and broke his
head on the concrete floor. I, who could always tell when he needed
something, missed his signal on that fateful day.

When you live in a joint family, your senses are always on high
alert. For over twenty years, his mother's steely eyes waited for me to
slip up, so she could regale the household with tales of my inappropriate
behavior... *she goes to her husband's room at odd hours of the day ...
she eats with her fingers ... she does not wash before bed...* little did
she know, her laundry list of accusations made me stronger, and, as a

matter of fact served to strengthen our marriage!

We talked less and communicated more by way of signals - the cologne he wore, to suggest I shut the bedroom door. The way he arched his brows when I wore pink. How he licked his upper lip to let me know how much he enjoyed the meal.

Ah! But I had my signals too. Pushing back a curl to let him see the new hoops he left under my pillow. Jangling my keys when I was running low on cash. Rubbing my temples to indicate I needed a break. It was a language all our own, nuanced, refrained and unutterably sweet, made obsolete by this tone-deaf generation, obsessed with noise and world-sharing, and it allowed us a sense of privacy in our congested home.

But that day. One moment he was laying down, the cold compress still on his forehead, in a bedroom no wider than the width of my sari, and I was in the kitchen, fanning the stove, coaxing a flame out of ash, and the next moment, he was up, wobbling toward the door. How did he fall on his back? We will never know. Like most young people, who tempt fate with their arrogance, we had no signal for 'I'm in trouble.' His head hit the concrete floor, and he was gone.

Time moved stealthily on and left him behind. I wish I had the cunning of Savitri. Or the protective instincts of a mother. I let my husband die. God forgive me, I also let my first-born die.

Malavika

Samir moved away to Dubai, or was it Kuwait, and I finally had the house to myself. But as it happens, with almost everything in life, the euphoria wore off, tedium set in, and soon, like the fishing boats that had all but disappeared for the season, I too felt the need to test new waters.

It was a silly little advertisement for coconut hair oil that drew me to the hills! "Pure as the driven snow", claimed the nonsensical headline. In the foreground, the smiling face of a woman with her glorious mane ascending to the heavens; in the background, were peaks of snow. I stared and stared at the majesty, the inextirpability, the ascetic calm of the striated mountains and was filled with longing.

All I seek, the heaven above

And the road below me.

Why not? I thought. I did some homework, found the best fare and there I was!

It was a magical time. I bathed in the midafternoon, along with the villagers, when the sun warmed the mountain stream like a benediction. And under the evening skies, I dipped mangoes in the very stream now turned frigid and bit into them, juice dripping down my freezing fingers. I sang without music (I had no need for it) in that remote shanty where gossip did not ripen and laughed with my new friends with the abandon of an afghan woman released from purdah. I picked up a thought and abandoned it before it stole its way to my heart. How wonderful it would be to share this experience with someone, I thought.

Then my son called.

'How long do you plan on staying?' Samir asked.

'I'm looking forward to the rigors of winter. They say it turns into a veritable fairyland.'

'Who says? Who are these friends?' he asked with customary suspicion.

'The shepherds, of course! They are my teachers. They inspire me. They live in the moment, you see. How can they not, when nothing in their lives is certain – not their fleet-footed dinner, not their sagging shelter, not the wrath of the icy mountain with boulders the size of a giant's fist, at the base of which they huddle…'

I continued to wax poetic, and it was a little while before he could interrupt. Apparently, the only two words he heard, that rang like alarm bells in his ears were "winter" and "rigors".

'You are not getting any younger. Winter in the mountains can be catastrophic!'

'Don't be a killjoy Samir!'

'Call me Sammy, for heaven's sake. And isn't it time you went home and cleaned up the place? You can always return next summer,' he said, assuming an obnoxious Captain-like tone.

I tried to explain.

'There is no backyard, vegetable patch or roof garden in my city. Every inch of space is flattened with brick and mortar. Gone the leafy trees, gone the heady bursts of jasmine and night transforming cestrum, gone the fragrance of cilantro and mint wafting through kitchen windows. And gone are the gardeners with tools as obsolete as their skills. Maybe they have put down their hoes and sickles, shears and rakes for a new trade, one that feeds the body and shrivels the soul – cutting stone for builders or carting lunch tiffins to office clerks, or hauling heavy, rope bound luggage at train stations for travelers who roam from city to identical city as if it is not the exact same concrete jungle, everywhere.'

I stopped to catch my breath when he jumped in in his abrupt way, 'What gardens? What gardeners? Since when have you ever concerned yourself with anyone but yourself before?'

He told me that cocooning myself in that cold mountain was just my way of getting as far away as possible from him, from the memory of his father and from everyone I had hurt and wanted to forget.

His words, edged with steel, did not hurt me. Unlike most mothers, I take the words of children for what they are – careless and without merit, flung like a soiled shirt in your face as they run out the door. But Sammy's tone of voice certainly caught me by surprise. There was still so much anger and resentment trapped beneath his fear for my safety. The thought saddened me, made me wonder if we would ever really . . .

'Ma! Are you still there?'

His voice jarred me back to the phone.

'I will write to you,' I muttered. Then he was gone.

⧗⧗⧗

Samir. *Sammy*. The confounding outcome of my first and worst mistake. Was I really trying to emulate the famed actress, or did I instinctively know that widow-white was the appropriate attire in a marriage as dead as ours?

You can be anything – a fashion model, an airline stewardess, an actor...under the awning of a tea stall, surrounded by bearded oafs lugging peace and love in the shape of guitars, I listened to my tawdry friends and let the heady mixture of flattery and hashish, influence my decision to leave Salil Captain. Declaring they were right, fool that I was, I told them I would repair the wrong immediately.

Breathless, I made my way through the dark and narrow streets leading up to our airless abode. As I raced, the questions raced alongside. *How will I handle it? What will I tell him? Who will take care of Samir?* A sneaking suspicion that I had not thought this through, that I was taking this almost as a dare, made me slow down on the stairs, just a little. *And what happens, after I make my big announcement that my marriage is over? How long before the shock fades from their eyes, the applause dies, and I'm forgotten by my hippie friends like a one-hit singer?* These things I thought, or maybe felt them roil in my stomach.

But, as it turned out, the decision was taken out of my hands. I caught Captain in flagrante delicto with a militant looking woman, teeth bared, riding him like a horse, almost making him neigh like one. Her uniform, still stiff, lay on the bedroom floor - a khaki tunic and pants. Once again, my thoughts raced, except this time I stood still as a statue. *A police woman. How ironic!* And then, *He's done this before. Our marriage is a lie.*

Quivering as much with rage as with relief, I shot out of the apartment. My life with Captain was over.

As a single woman, I worked sporadically. A receptionist in a hair salon, a substitute teacher (the math lessons came in handy) and a B-list fashion model, letting impulse govern all my career decisions. Still, I was not unhappy. There was the divorce money. Samir was sent back to boarding school while we pursued an uncivil divorce. A few years later, Captain remarried and moved away, leaving his volatile son during his dreadful adolescence for me to manage. Oh, how the boy hated me, forever crossing the line with his barbs and insults, certain it was I keeping him from his father, until one day, I told him to pack his bags and call his dad. They had a long chat. Bottom line, his father didn't want him. Since then, like it or not, it's been just the two of us.

Samir

She's hiding something. I can only reach her on my mobile phone, and when I do, I have the strangest feeling she is not where she is supposed to be, on the couch in the living room, her knitting at her feet, a book of Sufi poetry on her lap, or, before sunset, sitting cross-legged on her little stool in the balcony, communing with nature, her burgundy pashmina embracing a chair. I can set a clock to the banal busyness of her days, my mother. She who is so set in her ways and so fickle at heart. Oh, she can fool you. Bustling about in the kitchen, fanning the vegetables she so often manages to burn, the smelly evidence of past and present meals - potatoes, herbs, onions… trapped in the hem of her kaftan, then you might almost believe she is just another wife and mother – nurturing and selfless. You would be wrong.

There is a textural distance in her voice, a distance heightened by the absence of background noise – no frenetic TV announcements, no doorbell interruptions, no fruit or vegetable vendors rhapsodizing their wares, which is why for all her light chatter, I cannot shake off a sense of uneasiness.

At last, one day, I ask her point blank, why is it that I can get her on the mobile but never on the land line. Is she away? Is she with a man? And if she is, what's with all the cloak-and-dagger stuff? I am an adult. I can take whatever shit she doles out. That's when she admits she has stolen off to the mountains, to be with herself.

Be with herself. What the fuck does that even mean!

'I'm at Manasarovar,' she says. 'For the weather, I consult a yak. When it appears (she giggles), it's all good. When it doesn't, it means, we're having a stormy day. I love it here, Sammy,' she says. 'I wish I could live here forever!' Her voice rises like a flute and hurts my ears.

I am furious with her silliness. I tell her she cannot possibly handle the severe winters and make her promise to return.

She is blathering on and on about city dwellers and gardens, but none of what she is saying makes sense.

All I know is I don't want to have to pay the air fare and rush home to the intensive care unit because she's contracted pneumonia in the mountains or strained her heart with rock climbing! I need her at her post so I can roam free. It is my turn! I insist she leave at the end of the month, and she finally agrees, although, god knows, she is not one to keep a promise.

A case in point: ninth grade. Spring break. She was to pick me up from school and take me directly to the airport! She said we'd fly to Singapore, just the two of us and that she'd always wanted to take me there.

I had packed my stuff in a duffel bag decorated with peace signs, planes, smiley faces and other symbols befitting an international traveler and made sure all the cool guys caught a glimpse of it. When every single student, including Jai, left, and I was the last one standing in a cloud of dust waving a kerchief at car after car screeching out of the school lot, I knew she was going to let me down. Right on cue, a nun came running into the parking lot with a message.

'Samir? You are Samir, aren't you? Unfortunately, your mother is tied up with some business. You will stay with us in school, for the summer. Come along, then. We'll have fun,' she said, holding one hand out kindly when she saw the look on my face.

I ran away from school, early, the next morning. There was no way in hell I was going to stay there all summer, like some orphan, eating grits with the nuns. It took me thirteen hours by train, bus, and rickshaw to make my way home. At 11 p.m. that night, I rang the neighbor's doorbell, asked for our spare key and locked myself in our apartment.

Mother untied herself from "business" and came home the following day, banging and shouting and pleading at the door, saying she needed to talk to me about something important. I slipped a note under the doorway that pretty much ended the discussion:

I hate you. I wish you were DEAD.

I did not let her in for three days, subsisting on stale bread, jam, pickle and hot mix. Then I got hungry.

16

Annika

I have just returned from my first meeting (and probably the last) at the First Baptist Church. The support group sat in a semi-circle on straight back chairs in the dank basement of the church. Someone had made the effort to cover a side table with sheets of brown paper and arranged a tray heaped with dollar store cookies with gaudy blue and pink sprinkles that always remind me of the sad party hats they make old people wear during the holidays. A couple of Costco-size bottles of ginger ale and a few tubular boxes of unbranded potato chips completed the spread. There were no cups or plates but two rolls of paper towels, conjoined in plastic wrap. The fifteen or so members tried not to stare when I walked in, and one of them kindly shifted her chair to accommodate me. I sat down as quietly as possible.

The group coordinator did not sit in the exact center of the circle. Between her and the next attendee sat a small table, with a bunch of brochures fanned out neatly like a deck of cards. She was a brunette, although her beautiful shoulder length hair was streaked with blonde highlights. She made me feel at ease at once. After going through some house rules, she told me she did not want to put me in a spot, but she asked if I would like to tell the group a little about myself or my current situation, or would I like to wait? I said I'd wait.

It usually takes me a while to dispel the noise I bring in from without. I like to absorb the atmosphere, the brightness or dimness of lights, the body language of the attendees, the texture of the room or hall I find myself in before I can focus on the reason I'm there.

That day was no different. Finally, An African American raised her hand and said she had something to say. Something in her voice, vulnerability, perhaps, made me pay attention.

The woman spoke about an uncle who came to visit a few years ago, while her mother was still alive, and simply stayed on after she passed away. 'At first, I did not have the heart to ask him to leave and later found that I had grown attached to him. He is the only family I have,' she said.

She had tiny freckles across her nose. 'He does the yard work. I do the cooking. Except on weekends, I take over the gardening, and he makes these great roast beef sandwiches,' her eyes smiled. 'We have made a life for ourselves together. But now, he has Alzheimer's, and I feel like I'm being taxed for the couple of years of gin rummy and sandwiches we shared. My money, my health and my every ounce of energy is all spent. He is a big man, and this one time, nearly broke my ribs when he fell on top of me ... I was helping him out of the shower,' she explained.

A tear ran down her cheek as she spoke, and she rubbed her hands together as if they were cold. 'I don't have the courage to ask him to leave,' she cried. 'Where will he go, the shape he is in? I can't take the fear in his eyes. I think he knows what I'm thinking.' She sat down, head bent.

They gave her a few moments of silence. No one gave a suggestion, including the coordinator.

One woman got up and picked up the bottle of soda. She looked around for a cup, did not find any, and returned to her seat, defeated.

Then another woman raised her hand. She said she kept misplacing keys, glasses, even her pocket book. At first, she thought it was funny and even poked fun at herself, talking to her son, who was a doctor. But a couple of weeks ago, she lost her way around her condo complex. 'I felt like I was three, when we went to Great Adventure,' she said. 'My brother lost his hold on my hand, and for about ten minutes, the longest minutes of my life, I did not recognize anything! The world turned fuzzy, unreal. The rides, the happy people, the cotton candy stalls, so innocent just a minute ago, became booby traps, the moment he dropped my hand,' she said. Her eyes were enormous. 'That is how I feel these days. Any moment it can happen. I will lose my way. I will *lose my way.*' Her voice caught as she repeated the last words. She had rosebud lips and a smooth round face under a halo of fine blonde hair. She clutched the sides of the chair as if she was trying to stay tethered, afraid she would fall through the floor the moment she let go. There were a few murmurs when she stopped. The woman sitting by her side rubbed her shoulder.

The coordinator spoke at length about the resources available at the center and patted the leaflets by her side.

'I have *resources*,' the woman interrupted. 'My son is a doctor. I just … I just needed to talk to someone, preferably, people I did not know, people who … were not family,' she finished. Everyone nodded. One woman continued to nod her head like a wind-up toy that keeps spinning long after the battery wears out. The coordinator turned her eyes in my direction.

'Would you like to go next?' she mouthed her question.

'Okay,' I cleared my throat.

'My friend Anne Burke told me about your support group,' I said. 'She thought it would help to share.' I coughed. 'A few years ago, my mother in-law came to live with us.' My voice shook a little, I noted. It usually strengthens when I stop trying to listen to my own diction or gauge reactions while I'm talking. I've learned not to let it bother me.

I told them we had our minor, inevitable skirmishes, but in retrospect, everything used to be pretty hunky dory.

'However, in the past year, she's gone from being fully self-sufficient to needing help with her clothes, her shower, her hair. She's set a few minor fires, broken her wrist bone, cracked a couple of ribs, sprained her ankle, had a stent put in her leg and got a pacemaker for her heart,' I said ruefully. 'Lately, she's also lost most of her language and motor skills. She hallucinates and is sometimes paranoid.' I stopped, to catch my breath and rebuke myself for giving way too much information.

'The thing is,' I said, 'The thing is, every hour of every day, is different. There is no how-to guide because the program keeps changing. And emotionally too, the connection is sporadic, intermittent. As if the wire is corroded or … or the outlet has a defective clamping system or the connection itself, our connection … is too weak.'

I stopped again, thinking about what I'd just said, wondering if I was talking gibberish. But the coordinator nodded, *aha, aha,* as if I was making perfect sense, as if she knew the feeling.

I went on. 'We are adults. Older adults. My husband and I. We know our responsibilities and take them seriously. But I like walking in the rain. I like slipping on my shoes and running out for pie. I like having chili cookouts on the spur of the moment and taking the train to NYC on glorious summer afternoons. I like taking a day off and reading in bed all day, and I like talking to my girlfriends for hours on end over the phone. I like shrugging off my work load and simply being,' I said.

'And all of that, I can no longer do.

I cook. I clean. I monitor. *Chug, chug and chug.* That is the sound of tedium.' I said.

'Of course, there are times I'm still happy. Don't get me wrong. I still read, although not at a stretch, binge watch Netflix in the middle of the night and invite close friends over for chili – who has time for elaborate meals? And there are times when I'm truly grateful. She keeps me humble, you see. Grounded. It is like being allowed a peek inside some future-mirror and nodding to the person one might become, down the road, but then, I hear music drifting from a party across the street or the wind rustling through the trees or a goldfinch rocking madly from branch to branch and I am filled with hatred. For my life. For her.

Then there are times when I have a headache, or it burns when I pee, or I have a cold I cannot shake, and I'm fully aware how petty that is, for what is a cold when one is losing words, or losing a foothold on one's surroundings? And that is when I detest the sound of her phlegmy cough, the dentures gaping on the sink, her pee trail on the bathroom floor, the applesauce the color of excreta, and the never-ending pills, the overdrawn drama, the plastic face of Pat Sajak on TV, or the deafening, canned revelry of game shows and her passive aggressive silences.

Then I want to run away, lose myself deep inside a forest. Pay attention, once more, to my personal, picayune life. I want to be totally, unrepentantly selfish,' I said, and sat down, my head in my hands. Someone found a cup (miraculously) and filled it to the brim with ginger ale. I drank thirstily.

On my way out, avoiding pity-full eyes, I picked up a couple of brochures just to be polite. The coordinator said, 'It was a pleasure meeting you, and I hope you come again.' I mumbled something about time constraints and would surely try.

On the drive home, I thought there were a lot of stories out there. Perhaps I could arrange to meet some of those women in another, more casual setting, and blog about them. Then I was ashamed, maybe because that is not what I would want for myself – to become a minor character in someone else's story.

⏳⏳⏳

I peruse my journal before lights out:

2010: His aunt is supposed to come down to spend a week with Ma while we are away. She's had a wellness-check up and pronounced as well as she can be under the circumstances.

Abrupt change of plans. Heard a low moan that soon turned into a furious, one-sided argument. She was on the floor on her haunches, in a pool of urine, her hands attacking the air.

Adi tried to make her talk.

She pointed fearfully at the window, then without warning, started beating her chest. It took all his strength to pin her hands behind her back so she wouldn't hurt herself, until the terror left her eyes, and she fell into his arms, a limp and lifeless thing. We canceled the trip.

Dr. S. has asked us to cut down on the dosage for her trigeminal nerve issue. No mention was made of the psychotic episodes.

2012: Hurricane Sandy storming the East Coast, sinking its teeth into neighborhood trees like a wounded lion. My trees all dead…exposing their vital organs in a grotesque display. One tree crashed, a few hundred yards away from us, on the roof of a house, severing the structure in two, each raw and splintered half aching for the other.

No electricity for a day and a half.

Ma is in the ER, shuddering and retching after a fall. Back-up generators ensure the business of care-giving goes on as usual. I sat by her side all night and nodded off, chin buried in my chest.

A hospital trolley with a faulty, lagging wheel, clanged past the room. Drool in the front of my blouse! Ugh!

2013: I was still sniffing my birthday roses when I heard her cry for help.

She lay in a heap between the toilet and the bathroom sink! Cracked her head tripping over her pants, when she rose from the toilet, apparently.

Will I ever forget Little Martin Richard, with his toothy grin, on the TV monitor above her hospital bed? Two bombs detonated on Boylston Street near Copley Square at the 117th annual Boston Marathon. Dzhokhar Tsarnaev (so young) stared at the destruction about him like a poet. Horrendous!

Visit after visit, I bring her flowers. Duty, dressed as love.

2014: She was on Skype with her daughter when she started drooping, prayer beads still cuffed to her wrist. Something was off. Called the first responders.

Meanwhile, Malaysia Airlines, Flight 370, snatched out of the air and hurtled into the abyss. 227 passengers and twelve crew members lost!

2015: A nurse came in, yesterday, and asked me to wait outside while he attended to Ma. I could hear him cooing. *How are you, sunshine? Bet you would like a snack, eh? Oh... you are so cute.* He sounded tender and affectionate. When he was done, we spoke for a bit.

His name was Ed. 'I'm from Spring Lake, been in NJ all my life. Went to Monmouth University. Love my job. Like a mint?' I took the proffered candy and smiled my thanks.

'How about you?'

I mumbled something about writing and pottering about the house. He widened his green eyes flecked with sunlight and gold and smiled a dimpled smile. He talked easily, Ed from Spring lake, about rollerblading and guitar lessons, and using the extra cash for the monthly train pass, which works out cheaper if you feel up to clubbing in NYC... and while I was still blinking, he was gone. Sweet Ed. Gone like the last five years of my life. A rocket trail of dreams trailing behind him.

⧗⧗⧗

I can hear her furious rant as Adi tries to help her out of the bath. By the time they are done, he is red in the face. A vein on his forehead is popping alarmingly.

The visiting nurse is due to arrive. I clear up the clutter and position myself in my usual chair. She arrives promptly, shaking the outdoors out of her hair. She looks fresh as a lily, strong as a horse. As she goes about her chores, I jealously imagine trading places with her. I go to the deck, not reading. Chin pointed to the sun, eyes shut tight, I am blinded, but lack the will to change positions. Life ticks on.

Ma

I'm losing sight of my memories. Whole passages of time swirl behind the eyelids, obscuring logic. Perhaps it's from the fall. Or so she tells me. But I think I recall being pushed. Unless, that is something I saw on TV? They say it is normal, when you are my age, to confuse situations and conflate events, eras ...but what if I'm building a *new* set of memories, someone else's memories? I can almost see them, seeping into my brain and, like the roundworm, laying its eggs in the space reserved for my husband, my children, my mother! Can that happen? I am filled with nameless dread.

Family ties. Without them, the heart is just a muscle, the size of a fist, a *Lub dub, lub dub* performer that dies without self-knowledge, or a send-off.

Ah! A memory. Or maybe it was something that happened in a dream. *Is there a difference?* Two women minding the kitchen, where once, there was one. New Ma and I. The balance of power shakes and shifts so that each of us is affected in unexplainable ways.

How could Father not see that most fires begin in the kitchen before the flame spreads to the rest of the house?

If I suggested rice and curry, she insisted on roti and pigeon peas. If I asked for rice pudding, she felt compelled to throw out the rice because "it had weevils in it". One day, fed-up of her wicked interference, right in the middle of our tussle, I took matters in my own hands and plunged a heavy butcher's knife, straight through a chicken, so that it lay bleeding on the table, scraps of fat and tissue flying in all directions. New Ma, who was a strict vegetarian (I had not yet converted) went *aaaah*, as if I had plunged the knife directly

194

into her heart, and then thrashed about, screaming bloody murder all over the house. The servants ran out of the kitchen, followed by the pungent smell of burned garlic and blackened onions. Of course, I was punished. Father sent me away to visit an elderly aunt, a one-month sentence far worse than it sounds, for it was a place so dismal that someone drew a line across the name at the railway station and renamed it the Village of the Dead.

She was kindly and easy going, my aunt, but her kitchen was spare, and her home faced south, so we rarely had the pleasure of light. The walls, whitewashed with a rough hand, were bare of family pictures or embroidered tapestries with words like Happy Home or My Family, cleverly woven between green vines and purple fruit. Faded with time, barely furnished, the house sat in a perpetual state of misery, unwilling to accept change or furniture. Despairingly, I went from room to room, looking for a comfortable chair, a desk, writing paper in which to bury my thoughts. At last, I found, in a corner, by the stove, a metal stool, used no doubt to get to the cobwebs or colanders stuck for life in high corners. And on that stool, I served my sentence, facing the street, counting the days before I could go home.

Every stick of furniture in my father's house was handcrafted by local artisans.

I would lovingly stroke the mahogany arm of each chair and marvel at its worn dignity. You had to look closely and feel with the tips of your fingers the intricate carving on its fanned back, designed not simply to enfold the whole person, but also raise his status in magical ways.

Seated on his chair, my father, a man of considerable bulk, instantly turned into a king dispensing advice, justice, reason. Our servant, Ram, once had the boldness to sit on the very same chair, and I was astounded to see the difference it made in his manner. His back became upright, his neck elongated and he moved his head slowly from side to side, like a Minister. Even New Ma took on the elegance emanating from her preferred chair until she stood up, and shrank in status.

Every stick of furniture was a work of art, the loving hands of the artisan lending it shape. My father introduced us to the raw material, the grain, the *figure* in wood as well as to the artisan, his temperament and his history:

He is nimble.

He is blind.

He is strong as an ox.

He suffers from tuberculosis.

He is in debt.

He is a good husband.

He is a lovesick mule.

This is how we were connected to our furniture, the small business community that we cherished.

The furniture in my son's house is cold, untouched by time and circumstance. Certainly, it is far more comfortable than the grainy chair, my rollback desk (that often stuck whilst opening or shutting) where I hid my books, and the four–poster bed with corners that dug into my calves each time I crawled in or out of the flimsy mosquito netting that had to be mended, almost daily. But where is the designer, the carpenter, the man behind all this modern comfort? Where is his soul? Not in the over-lit, passages of Costco Wholesale, certainly.

Even after I returned from the Village of the Dead, New Ma, still anxious to prove her usefulness to my father, nosed her way into my life with the obstinacy of a woodpecker. One day, she came to my room uninvited, examined my unsupervised reading, her sloping breasts attracting the chalk dust on my desk, and swept the bookshelf of my *disgusting, useless* material. Before I had a chance to react, all my books (I had three) disappeared under her tunic and out the room. Enraged, both at the intrusion and the loss of my most prized possessions, I resorted to the no-fail strategy of pressing my lips in a tight line and refusing to swallow a bite until I had my way. Several uneaten meals later, the books reappeared.

But not the harmony.

I suppose I can understand now, although I would not go so far as to sympathize with her position. Displaced from her own home, married to a man twice her age, and now knocked over by a mere child - the littlest *shatranj* piece in the game of chess, New

Ma's anger bloomed into a firestorm that could not be contained. Increasingly, I feared her, the way one fears the flicking tongue of a garter snake, for what flowed out of her mouth was so full of poison. And although I never changed expression (*a woman must look serene and good tempered at all times*, everybody knows that) it was the slow accumulation, the drip, drip, drip of humiliations that made me hunch my shoulders and curl into a ball.

I realized then that I had no power over the adults who managed my life. I feared that everything I loved - my books, my father, my room - could be taken from me at any time. I lost focus at school and often spent whole evenings pleading a migraine until I heard the pipes vibrate in the wall and ceiling; her room was right next to mine and she took punishingly long, cold showers. Only then did I hasten out to the kitchen to put together a snack – a glass of milk, sweetened rice, listening all the while for her wet feet slapping on the hallway floor.

The very thought that our paths might cross as she hurried in for a scalding glass of tea, to soothe the complaints rising out of her wheezy chest, made my heart race, my fingers clumsy.

I suppose, over the years, we learned to coexist peacefully.

Maybe God was training me for my future life in my husband's home. Who knows! This much I have learned. Old conflicts often get swallowed by larger issues or, like summer insects, weaken and die in the wake of a healing rain. But the migraines, alas, became as constant as a nervous tick and plague me to this day.

Thankfully, very early on, I began to recognize the signs and was able to manage the pain with a host of home remedies collected from neighborhood grannies.

How strange I must have looked, I sometimes think, like a swami with powdered cinnamon or cloves drawn across my forehead in three parallel lines! Sachets of herbs with unpronounceable names were pressed to my nose; a glass of gingered tea, covered with a piece of muslin, sat on the sideboard and the room was darkened at all times. Small wonder that my friends became almost fearful of me and treated me then, as my daughter-in-law treats me today—with the distant courtesy reserved solely for the very old or the very sick.

In an unexpected way, the migraines brought me closer to

Father. He drifted to my room every now and again for a few words of comfort, an apple, a shy, how-are-you.

His presence warmed me like a pashmina wrapped around my heart on a cold January day.

Where is Father? Is he gone?

☙☙☙

On the screen, every day there are deaths. Some violent, some merely shocking. Almost everyone I ever knew is gone. Heart attack. Kidney failure. Cancer. Old age. Do people ever die of non-physical causes? Such as sadness or excess of joy? I am told a man died recently when he realized he had all the winning numbers on his lottery ticket. 'It was his heart,' they said. This is what I think. It got too full! In my case the end will not come because of fullness. Quite the opposite. My heart is a vessel, nearly seeped of all emotion.

How old was she? How did she die? They will ask my son.

'Oh, it was her heart. It died of emptiness,' he will say.

☙☙☙

There is a gentleman who comes to visit every day at 3 p.m. The moment I see him, all the noise in my brain quiets down. I press my hands in greeting.

I must be his cousin or aunt, or perhaps his sister. Why else would he visit me in my room and make small talk and have no one call it unseemly? I push my hand out. It whooshes through the air. I am a ghost. Or I am in a land of ghosts. Or I am a ghost lost among the ghosts of my ancestors.

The gentleman comes to visit every afternoon. But the thing is that *she* giggles in her annoying way each time I ask her to serve him tea or refreshments.

'Not here. On TV,' she says, with the finger pointing and clipped sentences one uses to clarify something to a child or a deaf-mute.

'Well,' I say to her, 'is it so hard to believe I can have relatives in high places?' She is very arrogant for one whose sister ran away and lived in sin! But then, my son does not disagree with her.

And I wonder, is the gentleman indeed a visitor on TV, or my mind playing tricks? Am I insane? I will call my daughter. She will tell me the truth.

The roundworm is also making me lose words. It is like threading a needle without your glasses on. The tip of the thread simply will not connect with the eye of the needle. The thread won't go through, and I cannot sew the words together to form a sentence. The worm is cruel. It turns language into shit and is turning me into a joke. I often hear *her* laugh, whisper about me: *She calls oranges buttons and zucchini a hammer!* Perhaps I do. Perhaps my daughter-in- law thinks *she* will never age.

Malavika

It was not the harsh winter that influenced my decision.

For weeks, I luxuriated in a dreamless sleep and awoke refreshed and excited, flinging open the windows, never tiring of my singular, mountain idyll.

I do not know what changed, but at some point, I started dreaming, almost nightly, of my apartment in the city. Unlike the usual phantasmagoria of twists and turns and plots within plots, I now saw brief, static images and small segments of my life, replayed in sleep:

I'm in my curtain-less bedroom, beams of sunlight strafing my eyeballs. Or,

I open the door, and a feral cat, lazily licking a spilled pouch of milk, is staring at me askance. Or, I'm arguing with my son, oddly, about a velvet couch donated by a friend.

Or, I'm holding my nose, skirting a puddle of dog shit on my driveway!

The following dawn, I thought I woke up to the sound of automobile traffic. I looked out of my window. A solitary lamb stood nibbling at long stalks of grass in the distant field. A river burbled at my feet, glittering like a platter of stars. So why did my heart not stir with gladness?

Disoriented, I tried getting back to sleep. This time I thought I woke to the sound of my neighbor tap dancing in the hallway during one of his drunken excesses. Of course, it was just a restless water pipe. Worrying the rheum out of my eyes, I made my morning cup of tea, only to find I was out of cream-filled biscuits. And just like that, I knew I'd had enough.

Home where my thought's escaping, home where my music's playing... I whistled, as I packed.

Samir

In the past, I always envied those goons on shows like Extreme Makeover. They start out behaving like Jabba the Hutt, lumbering in basements, reeking of fried chicken, only to resurface a few months later, all the lumps and bumps smoothed out, features re-molded, and confidence oozing out of their pores. If you can stand watching the final episode, you will see the camera pan over their hard, testosterone-rich bodies as they describe the boot camp months with deprecating smiles then sink into the waiting arms of teary-eyed wives, mothers, the whole freakin' human race.

What I envy most about these new "poster boys" for hope, faith and charity is their unflagging optimism, the simplistic belief (driven home, no doubt, by the makers of the show) of "lose the pounds, and you will gain the will to live".

The will to live - that is her gift to me. Uzma Habib.

I was pounding the streets, going door to door looking for a reason to wake up the next morning, bright with expectation, my manhood raised like a flag. Funnily enough, that's also what I saw in the eye of almost every woman I ever met, except of course for Mother (who wanted nothing from me and expected even less, certainly not a relationship).

Expectation. From the nuns in school, who offered to convert me with pictures of damnation and hellfire and a side order of grits, to Principal Spencer, who expected no more than my tight, round arse, to the ayah who offered her nuzzle-ready breasts like some overhanging fruit she was afraid might rot from lack of use, to the tribal women who offered to jack you off for a loaf of bread or a carton of milk. Then, there was Sherri, who wanted more than a friendship, but less than a relationship - a simmering ardor? A sleepy-eyed romance before she found her perfect mate? I never did figure that one out. And finally, Rama Jain, who pulled down her panties for every man I left bruised and bleeding at her feet - a favor for a favor. They made me who I am today – a fragmented creature, onanistic, and unwholesome.

But now, I have Uzma Habib. Even the sound of her name, a balm to the spirit.

We meet, and we meet.

The thought of her first thing in the morning floods my mouth like an almond cookie encased with chocolate, sprinkled with sea salt. There is a sweetness to her that is not cloying. A directness that does not prick, yet makes itself felt. She is Sherri, but clothed in modesty, my mother, but with the quality of constancy, and the complete opposite of the myriad women in public buses and busy streets that I have ignored in the past or used and promptly discarded because they either flaunt their beauty like auctioneers or subdue their intelligence with mundane lives.

Uzma without guile, you have my heart. Uzma without glitter, you shine so bright, I am dazzled. I am forever yours.

17

Annika

It is winter, and the skies are filled with prophetic silence. The clouds darken, hover low and disappear into inky blankness. There are flurries, then heavy snow, swallowing the low roofs of ranch style homes. Snow bowed branches brush against Ma's window. In the ashy light, her ashen face. I wonder how much she sees and how much she simply senses. The wind ruffles her hair. Memory flutters on her lids. The wooden blinds twist and tap against the window, their syncopated distress.

I bring in her supper. Her hand slips into mine, and there is an expression in her eyes I do not recognize. I sit beside her. Brushing imaginary specks of dust with her other hand, she tells me this:

When Yama swallowed my first-born child, I thought for many years that I had drunk from the deepest cup of sorrow. Like poison, it spread through my veins, and I developed immunity to the simplest of pleasures. I could not taste food, especially the foods that my son loved, and my skin became sensitive to color. I could bear only white and broke out in hives if I so much as held a bright fabric against my skin. My tongue grew heavy, and often, I could not speak except through gestures. I became uncomfortable and inept in social situations and began dropping tea, juice, water … things fell from my hands and drifted across the floor, not wishing to connect. Yes. He died on a tour of duty, but I knew it was my doing. The uniform that I starched and lovingly pressed and urged him to wear, was returned to me in a plastic bag.

She wiped a tear and went on.

'Witnessing a death, when it finally occurs, is like witnessing a yawn or a sigh. It is almost a non-event. What is indescribable is the emptiness that follows in its wake. No longer are you seated on a chair beside the spouse, parent, child or friend, vigilant and mute, thoughts ticking slower than the ticking clock. No. Now, you are seated by an empty bed, forsaken by the soul on its final journey, toward god. Still. You cannot let the tug of bereavement pull you into its abyss. Bewilderingly, all about you, life still abounds. Their eyes, jumping out of their faces, have never looked more alive as when a life becomes a death. You need to hold them close, the living ones, and help them move on. This much I have learned. Grief is like a tunnel. You walk through it and come out at the other end, sun-shy but ready to walk again. If you don't, it can become a burial ground for the undead. After a while, you would rather stay in the hole, derive solace from the darkness and find comfort in its bony arms. Do not get consumed by death, is all I can say.'

She was holding my hand now, in a fervent sort of way.

'Letting go of my grief meant releasing my son to Him, with a garland of roses on the white sheet spread above his stopped heart. I was not ready for a long time. But in the end, I did let go. You see, his wife was pregnant. Then the baby came. With her father's wide forehead and her mother's milky coloring, she shrieked into the night. And when her little fingers wound around mine, and her mother stood frozen by her side, her long hair undone, I knew it was all up to me. It was I who held her hands as the child took her first steps forward. And she held mine. Together we learned to walk away from death. Does that mean I love him less?'

She was looking at me dully, not looking for an answer.

Suddenly she is exhausted. Her hands flitting as furiously as her thoughts fall to her side. With a sigh, she rises, and then sits back on the chair. I know she probably wants to lie down but is afraid I might think she's being rude. Also, she will not lie down immediately after a meal.

I wait for her to tell me more, but she has either lost the thread or tired herself out.

'I'm sorry,' I say, gently.

She stares at me then as if seeing me properly for the first time.

'You must rest now. I'll sit here. Keep you company.'

She nods. Then she does something Gone-Mother used to do between my rushing in from school and rushing out to play; she traces her fingers across my cheeks.

'You are a good girl,' she says.

Then she takes to her bed. Soon, her mouth goes slack, and she is asleep.

I watch her face, corrugated as a hand-written note, folded and refolded before it is smoothed over. Her lips are chapped, and her once black hair now faded to widow-white. The walls of her room, painted a luminous shade of lavender, look gray in the setting sun, and her wheezing mutes all household sounds. One day, I think, with a catch, I will look at this chair or this bed, and instead of her body, I will see a slight, barely perceptible dent and a film of dust.

Perhaps, for the first time, I saw her that day, not as a show-and-tell example of old age, but as one who had outlived a father, a husband, two sons and most of her peers and looked into the maw of hell every day. I realized I had to treat her with more care, certainly more compassion. I could do nothing about the past, but surely, I could make the rest of her days a tad more comfortable.

Ma

At first, I thought she was a figment of my imagination, just like the gentleman who visits me daily. My son says he is not real. He lives on the screen. Then I touch her. She is real! And warm, and unbearably beautiful. She says she is my granddaughter. *Where is her father?* I want to ask. A memory lurks like a cloud over my head. I shoo it away. If the question fills you with dread, surely nothing good can come from knowing the answer. So, I hold my silence.

'Is your mother well?' I ask instead. 'Yes! I have gifts for you from her.'

My mouth starts to water. I do not remember the last time I have unwrapped a gift just for me. I could use a purse. A soft cardigan. Some lotion. Slippers. But it will not do to seem greedy. 'Later,' I tell her. 'There is no hurry.'

I cover my face with my hands. She looks nonplussed, then smiles and leaves the room. I take a nap. When I wake up, she is still there. Child of my child. For months after I lost my firstborn, I was spinning alone in a web of grief. Then this one grabbed my little finger and curled it in her fist.

There are packages under the coffee table. I point to them shyly.

At last, she brings them over. She draws close to me and sits at my feet. Then she pulls each gift out, one at a time, like a magician pulling scarves out of his hat. She removes the wrapping carefully. The paper crackles between my thumb and finger before it slides to the floor. She spreads a lap throw on my knees.

'Do you like it? Is it soft?' I pick it up and let it drop – I am gracious. 'It is beautiful. But I have three already. You must take this back,' I say. She nods and puts it away.

She pulls out a tube of something. 'Face cream,' she says.

I open the tube and sniff it. 'Mmmm,' I say, and she smiles, pleased.

'A teddy bear from my daughter,' she says. I pick up the toy. I ask her how old she is. 'Eight. Her name is Deena.'

'Thank you, Deena.' I shake teddy's arms and legs and then blow him a kiss. She giggles. 'Wait!' She says. 'Do that again.'

She is taking a picture. Her phone is equipped with a camera! I smile and blow a kiss for Deena. She gives me a hug.

Youth is beautiful, entertaining and awe-inspiring. It is its own accomplishment. She sees the awe in my eyes and is flattered.

I often think that when you are no longer a participant, you are no longer of any use. It is time to bow out with grace. But surely there is some merit to simply staying alive as a witness? To fold one's wings and rest and bless from a distance? This grandchild seems to think so. In her eyes, I see no pity, only love. I imagine it is a relief for her, too, not having to prove anything, simply to show up and be loved by this sagging bag of bones.

She pulls out a pair of slippers. They are lovely. Soft, padded. My feet go in all the way. 'Ah! Just what I needed.' I stroke her hair. She lays her head on my knees. I am suddenly afraid. *A woman must not love too much. It makes the gods jealous.* Everybody knows that.

Malavika

With prescription in hand and previous x-rays for reference, I awaited my turn. I have to admit, I was deathly afraid, my heart beating like an adulterer who fears detection. Still, I exchanged pleasantries with the female technician at the radiology center, until it was time for my mammography. Of course, I cursed, all through the process, the man who invented the instrument that squeezes your mammaries until you are ready to scream, and then squeezes some more. Finally, it was done. The technician handed me my clothes and directed me to the changing room. The report would be faxed to my doctor.

I didn't give it a thought until a few weeks later, when I received a note from my doctor, advising me to get a second mammogram and an ultrasound, just to be sure.

Sure, of what? Why are doctors always so mysterious?

So, there I was! In the waiting room, I tried to imagine my body a leveled field, a scarf around my hair, my eyes immense. *These things happen only to other people.*

I tried to focus on the chef demonstrating vegetable Manchurian on the food channel, and suddenly, inexplicably, for I had a decent breakfast, I was starving. I decided I'd go food shopping the instant I could leave. *While I can still eat.*

I went to the torture chamber once more, a little woozy with and possibly, the strange hunger pangs. Again, she handled my breasts like so much meat, which is what they really are, I suppose, and, as before, released the plates pressing into my flesh just one second before I passed out from the pain.

M is for mammogram ... and mother ...and Malavika, I thought for no good reason.

Will it still be me, when they cut them off?

On the way home, the hunger pangs gone as suddenly as they'd appeared, I found myself thinking of Shroff. Next to his bookshelf was a little prayer pamphlet with "*Nirvana Shatakam*" written on the cover, in archaic decorative font. The lettering took up the top half of the page. On the bottom half, the artist had drawn a simple line illustration of the sun rising between two mountain peaks. Inside, on the very first page was a six-fold shloka in Sanskrit. I do not have a photographic memory, but bumping along in my rickshaw, hemmed in on both sides by traffic, I could have sworn I saw the entire shloka run before my eyes like ticker tape:

I am not mind, nor intellect, nor ego,

nor the reflections of inner self

I am not the five senses.

I am beyond that.

I am not the ether, nor the earth,

nor the fire, nor the water or wind.

I am indeed,

That eternal knowing and bliss, Shiva,

love and pure consciousness.

I recited the words aloud, making the driver swerve and stare in confusion. Without batting an eye, I held my cell phone to my ears and continued in that vein for five more verses, as if it was the most natural thing in the world, speaking in a dead language, to the ghost on the other end.

By the time I reached home, I knew, whatever the outcome of the tests, it was time to make some pretty radical changes in what was left of my life.

Samir

We meet, and still we meet. And in between the compulsive touching, the rubbing of shoulders, the nibbling of earlobes, Uzma forces me to re-examine my life and gives me back my self-esteem.

'You have the opportunity, now live the dream,' she says, sounding a little like a keynote speaker at a graduation ceremony.

'Broaden your horizons, Sam. Finish Design School, or at least take some courses in commercial art.'

'But I don't think I'm very good,' I mutter.

'You were really good at drawing comic books, weren't you? And they called you a hero, if I recall correctly?' Her finger is on my neck button.

'I don't know. When you have no other means of entertainment in a boys' school, comic books are like gold, but outside…'

'Oy, don't sell yourself short, it is so not sexy.' She covers my mouth with her own.

And for my every why she has a *why not*, for my every nay, a *but perhaps* … steadily peeling a lifetime of doubts, like burrs off my skin. Then we continue where we left off, hands finding hands, lips tasting lips and, at some point, I find myself mumbling, 'Yes. All right. I will look into some online courses.'

Ah! It is so good for a while.

How naturally her body fits into mine. How, entangled in hotel sheets, we traverse whole continents. Her eyes, round and shining, lighting the way past the sloping hills and down the mossy valleys of her silken body, her fingers like drumbeats, shuddering down my back. Together we sniff out the best places to camp – the pillows of my lips, the junction of her breasts, the crook of my arm and the spot where her pulse moves to my will, like the throat of a frightened bird.

Sometimes, I pull away for minutes at a time, the distance between us like a gaping wound. I want to show her how it feels to be separate, exposed and vulnerable. Then slowly, with languorous design, I close the distance, warm her with breath and touch again. 'See how it feels to fit back?' I silently ask. 'Like two halves of a mandala. Closer,' I plead urgently, 'closer please.' Then she laughs, exuberant as surf frothing around a jet ski, 'If I get any closer, we will be stuck, like Siamese twins!'

'Umm. Siamese twins aren't really stuck, you know, they are...'

But she shushes me again, with a kiss, 'And here I thought you were just another pretty face.'

Then, just as it is getting comfortable, just as I'm beginning to draft a note to Mother, *I might have some good news*, we are "seen" at the beach, under a perfect sky, my hand cupping her breast, my face hidden in her raven hair ... and for that, my Uzma pays a heavy price.

'What is it?' I ask her, as she rushes into my arms, her hair in her eyes, and claps the door shut clumsily with the heel of one foot. She lifts her blouse and turns around to reveal the bruises on her back. 'We can never be seen in public again,' she says. 'Promise me.'

I try not to show the relief I feel, *she didn't say we had to break up*, 'I will kill them!' I rant against the men in her family, knowing full well it is an empty promise. This is not India. There are no policemen I can bribe, no friends I can ask for help. It is a foreign county, where a man in my position can, with one word, find himself unemployed, imprisoned or, worse still, deported.

18

Annika

On Tuesdays, she sits in the front seat of the car with her son, a spot of color on each cheek. On these half days, she, who is both mother and child, brims with lucid energy. He drives her to the GP, then her kidney and heart specialists. They, especially the nurses, make such a fuss over her, I wonder if she finds it embarrassing. 'Your mother is so cute!' 'How are you doing, sweetheart?' They say, lengthening the words and making the soft cooing sounds reserved for a child that I personally find offensive. Stop infantilizing her, *sweetheart*, I want to say to nurses and attendants everywhere, but of course, I hold my tongue.

After the visit, she generally makes a direct or oblique demand, depending on her mood, or simply holds her stomach, as if she's hungry, and he takes her out for a coffee and pancakes. When they return home, his step is lighter, the slump in his shoulders almost non-existent, a self-congratulatory smile hovering on his lips. She, however, slinks in guiltily, does not make eye contact and goes straight to bed. What does she think of in the moments before her eyes close? The warm hands of the doctor as he helped her into her chair; the dusting of powdered sugar on the waitress' apron, the steam rising from the freshly made coffee, poured like golden lava into her cup, the delicious, undivided attention of her son? Or does she simply pass out from sheer exhaustion?

I have my own routine – sun salutations, coffee and more coffee. Today, as I'm stirring my breakfast oatmeal, I hear Malavika's voice, as clear as if she is looking over my shoulder, 'Are you going to eat that? It looks like vomit.' Startled, I turn around, half expecting to see my pimply sister, who, I now know, was probably going through the difficult years when the body develops faster than the mind, skipping around the house, lunging at me with a spoonful of porridge, whispering eat snot, eat snot or something equally disgusting, with the sole intention of making me throw up all over the kitchen floor and suffer Father's ire.

The phone rings. The caller wants to know if I would be willing to make author visits to local libraries and rattles off a few dates. Still amazed, my first book is not only published but well received, I thrust the past where it belongs and attend to the present. Eagerly, I agree to the visits.

⌛⌛⌛

I knew the author visits would have to be canceled unless we could find someone to sit with Ma. When her granddaughter called to say she would love to visit, with heart in my mouth, I asked her if she could make it in the second week of the month. There was a pause as she checked her calendar, then, 'Yes, I can do that,' she says with certainty. I remember I had to sit down, weak with relief.

Which is how I got to be the sole proprietor of my car for a few short hours. Ma was thrilled to see her granddaughter. I was thrilled to iron a blouse instead of throwing on a t-shirt streaked with permanent stains, use gel to tame my frizzy hair and wear mascara again! With a final dotting of lip-gloss, I took one last look in the mirror, and the universe smiled back.

Shutting the door on the complex smell of Ponds cream, pee and vanilla candles, I stepped into a glorious afternoon. The air was crisp. Sunlight streamed through trees and splotched the street with puddles of light. Neighbors in light coats, cardigans and hoodies rounded the corner, some pushing strollers with pink-faced babies holding up their hands to the sun, exulting in its loving warmth.

I entered the library room, reserved for my book discussion, my senses on high alert. I can usually smell a critical, hostile or, worst of all, an indifferent temperament even before I've situated myself on the podium. In such a case, there is not much to do but present my work thoughtfully and neither invite nor decline feedback.

Today, that was not the case. The sight of forty eager faces greeted me like a gust of fresh air. Keenly aware of its magic properties, I reveled in the comments, questions and praise.

On the way home, giddy with happiness, although my mouth felt dry and my jaw hurt, I tried to remember the last time I'd talked so much.

Not willing to surrender the prized feeling just yet, I made an unscheduled stop at a Dunkin Donuts and sat facing a desultory parking lot with a Boston Crème and cup of java, mulling over all the kind things my readers said about my work. Then I pretended I was still single, pulsating with stories, scribbling observations on restaurant napkins, paper plates and homework books. I spooned out the foam in my coffee lustily, let it fill and stay in my mouth for a bit and drank down the rest. A couple of teenagers waiting in line giggled, tried to keep their hands off each other as they placed their order and reeled me back to adulthood.

Pierced by an unformed longing, I asked for my check. There were decisions to be made, at least one regarding Adi's mother. Soon, before she died of old age and I from dissatisfaction. I got into my car to attend to the rest of my life.

Ma

I ask her for breakfast.

'After you've taken a bath,' she says.

After my bath and after I've changed into the lilac, rayon tunic I received twenty-seven years ago as a gift from my sister-in-law, my hair, still damp, is pinned back in a bun. Tiny beads of water slither uncomfortably down the back of my neck.

'Where is my breakfast?' I manage to get to the kitchen without my cane, which is nowhere in sight.

'Give me a few minutes. I have other things to do,' she says. There is a lilt in her voice, lightness in her step. I wonder what she is up to.

She reinstalls me into my chair. As she positions my arms and legs like a doll, she bends closer. My cardigan is unaligned. She re- buttons it so that it falls straight. I can see the cords in her thin neck tighten like drumsticks and have a mad desire to wrap my hand around her neck and watch the life leach out of her eyes. But almost immediately, I want to hold her in my arms and feel her soft breath tickle my ears. Perhaps it is just my body reacting to unnatural closeness.

The last person who touched me was my husband, gone thirty years ago. 'Why do you return to me?' I asked him once, out of genuine curiosity. 'You, who go out into the world in your important clothes, making important deals with government officials, speaking in a language that leaves me in awe, what do you have to come back to? These barren walls, these humble meals and my inelegant ways?'

He laughed and ruffled my hair. 'Don't be silly. This is home.' Then he held out his arms as if embracing the walls, the house and the people. At the time, I thought I detected a note of mockery in his voice. Now I am not so sure. I think he was informing me of the true nature of things. Husbands led the life they chose, wives led the life they were handed; so it was written, and so it must be.

When she straightens up and leaves, I lean forward so that the water beads dampening my clothing does not make wet spots on the back of the upholstered chair. My one foot rests snugly in my slipper. The other hangs naked. She neglected to fit a slipper to my left foot. It feels cold. I stare at the metallic Buddha sitting cross-legged and tranquil at the far end of the room. A lizard, sitting on his lip, stares back in silence. 'There is no past and no future,' says the Buddha. 'I am all there is.'

She gets me breakfast at last. It is cold and bland.

Later that day, I decide I am done talking to ghosts and listening to faceless voices in my ears. I press back the memories like flowers between the pages of books and rehearse what I will say to my son: I have the right to the sun, the air and the sweet sounds of community, same as you. I am old and crippled but not yet dead. How dare you forget me between these walls, pinioned to my chair?

'What are you getting at?' he will ask, in his reasonable way.

'I want the temple out of my room.'

'Why?'

'I want to go to one that *is* real. A *public* temple. And, I want to walk there on foot. To touch the bottom most stair with my forehead, echo the "Om" of exulting pilgrims – men and women, like me, fashioned from the same brown clay. Through our collective devotion, we will honor the Goddess. I want to be part of something real. I want to go home.'

Malavika

There were two men, boys really, whom I knew in college. Shukla liked to draw his nails across my palm and tell me in his husky smoker's voice how I would always follow my heart. Then he would take my hand, kiss it and place it on his heart, so I could feel it flutter.

The other, Desai, would draw a vertical line and whisper, 'You have a fine brain.' He said *brain* the way most men say breasts and made me blush. After I caught Captain working up a storm on the four-poster, Miss Police Uniform, riding him like a virago, I tried seeking shelter with Desai, but he lived in the medical school hostel at the time and was not allowed guests. Perhaps my Samir would have benefited from Desai's influence, or perhaps not. Those were troubled times.

Desai went on to become a leading gynecologist and has the pleasure of sliding one cold, gloved hand between my legs, and one on my bosom, where he takes his time, as he accidentally feels me up.

The lump they found in my breast. Thankfully, it was scooped out with minimum scarring, then put in a mason jar and held before my face as evidence while nurses murmured at the size and shape of the evil thing.

At first, I simply stared at the fibroid. How can something so minuscule cause so much grief? I had lain in horror, night after night, ever since Desai told me about the abnormality, read lurid human body as it slowly succumbed to the deadly disease –the scarring from radiation, the violence of chemo. I thought of the years of reckless neglect, of bad habits catching up, and concluded in despair it served me right. Did I really think I could play fast and loose with my God-gifted body, ply it with bacteria-ridden food, tobacco and unsavory men and come out unscathed?

Naturally, I was not about to share the news with Samir. Who needs the cruel perspicacity of youth when you have Facebook. Sleep became a misery, much like first love. Dragging the pillow from one corner of the bed to the other, bunching up the sheets, I usually fell into a sort of stupor somewhere in the early hours, only to wake up icy cold and bathed in sweat, sure I was either dying or already dead.

It was benign, of course. The tumor. After they stored it away wherever lumps are stored, they said I could leave in a couple of hours, since it was outpatient surgery. Someone handed me a prescription for painkillers, *just in case*.

I made up my mind to make some positive changes in my life, but not while I was still racked with residual fear. I was especially afraid of going to bed. Then I remembered the bottle of vodka stashed behind canisters of sugar, flour, and seasonings so stricken with age, they all shared the same fetid smell and lumpy texture.

If I have a couple of thimblefuls of vodka in my fruit it would still be a healthy enough drink, I cajoled myself.

It was summertime. Fruit flies hovered thirstily over watermelons, strawberries, raspberries and mulberries. I bought them all along with tomatoes, cucumbers, limes, ginger, and a couple of cans of Duke's lemonade. Finally, I opened the vodka.

Every evening thereon, I sat in my aerie and raised a toast to the waning sun. I poured a finger of vodka in my watermelon or in my orange juice, stirred vodka in my lemonade or laced my berries with vodka; I juiced my tomatoes with a healthy dose of vodka, poured a refreshing measure over crushed ice and lemons and sipped my lemon-ginger vodka garnished with cucumbers and strawberries. At the end of the evening, I felt calm, refreshed and most importantly, sleepy. Samir called once and was pleased I sounded so mellow. Our conversation was easy, without uncomfortable pauses or traces of rancor. He made a tentative commitment to visit. I maintained a Zen- like stance, neither encouraging nor discouraging my peripatetic son.

Weeks later, plagued with acidity and heartburn, wincing at the ulcers in my mouth, and waking more than once during the night to use the bathroom, my enthusiasm for the cocktail panacea dissolved and then disappeared. Still, I clutched the bottle as a last resort and cut it out of my diet completely only when the season changed, the fresh fruit dwindled and the fruit flies migrated to other regions.

Too humid for a walk, too early for bed, I turned my attention, one unfortunate evening, to Father's collection of antiquated books and memorabilia. I had covered the entire bookshelf with a white sheet after he passed on and never looked at it again. It stood like an elephant in the room, hidden but not forgotten, and suddenly, after all these years, filled me with unease. I wondered what would happen if I drew the sheet aside. Like a child afraid to look under the bed after lights out, I dreaded the bogeyman under the sheet.

Of course, a part of me knew I would find no more than dust and cobwebs. I imagined splaying open each book, touching the crepe paper with the tips of my fingers, divining the words like Braille on the weevil-infested paper.

Perhaps it was time I throw out all his junk and create for myself a Shroff-like corner with only *my* books, *my* music and *my* meditation tapes, I thought. Excited, and before I could change my mind, I yanked off the sheet and examined the remains, holding my breath against the onslaught of dust.

I leafed through one book, then another and another, all of them familiar, although I was no longer certain which ones I remembered seeing in his hands and which ones were thrust into mine for moral edification. Just as I'd imagined, both cloth and leather jackets were punctured all the way through the book by feeding insects, and the inside pages so faded and stained by "liver spots" I could scarcely recognize the lettering. Motes, freed from captivity, filled the air, and made me sneeze. It was not dust or cobwebs, however, but the smell of the past that I wished I could ward off.

My eyes fell on a book that I did not recognize from Father's collection. *The Ordeal* by Aleksey Nikolayevich Tolstoy.

Yours or mine? I snorted. It looked newer, tidier than the others. Perhaps someone had lent it to him. Father was a magnet for relics.

I picked up the book. A scrap of paper from between the pages fluttered to the floor. It was a will. Dated, June 12, 2000.

Back in May, just one month before he put it in writing, I sat placing cold compresses on his forehead when he muttered, 'You can have this house in the very near future. Anika has no use for it.' I remember how full my heart was that evening, how I sat with him through the night, grasping my own hands as if grasping the olive branch I was offered, after all these years, as I watched him drift in and out of delirium.

In the will, however, he made Anika the sole beneficiary of his house and all the possessions therein. It was not signed, but the handwriting, small, mean and effortful, was surely his.

Somewhere between giving me his word and his difficult release from suffering, he reverted to his old opinion and let me know I was unworthy.

Over the years, I really believed I had forgiven him. I even thought I understood him. Of course, I repulsed him. They said her depression was a side effect of the drugs, that ultimately, it was the little white pills, tiny as mustard seeds that caused Mother to take her own life. But he made certain I knew that it was I who killed her as surely as if it was premeditated murder. I should have known. I should have known without having been told that my affair with Captain, my elopement and the subsequent disgrace were the real reasons she took her own life.

Her slow undoing – all my doing.

A big part of me, the superstitious part, believes that parents have supernatural powers. It is their blessing or their curse that directs the course of one's life. I believe I will never find happiness. My Father does not wish it. It is no longer forgiveness that I nurse in my breast, but the same, unhealthy rage that had me believe I was stuffed with cancer.

Samir

That someone would bleed for me. My heart is filled with gratitude and pain. Uzma. Her brothers think they have beaten the *kafir*, the non-believer, out of her system, but we continue our clandestine meetings, in tea rooms reminiscent of *dhabas* (except you do not get free dal with your naans), ignoring the leers of cab drivers, street vendors and winos. Then, as the sky darkens, we don our hoodies, and, cloaked in anonymity, duck behind a line of parked cars and hop into the nearest bus for anywhere. I am ashamed. 'You deserve better,' I mutter, hoping she won't agree. She doesn't!

'These getaways that we now call squalid, will sound so romantic in retrospect,' she says in her endearing way, taking a warm hand out of her pocket and slipping it through the open neck of my shirt. Heat surges to my face. 'Just think of the stories we'll tell our children,' she whispers, playing with a knot of hair on my chest, then laying her palm flat to feel the full force of my throbbing passion.

Then, it happens again. She is spotted outside my warehouse by her brothers' spies, and dragged kicking and screaming to a waiting car, her coffee spilling along the length of the driveway, her Styrofoam cup crunching under a wheel. My Uzma, taken, in broad daylight, to endure a stronger lesson as I struggle between a savage desire to squeeze the life out of the fanatic fucks who are hurting her, and a cowardly need to maintain a pristine visa status.

I stay where I am, cigarette convulsing between my fingers.

Hours later, she is at my doorstep. I let her in. There are welts on her back. I soothe them with ice, wash them with tears. I cut off a clean undershirt and wrap her like a mummy with the white strips. Swallowed by my sweatshirt, she waves the sleeves at me like drooping puppets and smiles a valiant smile.

'Say something nice,' she whispers.

'I love you.'

'How much?'

'More than you will ever know. More than life itself, Uzma. You are so beautiful.'

She smiles weakly.

'You are my inspiration. The journey and the journey's end. Without you …'

She's fallen asleep. I can see the top of her dark head, the rills between the tight braids. The black tears on her cheek. She has never looked sexier.

I used to be really bad at this game.

For all of her light-hearted confidence, there are times, my Uzma needs reassurance. Or, some sugar, as she called it.

'Say something sweet,' she whispered, that first time. I looked at her perplexed.

'I want to kiss you.'

'Obvious.'

'I want to fuck you?'

'Crude!'

'I love your hair, the way it uncoils itself.'

'Better.'

'Your teeth are so white. Your lips are soft pillows, meant for kissing.'

'Ummm. More.'

'I have to pace myself or I will be too exhausted to follow through with the obvious and the crude,' I grinned.

When she's awake, I feed her my specialty – runny eggs and weak tea. Somewhere during the meal, she nods off again. I carry her to my bed, cursing myself for the threadbare cover, the scratchy bed-sheet and the limp pillows. She sleeps on her side, exposing one shell ear, the dewy soft interior begging to be licked. A strand of hair falls on her face, tickles her nose. I brush it away, holding my breath, quiet as a thief in the night. My love for her is fierce. Boundless.

Fear fills my mouth. *What if we need to run?* I call Mother from the stairway, suppressing a familiar pang. *Here I am, still relying on my mother to bail me out.* I haven't really spoken to her, except via text message, in almost a year.

She says she's glad to hear from me. I tell her about Uzma. She makes a non-committal sound I hope is approval. I ask her for a loan. 'I need some cash. As much as you can drum up. Can you handle it, Mother?'

'Is everything alright?' she asks.

'*Just contingency planning*,' I assure her, the phrase feeling foreign to my own ears.

'Okay, text me, your current address,' she says, above the static. A rush of wind floods the receiver. I hold the phone away, then closer to my ear like a conch trying to get better sound quality. I suddenly realize she is in a bus or some moving vehicle.

'Are you traveling again?' I ask her, filled with misgiving. The words spring out, more sharply than I intend.

She sounds muffled. 'Yes. I'm traveling. There are some matters I need to attend to, Sam. Matters affecting you, affecting my sister…'

'Your sister! Since when have you concerned yourself with anyone, but yourself?' I retort, obviously incapable of keeping my mouth shut. Jai would say, cocking his head to the side, with mock seriousness, 'You have not long to live, my friend, you have chronic verbal diarrhea.' Then he'd sigh, press a solicitous hand on my shoulder and walk out of the room, overwrought. The ass. I wonder where he is these days. I wonder if I can touch him for a loan.

I don't know why she has this effect on me – my mother. I ought to remember, she is not getting any younger.

Fuck! I forgot her birthday. To compensate, I tell her, 'Perhaps

I'll visit soon. Bring my girlfriend to meet you.'

I talk some more, trying to get a fix on her tone of voice. She sounds lost. Fragile perhaps. Then I think of the sister she's going on about. Anika. I've always been curious about that big-eyed, under-developed creature who vanished from our lives like most of our relatives. Perhaps she can help Mother with whatever it is that's ailing her, making her run to the mountains, looking for nirvana. Yes. Now that I have my hands full with my sweet love, it's time Auntie-dearest did her share for this family.

At some point, we disconnect.

⧖⧖⧖

'Didi?'

I figured I'd call her while Uzma was still resting and I was still in the frame of mind to give someone, anyone, a piece of my mind.

Who's this?

'It's Sammy. I mean Samir.'

I grab a chair. It appears I need to steady myself. 'Ah! *Auntie* to you, then, not *didi*.'

'Yes. Of course. Auntie.' Now, I'm a little flustered.

'How are you, Sammy?'

'Fine... uh... I was wondering if you could call my mother. I'm sure she'd like to reach you.'

There is a long pause. Then, 'I will, *baccha*. I've been a bit busy.'

I find myself at a loss for words. Her voice is soft, well-modulated, kind. It throws me off.

'I remember you well, Samir, I mean, Sammy. Do you? Remember me, I mean?' she asks.

'Uh ... no, but I know you from ... Facebook.'

'And my phone number?'

'I think I found it on Linkedin, I'm not sure.'

'I see! Small world, isn't it?'

The pause stretches interminably. *What's wrong, man? Cat got your tongue?* I guess I take after my father. Mother is the only socially adept one in our family.

Finally, I squeak out, 'Uh, she's always off on these trips to God knows where... now she's in the hills again... I know she has something on her mind. I mean ... I think something is eating away at her mind.' The words spill out ungoverned, repetitive, but at least I get them off my chest.

'I will call her, Sammy. Can you give me her number, please?'

I rattle it off. She asks me to hold on. 'Tell me again,' she orders, and then notes it down somewhere, I suppose.

We call off making vague promises to keep in touch.

I wipe the sweat off my brow. *What the fuck is wrong with me?*

19

Annika

Such a strange call, such a bewildering start to the day.

The morning coffee went down my throat as I ruminated, sweet, hot and delicious. *Didi!* He called me.

Little Sammy né Samir. The shaggy-haired boy I longed to make a plaything of but could not. Father hated him with a vengeance.

Now, the boy was old enough to worry about his mother. How unsure, inept he sounds! Where is the spark, the M factor?

I write to her at last. My sister. I am distant. Polite. Afraid I will open a dam with a single, unfettered word. I tell her I plan to visit, have received her letter or rather her succinct note and will connect with her in the near future. I wish her well.

Then, I think of Samir again … his concern for his mother.

There must be a way to snap her out of this tendency to wing from pillar to post. But how on earth was I supposed to help when I barely knew her anymore?

For the nth time, I wished there was someone I could turn to for advice. A child needs a set of parents like she needs a set of eyes. *My father's eyes were blue. The kind of eyes that isolate your every fault and hold it up for public scorn.*

My sister was the unfortunate recipient of his scorn. I was exempt until I hit puberty. After its advent, I too became displeasing. His treatment went from silent companionship to frigid tolerance and deteriorated to humorless attacks on my manners, my cooking and my skin color, right until the time I was married.

Still, we cannot lay all responsibility on the past. Our actions are our own, fueled by intelligence. Thankfully, my mind was never neglected. Gone-Mother once told me, the only mind I should count on was my own. Hours and hours of homework on the kitchen floor on a woven floor mat that stuck to my damp legs.

And each night I waited in my room, the little bedside light on. She insisted that it was my father who read to us. Perhaps, it was more for his sake than ours. I think she saw the future and wanted to give him something he could call his own – a memory of those twenty minutes he spent reading to his children, so that, he might someday forgive himself, both for his destructive influence on our lives and her increasing devolvement. And he did read to us. Obscure books, impressive for their heft, otherwise as dead as the language they were translated from.

We sat through his pompous reading – I, ramrod straight, desperately trying to keep from giggling, and Malavika slouching, yawning and pretending to drop dead out of sheer boredom. After each one of his stories, featuring gods and demons, brave men and dutiful women with bowed heads and strong brows, I felt less perfect. How hard I tried to conduct myself with modesty and humility; to laugh less and smile more; to tread softly; to speak only when spoken to and to be like Gone-Mother on her good days. In the end, he was probably as disappointed in us as we were in him.

They say that lightning does not strike twice in the same place. But did I not lose Malavika, too, within the same year that we lost Gone-Mother? Now, nudged by Sammy's phone call and an unrelenting conscience, I wonder if I'm making a mistake, putting off going to India.

⧗⧗⧗

I thought I heard Ma call out.

She was on the bed, in her preferred death pose, hands crossed over her chest, staring straight up at a dark spot on the ceiling we forgot to paint over, when we replaced the builder's ceiling fan with a sleeker model.

'Do you need something?' I asked, taking a couple of steps in.

No answer.

'Can I get you some water?'

Her eyes looked glazed. Her face was splotched with bruises from one of her falls. Drool dampened the corner of her lips.

I picked up a tissue and moved forward to help her. Maybe my gesture was a little abrupt, or maybe in the shadowy room, curtains closed to keep the afternoon light out of her sensitive eyes, my hand took on an unfamiliar shape, or maybe she was still in the throes of a nightmare, when I walked in. One can only conjecture.

With surprising strength, she pulled herself up and struck at my face once, twice, and as I reared back, she found a chunk of my hair and yanked with all her might so that I screamed, twisted and fell forward almost on top of her face. Then she thrust me aside, knocking off a vase quaking on the side table, with her elbow. It hit the floor and split apart like a jaw. She pulled herself up, staring at the damage and massaging the ropey tendons of her neck. Her face, lined from right to left, fine as an Urdu verse, was sodden.

I was still struggling to catch my breath, when Adi, now in the room, almost lifted me out of the room, his hands under my arms. He put me on a chair in the kitchen and rushed back in to his Ma, who was now wailing piteously, telling her son she was being attacked.

I alternately rubbed the tender spot on my scalp and my neck, checking for torn hair and torn skin and trying not to cry. When she was upset, my gone-mother used to make tea to give her something to do.

Now, I turned the kettle on and busied myself looking for mugs, milk and sugar. Slowly, my hands stopped shaking. In the next room, too, the god of silence finally waved his blessed wand. When Adi returned to the kitchen, I handed him a tray with two mugs and Ma's eggless biscuits.

'What about you?'

I pointed with my chin at my mug.

'Yes, you better wait out here until she is back to herself,' he said. I wasn't about to contradict him.

'How's she doing?' I asked, careful to keep my voice neutral. In the past, he's faulted my tone, told me I sounded dismissive. Or cold. Or something.

'You can go in now.'

She was sitting up, her face pink under the purpling spots.

Her hand reached out to stroke my head lovingly. *What a difference a cup of tea can make.*

'What did you do? Do you realize you grabbed my hair and hit me aswell?'

'I did? You're joking!' she giggled.

'I'm not joking! Look, look at me.'

I brought my stinging face closer to her. She traced a tentative finger over the slash running diagonally from my eyebrow to neck.

'Do you have any more yarn you need to wind into a ball?' she asked, dropping her hand, obviously tired of the subject. Nonplussed, I let it go.

'No. But I can help you with your writing,' I said. I pulled out a pad, a sharpie and my activity pad from my tote.

'Use this pen. It will help you see what you are writing.' I put pad and sharpie on the activity pad and handed it to her. She placed the pad on her lap.

'Oh, I like this tray,' she grinned appreciatively, and started doodling on her pad.

The rest of the afternoon was blissfully quiet. Occasionally, she lifted her head to admire her handiwork, ask me how she was doing and went back to it, tickled pink when I gave her a big thumbs-up.

When Adi came up to our bedroom, his hunch looked more prominent as if he were carrying a weight he could no longer support. Now, behind closed doors we discuss her future and ours.

'She wants to go home to India… to die,' he said, his voice betraying emotion.

'And so…?'

'I cannot let her.'

He climbed into his pajamas and thrust both hands impatiently into the sleeves of his shirt, trying to draw it over his head. Too late, he realized he hadn't unbuttoned his collar. He thrashed about like a rooster with his head cut off, obviously stymied.

'Wait.' I inched my finger through his collar and released the button. He came up for air, red in the face and mad as hell. It would have been quite funny, really, under any other circumstances.

'Perhaps we can go,' I tell Adi when he looks calmer. 'Just a few months from now, it will be cooler in India – the weather is so much nicer.'

Because between each heartbeat, I miss you – my sister.

☒☒☒

Gone-Mother was not comfortable with her beauty. Every Saturday, we visited our grandparents. It was the only time she spent a few moments over her appearance. But despite the starched, earth-toned sari, the hair pulled into a neat bun, high over her head so that it made her collar bone jut out, and the newly polished gold earrings she wore in her torn and sewed up ear lobes, her most distinctive feature was her eyes – not their color or shape, but the fire that burned in them like hot coals.

I don't think I ever saw her laugh. At least not in a joyful, spontaneous, over the top way. Sadness darkened her face like rain clouds in a yearlong monsoon. Wanting to erase her sadness, I rubbed my body against hers. Instead, it spread to my heart, and established residence there before I knew its name.

It took many forms, her sadness – mute and dull-eyed in social settings, shrill and virulent within our walls and pensive and tear-soaked in the dark.

Only when she looked at me, was she radiant. Sometimes, the love shone so brightly, I had to look away, blinded. How to reciprocate that intensity of feeling? I was a child and never did learn what she saw in me.

Ma

My husband is at my bedside. He will not leave. 'Come, *Devki*, let us go,' he says, happy as a lark. Up, up and away! He wings his arms like an angel. I hide my face with my shawl. He pulls it away. There is a weight on my chest. Somehow, I roll over. *Who is smothering me?* My shoulder hurts. I cannot move my arms. I cannot breathe... I cannot brea... I can... not...*help*!

Malavika

I thought nothing could be worse than the fear of cancer and impending death. But this was worse. His final betrayal. I love my apartment. I kept my promise and never once set foot in his house until Father got sick and was forced to take to his bed. *Here we go again* ... I remember thinking, when my aunt, the only one of Mother's many siblings who still corresponded with me, relayed the news of his illness.

Where was little Anika when he was wetting the sheets, swiping at his breakfast tray with wily hands and beating the side of his bed with his fists as if he wished it were I he was pounding?

My baby sister, who stood like a poodle beside him when Mother left us, looked everywhere but at me, spoke to everyone but to me and simulated his disdain as if it was a game and not a deep, scathing insult! Where was she in the middle of the night to direct him to the loo? In her little brick house at the other end of the world, is where, playing at normal.

Well, she played a good hand, little Ana-banana, with her awkwardly assembled limbs, her tender-than-thou ways, and her unoriginal mind.

I was so wrong! I thought he had come around when he finally took the toast or the poached egg or the *khichree* I offered with a gracious smile and declined what he could not hold down with a gentle wave. I thought he was happy when I lured a Myna to his window just for his amusement, or when he sighed with pleasure as I rubbed his heels with essential oils to help him sleep.

It was the closest we ever came to coexisting peaceably. So, when he said, '*keep the house,*' I thought what he meant was, 'You are my daughter and I forgive you.'

Obviously, I heard what I wanted to hear, forgetting who he really was - an unrelenting, immovable stone.

I was living a lie. Anika, fashioned in the image of his (now exalted) wife, was the star pupil, the one who always lived up to his expectations. Whereas I, like an unwelcome addition to a house, did nothing to enhance his property. And even as I sat by his bedside, easing him into his final abode, he was retracting his word. *He giveth and he taketh away.*

The fault was mine. I took refuge in fantasy. When Anika was still little, and Mother just gone, I tried to help, although only at aunt's bidding. A part of me wanted to show them - the cousins, uncles and aunts - how I'd risen in life, how I had the power and the means to care for my family. But there was another part, the secret desire to win his gratitude, his approval. That is what really drove me home. Clearly, I'd read too many books with happy endings.

I took care of Father and Anika, going back and forth from my husband's flat to Father's house for months at a time, neglecting Samir, neglecting my studies, neglecting Captain, clearing out cobwebs, making fresh meals and making sure Anika did her homework so that there was a semblance of normalcy and she felt safe again. And what did I receive by way of thanks? A verbal whiplashing seared in my brain like a branding iron. Samir did not go unscathed either. Perhaps somewhere in his heart, the boy still believes he is the bastard child of a wayward mother.

20

Annika

I thought I was quite calm. My heart did not flutter, my hands did not shake and my eyes were not bleary. There was no vertigo, no twinge of pain anywhere.

I came down to check on her. She was on her belly, hands stuck to her sides. I noted with interest that despite the fact that her legs stretched out stiff as boards, she looked very little. Almost diminutive. Her nose and lips were buried in a cushion, as if locked in a kiss. I thought of SIDS and wondered if it could happen to the elderly and if so, what did they call it? SEDS? Perhaps I should call a doctor, just to be sure, I was thinking, when I heard a scream. SHE's DEAD!

I'm told it came from me. I heard another and discovered it came from Adi. And then, for the second time in my life, I lost my hearing.

⛫

I was flying home to attend Father's funeral when the pilot announced we had to make an emergency landing. The plane was running out of fuel. There was a great deal of movement after the announcement. A pale looking stewardess was gesticulating urgently, pointing at exits and reiterating the rules one habitually ignores at the start of every flight. I could not form a single, coherent thought. Despite the chaos, it was eerily quiet. That was the first time I went deaf. Of course, I was also convinced we had drowned, every one of us, and what I was witnessing was a scene from my afterlife. I'm told, stress can do that to you. I did not make it to Father's funeral. We returned to Newark in the middle of the night, were offered a free hotel stay and scheduled to leave the same time, but on the following day.

I declined the offer. *It was Malavika who handled the funeral and everything else.*

Ma

A tetragon of light cuts my empty bed in half. The curtains are flung apart to expose the windows. Sunlight floods the room and changes the colors of the upholstery. My room, despite the light, looks abandoned. It is as if the housekeeper, in the process of cleaning up after a tenant, has hastened off to another appointment. The blinds are rolled up but not locked in place, so one corner sags unevenly. My bed sheet has been tucked in at the corners, but not smoothed flat. There are cracks and wrinkles where my body used to rest. My shawl, draped around the armchair, is skimming the carpet, gathering dust. The bathroom door is ajar. The box that holds my dentures still rests on the sink, caught in an eternal yawn. I always kept it shut.

Old Coot, the bane of my life, now the rightful owner of my habitat, wanders in and sniffs the air like a policeman. He rolls around fighting invisible fleas, pillows his impertinent head on my slippers at the foot of the bed and claims them for his own.

Light everywhere. Light and loss.

Malavika

Happy Birthday, Malavika. I bought myself a birthday cake and watched the candle melt to a nub. I wiped my hands on my faded cotton nightgown and thought, with grim amusement, *I have seen this done, 49 times in the past!*

Admittedly, my most memorable birthdays were spent with Captain. Let's just say he was overly enamored with lacy underwear, and the supply never ran out while I was married to him. Birthdays, in my parents' home – Mother with shy pride, plating a thick slice of pound cake for each one of us, Anika hopping from one foot to the other as if she needed to pee (little Ana-banana now 42) and Father saying a mantra or two before he gorged down his share. It was almost nice. Birthdays with my hippie friends – brownies followed by ganja and the extraordinary feeling of dancing on the edge of a cliff. Birthdays with Samir - his serious face lighting up at the sight of both cake and the parental unit, all in one room.

I closed my eyes to make a wish but saw only the scrap of paper resting like a murderous piece of flora between the forgotten pages of *The Ordeal*. The flame shuddered. I cupped my hand to the candle so it wouldn't die out. A shadow of my cupped hand grew on the opposite wall. I withdrew my hand and rested it lightly on my lap. The flame died. Bathed in near darkness, only the moonlight filtering through, I sat inert, simply observing the ebb and flow within and knew at last what it was I really wanted –a Bodh Gaya of my own making, deep and silent as a cave but open to light; a cocoon that beckons your soul, like an unending forest trail.

I had a foretaste of peace – the massive, un-nuanced quiet

of the mountains. Without *raga*. Without *dvesha*. The sense of simply being. If only I had the courage to follow through. Samir's rant about fierce winters and fearsome terrain, combined with my own fickle nature, had me convinced that a city dweller could not thrive in that Utopian setting. Perhaps he was right about the Himalayan Mountains. But there is a nest for every bird, a rock for every insect, a tarp roof, a tepee or a castle fashioned for every creature, is there not? One simply has to look. And, without the apartment to fall back on, that is, *if* I accede to the terms in Father's will, I would have to commit to a new place, a new life.

A *guilt-free life*, free of Anika and her wide, discomfiting eyes that follow me like a shadow. The thought gathered momentum, filling me at last with a new emotion, a synchrony of joy and trepidation that I welcomed with eyes wide open. I lit the birthday candle one more time and made my wish.

Samir

They are after me... I will live to tell the tale ...*Hai Ram!*

Uzma

Samir is gone, and I cannot breathe. They did this to him, I'm now sure of it – Munir, Adar and Galib. My own brothers. The three faces of misdemeanor. Who do I call? Where do I go?

Samir. Be well. Stay alive. Come back to me.

21

Annika

There was some talk of traumatic asphyxia and smothering, but of course there was no post-mortem. She was 90 years old and had been dying for a very long time.

A week after we lost Ma, Adi and I, filled with inexplicable guilt, flew to India to cast her ashes in the Ganges. But before we left, I managed to keep my hair appointment with Maddie.

I loved Maddie. Underneath her purple hair, heavily mascara-ed lashes, flesh like pillows draped over an extra-large mattress and the tiny puddles of sweat where her cleavage dipped was a generous heart and a razor-sharp mind. She was also a great stylist, and like every great stylist, treated her chair as a sort of confessional. She let me do all the talking, all the while, maneuvering my head with her hands. In the years since I have known her, only once did she break her rule and reveal a little of her own life's drama.

She had been trying a new weight loss program, and obviously it had done wonders for her. But when I told her how amazing she looked and how proud I was of her resilience and discipline, she looked pensive. Then with a catch in her voice, she told me, when she went home to visit, her sister Brea was upset because she said now she, Brea, would be cast as the *fat sister*.

Seeing the dismay on my face, Maddie at once switched gears and asked me how things were at home, with Ma and all. I told her she'd passed away, and we were going to do the last rites in India. Then Maddie, who is the soul of sensitivity and also a wonderful actress, gave me a present. She did her impressions of Lucille Ball, Carol Burnett and Roseanne. This was no mean task because all the acting had to be done with the mouth, eyes and small head movements, leaving her hands meticulously occupied flat ironing my crazy hair. Soon, we were doubling over with laughter, which brought other associates over to my chair wanting to know what was going on. 'Her mother-in-law passed away,' she said, guffawing again. They watched in horrified silence.

'Thanks for making me laugh for the first time in weeks,' I said as I wiped my eyes and got ready to leave.

'Listen, why don't we do a girls' night out when you return?' she asked, kindly.

The realization that I could now do that – go anywhere, anytime without looking at my watch - hit me with gladness and guilt.

The only other person who could ever make me laugh out loud was my sister, Malavika. She knew about the tickle-spot on my neck. All she had to do was wiggle her fingers in the general direction, and I would explode with giddy laughter. She, too, had a rare talent for accents and mimicry. She'd sway her hips like the cleaning woman and threaten us with a broomstick and a nonsensical regional accent that reduced me to a puddle every single time. She could also kick her legs and make her heels touch her spine, Chaplinesque style and make slits of her eyes that were at once terrifying and incredibly comical. She was my hero.

I sat on his mother's chair one last time before we headed for the airport. The curtains parted an inch or two, and I was struck once more by her pinhole view of the world.

In one corner, hiding behind a door, her walking stick; at the foot of the garage, her slippers; Inside the garage, her wheelchair. A walker. Creature comforts designed for mobility, now stilled and without purpose. Perhaps we can donate them, I thought, idly.

Desultorily, we swiped at the messages of support from friends and extended family, some straightforward sorry-for-your- loss texts, others sprinkled with emojis that seemed to trivialize our grief.

※※※

Back in the day, seeing someone off at the airport was almost mandatory. The anxiety of parting, the fetid, humid air, the bulging luggage threatening to writhe out of trolleys and squeezing past surly officials was simply quotidian life. I can still see my family at the airport, my father, adhering to social norms, present and accounted for, sandwiched between overwrought passengers; my favorite aunt with her right hand capped against the sun, her face a little puffy, BP high perhaps, foundation trickling down her neck, the color of Pepto Bismol; friends and cousins waving handkerchiefs, arms jiggling out of their sleeves, swiping tears, or was it dust, spasmodically. I stared and stared at the geography of their faces, memorizing all the ridges and slopes, honoring the distances we had travelled together. We took the fork for the Departures line. Their faces blurred and faded like scudding clouds. A final wave in their general direction, and then we were off.

Still, I was a little over twenty-one and just married. Hope flew with me on the wings of that plane. On the flight, Adi was solicitous, holding my hand even when he was asleep, his head lolling on my shoulder like an infant's. The stewardess, envy written all over her face, asked me if I was a newly-wed.

I nodded.

'How did you meet?' she asked, vicarious excitement, sparkling in her eyes.

'It's a long story,' I smiled pretending to shut my eyes.

She bent across him toward my corner, tightening my seat belt, her bosom spilling, the powder dotting her forehead flaking off and settling like pink dandruff on my skirt, her silken sari feathering his thighs, so that he twitched and responded. Only then did she straighten herself, a small look of triumph and a half-smile, like a single quotation mark.

⧖⧖⧖

On the flight, Adi, frozen in front of a TV monitor watched a movie play out, each actor adrift in the exosphere without a unifying force; on his lap, a newspaper folded neatly to a square, displayed a crossword puzzle that he left untouched. I too held a book in my lap but could not muster the energy to open it. Other people's stories are only interesting when your hours follow hours and days follow days, predictably. I had called no one, personally, but knew that news about our arrival would spread like birdcalls throughout the community. This time it was I who held his hand and slept exhausted for a few jerky hours.

A sudden turmoil shook me awake. The plane settled down, but of course, I could no longer get back to sleep. I let my mind fly to the past.

The first time I met Adi, I was at the beach with a gaggle of high-spirited friends. We'd just taken a dip in the ocean and were hurrying off to the beach club, where one of them was a member, in order to rinse off and change into dry clothes. Huddled in a group, we wrung out our skirts and did the best we could to shake the salt water out of our hair. That's when I spotted a man in a bowler hat who looked as if he'd rummaged in the bin behind the hotel and wore everything he found in there, head in our direction.

'What do you want? We're not buying,' my girlfriend said.

'You should see a *hakim* for that,' he pointed at the vitiligo dotting her exposed leg like a road map.

She colored and pulled down her drenched skirt. 'What's it to you? Please leave us alone.'

We had come to the beach at her suggestion, and I guess she felt like the leader of the pack.

'I can read your face. And your palm. For free …or whatever you can offer.'

'No.'

'Why don't we let him?' I mouthed, 'The chap looks hungry.'

We were still trying to decide whether we should let him read our fortunes or just send him off with a buck or two, when a voice behind us chirped, 'You girls should watch out for strangers and con artists.'

It was Adi. In sneakers, sports shorts and a cap, he smiled easily at us.

'And who are you? Our father?'

The words spilled out, defensively. I felt a pinch on my arm. 'Shut up,' my girlfriend whispered.

'You are Adi, aren't you? Visiting from New York? My parents know you,' my girlfriend smiled in her winning way.

'Yes. Well. Take it easy, girls. Don't want to spoil your fun.' And he loped off.

'You're an idiot. You will never get married!' she hissed the moment he left.

'Huh?'

'Never mind.' She shook her head, obviously writing me off. I followed her, thoughtfully.

It was a few weeks later before I met him again. This time, in my girlfriend's home, where he had somehow wangled an invitation for himself as well as one for me. I made sure I was on my best behavior.

'Would you like to grab a cup of coffee?'

'No thanks. I just had a cup.'

'I mean, outside. With me. In a restaurant.'

'I can't. I have to be home soon. I have to get dinner ready for my dad.'

He digested the information in silence.

'I'm going away for a year, but I would like to stay in touch,' he volunteered at the end of the evening.

'Who knows what …' I started to say and then paused when I sensed my girlfriend glare in my direction. 'Sure. That will be nice.'

A year goes by slowly when you are watching the clock. Tick follows tock follows tick. I had no boyfriends. I did not date. What with Malavika's elopement, Gone-Mother's drastic passing and Father's dramatic despair, I grew up, clueless and frigid in social settings. In fact, I was once told, by a well-meaning friend, 'You come across as cold, abrupt and lesbian-like and can do with some serious, feminine graces.'

Still. He came down, as promised.

'I was looking for you at the beach,' he said.

'Huh? Yeah,' I mustered, after a great deal of thought.

We were married that same year. My girlfriend, who introduced us, wanted a present.

'For setting you guys up,' she said.

'So, what do you want?'

'Get me one just like him when you are settled abroad,' she grinned.

On that first flight, I looked enviously at Adi, sleeping like a baby, and I too tried to nod off, but like particles of dust going past a window, my friends whooshed past. 'Don't argue, try to adjust, and don't forget us,' they urged, making it impossible to sleep until, rummaging absently through my purse, I found the envelope I'd extricated from the wedding gift box, with the words *For Ana-banana* written in mischievous cursive on the cover. Holding it to my heart like a security blanket, I fell at last, into a deep and dream full sleep where she visited me, my sister, in a robe spun out of stars, relaying messages of love with semaphore arms and closing, forever, the chasm of loss with newfound joy.

Malavika

The first order of business after I'd made my decision was to connect with Anika. I did not have her home address, but that was easily obtained. Being the goody two-shoes that she was, I was certain she was still in touch with at least some of the old biddies related to us on Mother's side.

I stopped by to visit one of our least offensive aunts, and sure enough, before I had downed two sips of tea, she began displaying the New Year cards she'd received, like proofs of love, from my darling sister. I could see the return address on the envelope from where I sat. When I was done with my tea and nibbled at the rusk and the hot mix she'd spooned into a miniature wooden bowl, I made a show of taking back the tray to the kitchen.

'Absolutely not! You will sit right here,' my aunt admonished, as I knew she would. Meekly, I let her take the tray out of my hands and waddle off to the kitchen. As soon as her back was turned, I wrote down my sister's address, noting with surprise that she now spelled Anika with two ns. Was it a slip of the pen, or like Samir aka Sammy, had my sister anglicized her name too? I snapped shut the diary and left as soon as it was deemed polite.

It was when I found the onionskin notepad with the embossed quill that my mood shifted from euphoric to curious. *When did you design the letterhead? Do you know your nephew has inherited your love for design? What else did you have up your sleeve?* There were so many things we did not know about each other. With that knowledge came a growing sense of sadness, and with it, yet another question, probably the most pertinent one. How does one reintroduce oneself to a sister?

When you slipped out of her womb, Ana-banana, it was I, not she, not our father, who cradled you first, made the first cooing promises to love and protect your little body, delicate as a quail's egg, skin the color of condensed milk freckled with brown sugar.

Since then, between all I have done and all that was done to me, separated as much by time as by distance, I am rendered speechless.

In the end, I managed a few airy lines, hoping we could connect as soon as possible, suggesting it was time, didn't she agree? I did not mention Father's will, my health scare or my plans for the future. I realized, after I'd already mailed the letter, that I hadn't asked after her husband or her children. *Did she have any?* I hoped she would not notice the oversight. Meanwhile, I took stock of everything I owned and everything I wanted to be rid of.

Samir

There is a man, seated cross-legged on the floor, a snake around his neck. Also, a bubbling sound, curiously relaxing. The smell of strawberries mixed with smoke wafting through the walls. Flavored tobacco! There's a man smoking a hookah in the next room, I put two and two together at last. From where I lie, my one eye stubbornly shut, the other twitching uncontrollably, the hose looks alarmingly like a snake. Who is he? A kidnapper? A guard? Fear oozes out of my every orifice.

I cannot help it - I stink.

Voices. Rising and swirling and settling like cannabis in the air. The phlegmy, nauseating sound from his chest, just before he spits. Occasionally he urinates, longer and louder than a freakin' horse, followed by belching and more throat clearing. *You are wrong, Principal Spencer. Hell is not fire and brimstone, situated below ground level. Hell is this earth, teeming with men, built like apes and behaving like wanking gorillas.* Maybe there's a toilet behind me, maybe he takes a leak on the same floor he sits on. Oof, the stench! I retch at the sounds, the imagery. A thin line of vomit trickles down my chin.

They cracked my ribs like walnuts. The fuckin' sadists.

I try not to breathe. Pain ratchets through my body. Was there a hammer raised, or was I shot with hallucinogens? Hands bound above my head, I focus again on the sights, sounds, smells, and finally, on each of my body parts, like a forensic technologist, examining evidence.

My bruised and broken body has a hell of a tale to tell. Alas, Uzma! You did warn me.

22

Annika

Dawn peeks inside my window, wakens me like a mother, tender and gently smiling. My first thought is a prayer. *Help us get through the next few days. Om shanti.* I pour water into the kettle, and then pour some more when I see Adi shifting and stretching.

From my window seat, I watch Mumbai rise with small bursts of sound, gaining celerity like a local train with every passing minute.

Outside my window, crows perch on the branches of a solitary beech tree, proud survivor in an ever-widening parking lot. A cabal of housemaids convenes in an open lot in front of the shanties across our street. Heedless of the sanctity of the hour, strident and intrusive as the crows, they gossip about their mistresses. Stray dogs and children watch the theatre of expressions with incurious eyes. I push the curtains close and turn inwards.

We have our tea quietly, Adi and I, not yet ready to make plans although there is much to be done. The flavorful aroma of loose tea leaves pervades the apartment, and slowly, the other lumps on the couch, the beds, and the floor, stir under their sheets. Cousins and aunts from near and far have arrived a day before us, to guide and comfort us through the four days of mourning, followed by prayers.

Her scant hair wound and pinned efficiently out of the way, Adi's aunt tugs at a knot buried in the hair brush, gathers the torn strands tightly and drops them in the bin, shutting the lid with a bang. 'Can't have stray hair floating to the stove and into the lentils, can we,' she says, smiling, seeing me stare.

When she didn't have the strength to reach behind her head, I tried to help Adi's ma with her chignon. But I never could coil it so that it sat like a snail attached to her scalp, the pins artfully concealed. In the end, she had to make do with a braid, skinny as a mouse tail, the ends held together with a beret. I think of the hairpins, knitting needles, hooks and hankies, prayer beads, activity pad, sharpies and small toys– freebies found at the bottom of cereal boxes, she was saving as presents for the servant girls – and to my surprise, I find my cheeks dampen.

Someone leads me gently to a chair, murmuring inanities. I am enclosed in a circle of love.

'I still have all the scarves, receiving blankets and cardigans she ever knitted for my children,' shared one cousin, assuming correctly, it was Ma I was thinking about. Nods and grunts, followed by more sharing. 'She loved pizza. I remember, she sneaked into the kitchen one night, did not turn on the light for fear of being found out, and almost gagged on a piece of chicken smothered with cheese,' declared someone. The aunts, every last one a vegetarian, covered their respective mouths in dismay.

Then they were all looking at me, as if I was the one now holding the conch, willing me to share a story, an anecdote, something. Instead, I tell them how guilty both Adi and I feel.

'About what?'

'I think we ought to have taken her to Varanasi. She was always talking about real temples, a real pilgrimage, the holy river and once, in a fit of temper, even asked us to remove the brass idol from her room.'

'Why is that?' asked Adi's aunt.

She told us, 'When a wanderer or a seeker happens upon a temple, he understands it is fate, pointing him to his journey's end, pointing him toward the final rest stop. It is time to visit a real temple, not sit idly before a solitary goddess in a solitary room.'

'What an extraordinary notion for one who sat before an idol with her rosary, twice a day for over half a century!' Adi's aunt laughed. I looked at Adi out of the corner of my eye, but he was immersed in an email and, I thought, not paying attention.

'And would you still be racked with guilt if I were to tell you, that she hated the sun, the rain, the wind, and the cold in equal measure?' asked his aunt with a twinkle in her eye.

I frowned in confusion.

'Adi's mother, my dear, was a homebody, a hothouse plant always at loggerheads with nature. Trust me, we've travelled together often. More often than not, she would about-face, a third of the way into the pilgrimage because she couldn't bear the heat or dust. *"God resides within us, why do we need to climb a hundred steep stairs to get to him?"* was her excuse, at the time,' she said and laughed uproariously.

Adi, who apparently heard every word, now asked her to stop mocking his mother.

'At least she tried,' he said.

'I...' his aunt, started to say something, then tugged at her knot and left the room.

Then, someone else pitched in, pacifically, 'She nursed me through so many fevers. She was so tender, I would feign illness, just to feel her touch.'

I allowed myself to drift off, much like the train, the crows and the noisy housemaids outside the window.

A kindly nurse once called us a *"Beautiful family."*

At the time, I thought only in terms of how little we had in common, Ma and I. Now I reflect on all those things that we did have in common:

The ability to interpret silences.

The belief in a higher power.

Resilience.

Sporadic bursts of generosity.

A distrust of excessive emotion.

Good pizza.

Love for her son. I guess it took her death for me to realize that we were, indeed, a family.

Malavika

I did not expect to hear from Ana-banana the moment I reached out to her, but after the first week, then the next, and a few more nexts, her silence was beginning to affect even my sanguine nature. I grew mean spirited and cantankerous. On a flight to Shillong on a mission to check out a Buddhist monastery, I turned around and threatened a little boy kicking the back of my seat with bodily harm. The fact that his eyes welled up and he stuck a thumb in his mouth for comfort did not move me at all. His mother, startled out of the paperback romance pressed to her bosom, drew the child close, muttering darkly about *nasty old biddies* and *where they belonged* until she caught the look on my face and pressed her lips in a thin, tight line.

In Assam, my cab driver and tourist guide, hair ruffled by a pleasant wind, standing on the side of the road to slurp from a flask of fragrant tea, suddenly, overcome with nature's bounty, burst into song. I gritted my teeth for about five minutes and then told him to pipe down, he was frightening the birds.

In a crowded public bus, en route to Shimla, nauseated from the hairpin turns in the road, I politely asked a peasant to snuff out his *bidi*. When he gave me the same attention as one would give a cow in a field of cows, I snatched the bidi out of his curled lips and crushed it under my pointy heels. Intakes of breath and low grumbles in the bus. Then, 'People travel far, and their ugliness travels with them,' observed someone at the back of the bus. I opened my mouth, then shut it again. The phone rang, just then, to my extreme irritation. I was not expecting any calls, having Whatsapped my friends about my whereabouts. It was Samir, going on about a girl, a loan, a homecoming. I agreed hurriedly, not wanting him to catch on that I was traveling. But he did guess. I tried to explain, then hung up on him when he got irate. Like mother, like son.

The peasant was right, of course. Wasn't it Confucius who said, "No matter where you go, there you are"? Maybe it was time I ventured inward rather than farther. I did not turn around to look at my tour-bus philosopher, but I did take the next flight home to rethink my life and try to connect with Anika, one more time.

⧖⧖⧖

I unlocked first the grill and then the door, taking care not to step on the mail accumulated around the doorway. The card with foreign stamps stuck out like a white face in a sea of brown. It was Anika with two ns.

From time to time, I stared at the letter, sitting on my windowsill, held by a paperweight. Chores done, I wiped my hands and slit open the envelope. I passed my fingers on the folded sheet and realized I did not have my reading glasses on. I found them in the kitchen by the sugar pot. The tea I was making and had forgotten about had boiled over. I swiped the pool of water in and around the cooktop half-heartedly with a dishcloth, dried my hands once again and returned to the letter.

She was "happy" to hear from me, she said. She might plan on a visit in the near future as her mother-in-law was getting increasingly homesick, and perhaps, we could catch up. It would be nice to hear about your last twenty-two (underscored) years reminisce about our time together, she said before she wrote "My best to you and Samir" and signed off.

I read the note again with a pang. Twenty-two years. Longer, if you do not count the brief glimpse I had of her, at her wedding.

How polite she is. Polite and distant, pointedly ignoring the need for urgency, mentioning a meeting *in the near future*, as if exchanging platitudes with an acquaintance.

We will go to Singapore in the near future.

We shall move to a new building in town with two elevators and a pool, in the near future.

You can have this apartment in the near future. Anika will not want it.

The near future, in my experience, is like the weather report –
it changes daily.

Uzma

'But Uzma, how can you be so sure? And would you please stop pacing?'

I'd come to ask for help, but I could see she was already getting antsy, my brother's girlfriend. I pushed up the horizontal slats with thumb and index finger. The car was still outside. It would not leave without me. This was my life, now: being driven everywhere and monitored round-the-clock.

'I went to his place,' I told her. 'Samir wasn't there.'

'But that doesn't mean anything!' She stamped her feet a little.

Her lips were glossy, the color of cotton candy.

'Tell me exactly what you think is going on.' She softened her tone when she noticed I was sniffling.

I began at the beginning.

'I rang the doorbell. More than once. He was supposed to be home. When he didn't answer, I called him on his cell. I thought I heard it ring in the recesses of the building. But he didn't answer the cell, either, and I just had this really bad feeling, you see. Then, as I was about to leave, his landlady, who I have never given any reason to be annoyed with me, opens the door, her hands on her waist and glares at me like I've pooped all over her doorstep.

"He doesn't live here anymore. Samir," she tells me. I had to wipe her spittle off my face!

I asked her when he left. She says he left the previous night, but you see, she wouldn't make eye contact when she said that.'

I couldn't help it...I told her what I thought, that she was lying through her teeth. Then she got all huffy, told me she'd call the police if I didn't get off her doorstep this minute, and I just, I kinda lost it. I begged her to tell me the truth, and I would never bother her again. I went down on my knees, Sheila, I was actually groveling.'

My hands wouldn't stop shaking. I shoved them in my pockets.

'She kept insisting that Samir left the night before, and she had no idea where he was, but then I saw her look at my pocketbook - in that furtive way, you know, so I opened it, took out a clump of notes and just handed them to her. I guess the money changed her mind. She tried to look insulted, failed, then balled up the bills, tucked them into her bra strap, and admitted she saw three men drag him by his feet to a black car at about 11 p.m. last night. They told her that if she squealed, they'd rip her tongue out. She got quite hysterical remembering the terror.

"They threatened to cut me up!" she said. "This is a good neighborhood. You are all trash!" She'd begun screeching. It was hideous.'

While she was ranting, it occurred to me, surely Samir would leave some sort of a clue, make one last-ditch effort to let the woman he loves know he was in trouble? I inched forward to obstruct the door, and when she calmed down a little, I told her that I might have a couple hundred dollars in the glove compartment of my car, and she could have them as well, if she'd just let me into his room and answer a few questions. She sighed and rolled her eyes a little, but of course, she acquiesced. Money talks, right! When we got as far as the hallway I asked if they'd hurt him before they dragged him out. She just puffed her cheeks, blew out her breath and went *Oof*, her chest rising and falling, her breathing irregular, as if it was all so unbearable, she could scarcely recount it.'

I could feel my knees buckling. I asked Sheila if I could have some water. I sipped at it slowly and continued, 'Anyway, by the time I got to his room, the landlady was actually patting my back in a sudden show of magnanimity.'

Sheila was leaning in, her face a study of attention as if watching one of her favorite soaps. I was glad I had her enthralled. Still, it was sort of distasteful.

'You are so right. Money talks every time. Go on,' she prodded.

'I could see he'd left in a hurry. His bed was unmade. His clothes, extra pair of shoes, everything was there, untouched. I folded his stuff and put it all in a duffel bag I found in the closet. Oh, I emptied the bath closet as well. Imagine! His whole life fit in the little bag, with room to spare. I sat on his bed and thought, *this is all we have. Why would they grudge us even this?*'

My voice cracked a little. Sheila placed her hand on my wrist.

'I was still sitting on his bed when I heard his cell phone ring! I found it stuck between the mattress and the bed frame. Obviously, he couldn't have made a grab for it when they crashed through the door. It grew quiet before I could pick up, and then it rang one more time ...an unknown number, I could almost feel the caller's anxiety shrilling through the ring tone.

I found just two numbers on his contact list. Mother and Uzma. He doesn't even have a password.'

'Did you answer it?'

'No. I wimped out. It was his mother. What could I possibly to her? Lovely to meet you. I think your son has been kidnapped!' I hiccupped.

Sheila nodded thoughtfully. 'And then...?'

'That's all! There was nothing else in the room I could go on. Sheila, you are the only one who can help me. We are practically family, already.' I was beginning to sound pathetic even to myself. Fortunately, it worked.

She raised herself to her full height, presumably impressed with her own role in this drama.

'I will do what I can. Adar listens to me. You are right. We are practically family. We are getting married, you know.'

She smiled brilliantly and then made an effort to rearrange her features to fit my mood.

'I know. Congratulations,' I said, as sincerely as I could.

'Oh, thank you!' She was so grateful, I decided to continue in the same vein. Milking the moment, I suppose.

'I know he loves you. I've heard the mushy poetry he composes for you every night,' I said, exaggerating shamelessly.

She bloomed like a freshly watered flower.

'Wawa! Thank you for sharing that. That is just so...' she puffed her cheeks and shuddered with delight.

'I *will* help you. You *can* count on me, Uzma. You'll see. And when your boyfriend returns, all in one piece, he might even add another number to his contact list. Moi!' She piped girlishly, striking her chest with each thumb.

I smiled weakly, leaned over and kissed her hand.

Now, we wait.

23

Annika

Adi holds the urn in his lap. To him falls the sorrowful task of wading in the river, chanting the appropriate mantras and overturning her ashes in the rushing water. Her remains spill out of his hands and drift into oblivion. Does the urn in his damp hands feel any worse than seeing the life drain out of her eyes? Or does it give him some comfort, this solid observance of ritual and tradition? I do not know. Grief is a private journey and must be endured alone.

I am out for a walk. The air, tinged with salt, mad with memory, whistles and weeps, rages and sighs until I find myself in my old neighborhood where it finally stills as if listening. I take in every park bench and fill it with my father and his cronies, their argumentative voices disturbing the sunset hour. A solitary sloop hangs motionless in the ocean, becoming one with the seascape. The water froths whitely against the gargantuan black rocks. I study every building, populating it with the ghosts of neighbors and friends, long gone. Then I take a bend in the road and freeze at a memory:

Malavika is walking towards me. She does not see me. Her one hand is tucked under the arm of her seducer husband. Her face is lifted to the sun. Her mouth is wide open as if attempting to swallow the ocean air in great big gulps. She walks right past me. She looks so happy!

'Oy, Auntie, you are in the middle of the street!' Shouts, laughter, tooting of horns. I pull back with a startled shriek and pat the perspiration beading my neck and face with my scarf.

I can simply walk the two hundred yards to my past, ring the door bell, remove my slippers, and step inside that strip of space we once called home. Or I can leave. But do I have the nerve to make it to the apartment? How will it feel, the ground beneath my feet? Like a block of cool tiles, scrubbed to a shine, ghosts fulminating under a false new floor? Or like a playground of childish delights, I will eagerly explore *even though between the hallway and the kitchen, she lay stretched, with unseeing eyes?*

I cannot make a decision. Yesterday is a troubled country, riddled with threat, inhospitable at best. I'm hopelessly unequipped for this particular terrain. Best to turn around and return to Adi. Later I will make an appointment with my sister and have her meet me in a restaurant, stranger to stranger.

In my eyes, a sudden bite of dust. In my ears, the plangent sound of waves. Prodding out the grit with one finger, I hail a cab.

Malavika

My maid disapproves of me. She shows her displeasure, not with rude language or subtle disobedience, nor does she slam the tea tray on my table or direct debris in my direction with an overzealous broom, but with slight, barely perceptible shakes of her head, a cocking of the brow, a blank stare fixated somewhere past my shoulder. A few days ago, handing me a glass of water after I huffed up the stairs, she demonstrated her disapproval with a robotic stance. 'A *man* by the name of Aziz Raja called twice. From some foreign (*phorun* she pronounces) country. I have left his number by the telephone,' shemotioned.

'*Raja*! Maybe he will whisk me off to his kingdom!' I trilled, just to get her goat. It is how I always handle idiots who insinuate every male caller is my fornicator.

No response, except for the merest suggestion of a sniff.

I was not impressed by the fact that this Raja was from "a foreign country" or that he had called me twice on the same day, and I ignored his calls.

A week later he called again, and this time, he found me home. In the polite but pompous manner of a "suit" he said he was very sorry to inform me that my ex-husband, his client, Salil Captain, had passed away. After a brief pause, allowing for emotion, I suppose, he went on to say that there was the matter of a will, and he had some questions. When would be a good time?

I told him to call in about two hours, for I was getting late for a hair appointment. I don't know why I chose to minimize the news of Salil's passing, and sound so blasé. Maybe I did not want to let on that I was at all frazzled.

When he called again, I picked up the phone carefully as if it was a religious artefact, and we were about to perform a ritual.

'You have a son by Salil Captain,' he confirmed with a question in his voice. I responded with an "mmm". He asked Samir's age. I said he was thirty-two, would be thirty-three in a couple of months.

'That sounds about right,' he said, as if there was ever any doubt.

'Your son will be coming into some money soon. Just a little paperwork to sort out,' he told me the amount in a precise, even tone.

'Oh, enough for a dowry!' I scratched the number on a pad, laughing a little too long as I did so.

'A dowry ... isn't that what women give...?'

'It's a joke, Mr. Raja.'

No answer. He probably didn't believe in joking with ex-wives of dead clients.

'Do you have any questions for me ... funeral arrangements, cause of death, etc...' he let his voice trail off.

'No. Thank you. My son will reach out to you if he has any questions. You have my number. Do you need an address? My bank information? Samir's contact information?' now I matched his tone so closely, it gave him pause.

He cleared his throat, said he would let his administrative assistant, Ms. Munsi, handle the details and that she would be in touch within the hour. Then he hung up, clearly too busy for goodbyes. I put the receiver down, his foreign accent lending an anomalous quality to the words still ringing in my ears, so that for some time after the call I wondered whether I had imagined the entire conversation, after all.

So, Captain is gone. It saddens me that after the initial shock, I detect no more than a slight change in pulse rate. I touch my face. It feels flushed, but only momentarily.

A seasoned actress, once asked by a Stardust reporter how

she managed always to remain so positive, stated that she never looked back, stayed focused on her greatest roles and erased from memory every bad audition, every early-on movie that gave her more notoriety than praise.

I buried the years spent with my ex-husband years ago. Dredging up the past would be tantamount to exhuming the body of my mother. I have no taste for it.

My marriage, *her* death. Cause and effect. Action and result. It does not take a rocket scientist to see what I had let happen. The two momentous events still nestled beneath the surface of my brain like two hissingsnakes.

I'm buried so deep in the past, I do not hear the doorbell. My maid sticks her head out of the bathroom, lather on her hair, red in the face from beating the dirt out of laundry.

'Oy, auntie, I cannot open the door in my state.'

I look at her as if she has two heads. Then the bell rings again and understanding dawns.

'Sir is dead.' A servant is looking up at me pleadingly.

I stare at her fluttering hands.

'Shroff Sir. Went in his sleep. Do something, please!'

'I can't rouse him if he's dead!' I shout furiously at the crone. She doesn't say anything, but takes my arm. She has been on this planet long enough to know that anger is just another reaction to the death of a loved one.

I go down one flight of stairs and go up another to Shroff's. I pass my hand across his beautiful face and press my lips to his creased forehead. He still smells fresh. Then I take his hand the way he once took mine and guided me toward sweetness and light. It is heavy and stiff, but surprisingly soft. I remember how it trembled like a bird in distress when he was paying the cabbie. I had an inkling then that it would not be long before he left us.

His books, the pressure of his hand on my shoulder, his old- person jokes, the portrait of his wife, *she was a lovable woman,* suddenly it's all too much…I keel over.

He was my haven away from home. My father and my mother.

My teacher and my friend. Of course, he did not know me in the end, crushed under the weight of so many ailments, but he was the unforgettable one. I cherished him.

It is only when I get back to my apartment that the tears begin to flow, and just for a while, with news of two deaths on the same morning, I'm no longer sure who or what it is that I'm mourning.

The following day, I'm a little more pragmatic. Shroff's only surviving relative, a niece, has been called and funeral arrangements are made. The neighbors gathered in a clutch to praise and cry. 'Not a wicked bone in his body,' someone is saying. I realize it's not Captain they are talking about.

I thank heavens that Samir, except for his little idiosyncrasies, is not like his father. At least, dear *Barker* does not have a Lolita complex. Yes, I call my son Barker, but only in private. Ever since that awful summer when Shukla referred to him as a mongrel and Samir, *who knew he had a sensitive streak*, decided he would turn into one!

Shukla. All those literary allusions and highfalutin language, in college, designed to make a girl's head turn. I wonder that had it not been for his encouragement, would I have ended my marriage so readily? When we split up, I couldn't go to Father's house and I didn't want to be alone, so I knocked on Desai's door. But Desai made it clear I couldn't live with him; he was rooming in a hostel. Then, Shukla took me in.

We were good together, at first. Until, something changed. He became careless about his appearance, even slovenly. Left the bathroom door ajar when he peed, answered the door with a toothbrush in his mouth and didn't bother to get his shirts ironed. Some mornings, he woke up and did not seem to recognize me. He became, in turn, condescending and eerily quiet and finally just left the apartment and did not surface for days at a time.

One day I asked him what was wrong.

'You used to make me feel like Cinderella, I said. Now, I don't know...'

'You don't see it, do you?' he said, cruelly. 'You are a kept woman. I can treat you any way I want.'

After he left, I studied my face in the mirror. It looked the same as it always did, only a little perplexed.

Then I brought Samir into his home, Shukla called him a mongrel, and just like that, my son started barking! Shukla couldn't handle Samir's weird behavior. We moved out before he could throw us out. And, at last, spring break was over.

I met one of the school parents, years later at a charity function, raising funds for autistic children. When I introduced myself, she asked me, not even pretending to hide the malice in her voice, 'Aren't you the mother of that boy who used to bark?'

Her idiot husband stood by her side, quiet as a mouse.

'Oh, is that all he did? When I was his age, I did more than just bark, I would bite, like this...' Then I pushed my face within inches of her husband's neck, licked my lips and clicked my teeth like a vampire.

That worked! I didn't see her again, all that evening.

We have never once discussed my marriage or my separation, my son and I. What sense does it make when everything I remember, he may remember differently? Memory is a hall of mirrors, distortions at every turn.

Still. I look at the digits scribbled on my note pad. The money Captain has left for Samir is certainly not a figment of my imagination. Should I accept it? Or should I make a grand gesture and tear up the check when it arrives?

In the end, I decide not to cut off my nose to spite my face. Samir, poor boy, should get what he is owed. I pick up the phone one more time, this time to pass the information about his father's death to his first-born, coaching myself as I wait for him to pick up the phone, to: (a) give him the bad news first, and (b) BE SENSITIVE. He doesn't answer. I continue to try.

Uzma

Samir. Brash but unsure. Handles situations, women and relationships in the same one-size-fits-all manner. Still. It's the way his face lights up when he sees me, you see. There are times I have to look away, embarrassed by that naked want.

When he folds me in his arms, it is as if we are encased within the soft pink center of a conch, and the rest of the world, is simply white noise, beating against the carapace. And upon his touch, I turn into a glass figurine - precious. Fragile. Owned.

When we separate, I am hollow, aching to be filled. And when I say goodbye, his eyes turn empty as a desert spring, except for the brief glimmer of fear.

The first time we made love, there was a look in his eyes I could not fathom. Was it a question or a demand? Was it a longing or a complaint? His hands were slick from gliding inside me, his kisses deep, his body moved beneath or above me as if he had done this many times before, but only just gleaned the significance. Yet, the question (or the demand) lingering in the space between us, detracted me from surrendering to a deep, free-floating happiness.

When it was over, we lay side by side, in the sated tranquillity of lovers, not talking, except for the occasional sigh, moving in and out of consciousness. There was a heaviness in my belly, and a burning between my legs, deep and sweet. I turned to him and examined his face, his unreachable eyes, and needier than I have ever felt before, asked if he was disappointed.

'Why in the world, would you say that?'

He was genuinely surprised.

'You have this look, I can't figure out, as if you want something from me that I cannot give...like maybe I am not enough,' I dithered.

He took my face in his warm hands, prying open my mouth with his finger. I kissed and licked it the way I thought he liked, the smell of sex still on him. Then he rubbed my lips, raw and bitten, with the ball of his thumb, and said, no, he was not disappointed. He was simply afraid.

'Of what?'

'Of losing you. Of losing the one sane thing in my life,' my lover said.

Samir. I am right here. Come back to me.

I open my pocketbook to find a tissue when his cell phone rings, scaring the daylights out of me. It's his mother again.

24

Annika

In the early evening, when the sun-struck city did not feel as punishingly hot, I shopped for light, cotton tunics and airy, flared pants so that I could both roam the undulant city in local dress and avoid needlessattention.

Still, it took a few days for me to feel less dépayse. I believe it was only when I found myself sharing a *gali* with a herd of goats and ignored their bleating as I would any other noise, that I felt and smelled like a native.

With the imprimatur of sophistication shrugged off, my shoulders relaxed, my feet sprang off the curb and flew through the concrete rills of the suburbs with rollerblading efficiency. And, in the known alleyways and hidden passageways, I discovered fragments of my former self that I took home to examine with the painstaking care of archaeological digs.

Ignoring the new eateries with no history and little charm and names like OMG Burgers or Souper Cool, we ate in unknown places, Adi and I, local holes where the hygiene was suspect but the aromas evocative. Our palates welcomed the distraction, and our stomachs adjusted accordingly, making more space. Large glasses of lime sherbet or salted lassi eased the spicy meals down the digestive tract, giving a clear pass for the next day and the next. Full of vim and new vitality, I smiled at strangers, told them they looked familiar, and they said, yes, you look familiar as well. It seemed, India, like a jilted lover, had forgiven me at last and extended a hand in friendship.

Finally, one day, Adi showed me our return tickets and told

me it was time. 'What are you talking about?' I asked, avoiding his eyes.

'Call your sister. We will meet her together, if it makes it any easier,' he said. I told him I needed one more day to think before I did as he asked. Reluctantly, my husband agreed.

I made a mental flowchart of our conversation before I called Malavika, the following day. Keep it short and decisive, I warned myself, and the tone – formal and respectful, without a hint of intimacy. I dialed her number, cursing myself for not making a hard copy of the talking points. She answered the phone in two rings.

'Hel-lo,' the voice at the end of the line trilled, stressing on the second syllable. I... I said, and lost the ability to produce sound. It was Adi who spoke to her and set up the meeting.

Malavika

We are to meet in a restaurant, like strangers, but nervous as a kitten, I wake up at 5 a.m. Since I'm up anyway, I start shining my home. I replace all the cushion covers and put up the curtains I was saving for Diwali. I move Father's bookshelf, his worm-eaten book of Sanskrit Grammar, and the wall clock above his desk to my bedroom, vowing to rid myself of all his belongings, the following week. Then I pick up his photograph, put it in a box, wrap the box with an old shawl, and store the lot in the attic, for what point is there in holding on to someone who evokes neither pleasure nor curiosity, but occupies a space in your living room, like a surly proprietor, his feet on the couch?

I take special care with my appearance. I am the *didi*. I want to look serious but not stern, glamorous but not overstated, and all those things I was to my Ana-banana before we grew up and grew away. In the end, I fall back on a favorite white-for-wisdom eyelet tunic and pants and silver hoops in my ears and hope for the best. With a feeling akin to nerves before a job interview, *Uh, I'm here for the big sister position*, I go to the restaurant an hour early, ask to be seated facing the entry so that I will see her the moment she sees me and the burning in my breast I once thought was cancerous may be assuaged at last.

She arrives at last. Two minutes before our set time.

Unaware of the water in those wide, wild eyes, she attempts a hello, a hug, a handshake, knocks against a chair along the way and then sits on the edge of her chair. Her bag drops with a thump. Her face is a mess – sodden, crumpled and in need of a good wring.

'I … ' she says. 'You…' she whispers, and then struck, as I am, with the blunt force of memory, she simply stops trying, her mouth still open.

I do what comes naturally. I cup her little face with both my hands, bracing myself for the possibility that she might flinch, and keep her still, until the tears subside. Her cheeks feel warm on my palms and a smile, shy as morning dew, hovers in the corners of her lips, instead.

'My Ana-banana,' I say. Then I watch her smile grow and grow until it infects the whole world, and the sun takes its head out of the clouds and beams on cue. And within its healing light we sit.

'Are you ready to order, Ma'am?'

Only then do I release her face and let my hands rest on my lap.

'Coffee,' I tell the blousy waitress.

'And for your daughter?'

'I'm not actually her …' but the waitress is already moving away, her eyes darting towards another customer.

'Coffee will be just fine,' Anika says, instead.

Samir

Then, one day, there is an argument. Voices, more than two, at first, scarcely above a whisper, then raised. The volley of expletives increasing exponentially is scaring me shitless. It is not illogical to assume any one of these thugs can, without ramifications, burst into my room and plunge his frustrations into my already broken sternum.

On a positive note, although I have been lying in a torpor for more days than I care to count, my vision seems to have improved. The skin on my face not as raw and tender, the throbbing in my head not as constant – more like distant thunder than a crashing drumroll. My chest is still bound, but I can breathe a little deeper. My voice is coming back. I wiggle my fingers under the athletic tape. At this rate, I might soon be able to sit up and even give the arseholes the finger, I think wryly. Two weeks ago, that would have been a pipe dream.

The voices have died down in favor of heavy breathing and occasional yawns. Then just as I'm about to sail off to coma-land, a ratatatat of fuck-related words foul up the air so heavily, even I feel compelled to bleep them out of my narrative. Until, improbably, the nervous clicking of high heels and wafting through the walls, a pleasant scent—definitely female, - freshens the room. My heart is bursting out of my chest.

'What the heck is going on? How long do I have to wait out in the car?'

'Uzma! My love!'

A sudden silence, so all-encompassing, I may as well have

been a corpse, shoved six feet under. 'Uzma, please get me out of here, Uzma, I'm here!'

A rush of wind as the door opens and a fist lands on my jaw. Blinded! Blood fills my mouth, as well as something solid, microscopic, like tittles of rock. I feel around with the tip of my tongue. Gashes on the inside of my cheeks. Broken teeth.

Then a high-strung voice: 'Did you hurt the chappie, you moron! I will tell Adar...'

The scented woman is in the room. It is not Uzma.

Uzma

We all have a role to play.

Mother, well-coiffed, with a propensity for tailored designer suits, teeth whiter than bone, supervises the staff, supervises our comings and goings, a wistfulness in her eyes that breaks my heart, (and also makes me impatient). Allows herself to be nudged gently in the direction of the latest visiting tycoon that Father is trying to court. You will find her on the terrace, in the twilight hour, sipping watermelon juice out of a champagne glass, and listening to Sufi music.

Father, the wheedling, politicking, head of our proud familia, was born, as they say, with a silver spoon in his mouth. Lost everything he inherited, at the spoiled age of twenty-three, betting on horses. At twenty-nine he won all of it back, including a wealthy wife, young enough to raise eyebrows and boost his ego. Today, I can say without bias, he is a staunch member of the community, loved by all, his sub- rosa deals notwithstanding.

My brothers, dubious viziers, contemptuous of women, publicly boastful of their exploits: *take her doggy style, pin her arms behind her, grab her by the pussy*...

Each one of them averse to work, or college or sports! They kiss my mother's hands reverentially and protect my honor, like a piece of prime property in the hustling heart of Kuwait.

And I, Uzma Habib, am just as accustomed to my designated role, angel of mercy to the tired and the poor, hair trapped in a beret, passion locked behind my black eyes, waiting, and waiting.

In comes Samir, an immigrant more pathetic than a limping horse, *he owns two pairs of underwear and worships a stone idol with many heads tucked furtively behind his almirah.* The one time he dropped by to our home, there was a slight mix-up. He was ushered in through the back door. They thought he was there for the chauffeur position.

I gave myself to him. And nothing is as it was.

☒☒☒

Three times I reach for his cell phone, where her number is saved, but, coward that I am, I cannot bring myself to call her. How do I introduce myself to his mother? More importantly, how does one tell a mother that her son is missing and presumed dead?

I'm staring at the phone still, rehearsing my little speech when my pocketbook comes alive, making me jump. This time it's Sheila, buzzing me on my personal phone.

'He is okay. I just saw him.'

'SAMIR!'

'Shhh! Yes. He will be fine. *I think.*'

'What do you mean, *you think* Sheila! Where is he?'

But she hung up.

25

Annika

I step inside her apartment, once ours, gingerly. It is a foreign country, with familiar landmarks. The couch. The dining table. I look at the floor. I don't recognize the tile. We have left our slippers outside the front door. The floor feels cool. I'm pretty sure there are no fissures. No cracks through which their cold hands will reach out and pull me into the mire. Still, I hold on to Adi.

Malavika

She is holding her breath, her eyes wide as saucers. Breathe, I gesture, expanding my chest, circling both hands upward and outward. She looks like a bird, smiling, tremulous. Adi takes her hand, squeezes her fingers, *I'm here*. Together, they enter.

She looks frozen. I let her take her time and focus on Adi instead. I scarcely know him, having seen him just once, dressed like a doll at their wedding.

'How've you been? Has it been a comfortable visit?' I smile, inviting a response, hopefully, a longish one.

'Adi lost his mom. We came here for the funeral,' Anika interjects softly, then goes back to being a statue.

I cover my mouth with my hand. 'I'm sorry!'

He smiles gently. 'It's okay. She was hovering on the edge for a long time.'

Then he tries on a jocular tone. 'Apart from a nauseating proliferation of biryani lunches, we've been doing quite well, thank you.' He strokes his belly.

I've made lamb biryani for dinner. At some point, I must sneak into the kitchen and stow it away in the freezer. But there are plenty other dishes they can have. I hadn't cooked in a while, but once I got started, it was not so daunting after all, cutting the cauliflower into florets, chopping the chicken legs, grinding and roasting the spices... I have hot sambhar, Mughlai chicken curry, dum aloo, roasted cauliflower and cucumber raita, with tandoori *rotis*, and semolina pudding with a strand or two of saffron for dessert. I will now make plain rice tempered with cumin, in place of the biryani. Oh, dear god, I have nothing for them to drink!! I can send the servant out for some beer.

'I like your home. Nothing jars. Everything flows the way it is supposed to,' Adi says, nodding appreciatively.

'Towards the ocean, you mean?' I joke, pleased nonetheless.

We look at Anika. She is still frozen in place, her ear cocked to one side, as if watching an opera unfold in the nether world because there is certainly nothing of *him* in this room. A table empty of his glasses, notepaper and other paraphernalia. A clay water pitcher, hopelessly out of place, in the area where his bookshelf once stood. The naked wall, with a faint outline of his framed photograph in the attic.

The floor replaced, his clothes given away to the poor. Now I wonder if I'd made a mistake tucking all his things out of sight. Maybe there was a part of her that still missed him, that never did get closure. Had I left things the way they were, at least, she wouldn't have to slip into another world to look for her father.

Annika

As rooms go, it is clean, airy, its shabby truth concealed under embroidery, made cozy with handloom cushions, jute rugs, Chinese lanterns and rosewood tissue boxes, for a touch of budget exotica.

She has assiduously swept away every proof of their existence. And still he breathes uneasily, above our heads, Father, behind the new paint, beneath the new floor, around the attic with the cobwebs and the squirrels. I can feel him, like the smell of furniture and rodents and mothballs in the attic.

But where is she? My stomach hurts as if I've skipped a meal.

Ah! I see her now, wedged between the kitchen and the hallway, the blanket of death drawn over her eyes. Secretly, I always wished she had chosen a better time, like when I wasn't home, or when Malavika wasn't out carousing with her ex. Instead, she had lain on the floor, unmindful of how it would affect me. All of us. Still. How peaceful she was in death!

I'm sorry, Mama. So sorry this world was too much for you. We were too much for you.

And there *we* are, in the comfortless kitchen, Father and I, intrepid survivors, cooking for two, washing for two, fighting for two, the *good* man and the *earnest* daughter versus the *whore* Malavika, the *evil* Captain, the *bastard* son.

And every evening the scrubbing and cleaning, the inventory, the math homework, the reciting of shlokas and my petrified prayers cast into the darkness. *Please, dear God, let him stay mad at them, let him forget about me.*

And here is the balcony, where I waited for her, night after night even as the skies, whipped by lightning, raged and burned. Malavika. My sister who left and always left.

Yet, here we are.

Malavika

She is in a sort of trance. I get a glass of water. Adi is shaking her, patting her face, rubbing her hands. In the midst of all this chaos, the plangent cry of the phone.

'Yes. Hello.'

'……..'

'Hello.'

'Is this … Samir's mother?'

'Yes. How can I help you? Who are you, please?'

'Auntie, my name is Uzma Habib. I have Samir's cell phone. I see you called him a few times.'

'Uzma. Where is Samir?'

Anika and Adi are looking at each other, trying to appear deaf, concern flitting across their eyes.

'To tell you the truth, I really am not sure, but…'

'Uzma. Listen to me. Are you his girlfriend? He has mentioned you once or twice.'

'Yes. You could say that.'

'Where is he, my dear?'

That's when the girl breaks down.

26

Uzma

'She wouldn't give me the details. But she said he was definitely alive, and they were simply waiting for further instructions from Galib.'

'Who's they, Sheila?'

'I don't know. I guess, your brothers asked a couple of goons to hole Samir up in this warehouse like place until they decide... you know,' Sheila frowned with distaste.

'No, I don't know. What is it they plan to do to him? How do you know it's a warehouse?'

Fear makes my voice sharp.

She takes my hand.

'Adar told me. I've convinced Adar, to let Samir go, and he will. Don't lose heart, Uzma.'

She rose to inspect herself in the mirror and brushed a stray lash off delicately with an index finger. There is something she isn't telling me, but her face is closed off like a Stepford wife's. I thanked her and walked her to the door, making a mental note to have a box of Swiss chocolate delivered to her doorstep that afternoon with something mawkish like *Counting on you. Your sis*. As for the bile rising in my throat from all that sucking up, I will just have to swallow it.

I couldn't put off calling Samir's mother any longer. She picked up the phone almost immediately.

Despite some trepidation, I started off strong. It was when

she addressed me as 'my dear,' that I couldn't hold it together. Who was I to deserve such kindness when her son was lying somewhere, possibly with his head and other body parts disassembled, simply because he loved me?

I told her he was in trouble, and it was my fault because we loved each other, but my brothers, racist pigs, couldn't get past the fact that Sam is not a Moslem. But he was safe; I had reason to believe that he was, and the moment he was home, I blathered, I would make sure she was the first person he called.

She told me we'd talk again after "I'd settled down" and sounded calm as a family doctor, as if I was the one who needed reassurance.

Two days later, it was my mother who wanted a chat. We were on the terrace, before sundown. She had a good hour before she would dress for dinner and go out with my dad.

Even though it was just the two of us, my mother had made an occasion of it. We sat down, to an ebonized oak tray with petit fours, sliced melon, and cappuccinos for two. Birds chirped in the background, or was it Sufi music? Quite pleasant really but for the fact that I could not take a solitary breath without worrying about Samir. If he was safe, why hadn't I heard from him?

'Uzma. First of all, Samir is safe. I want you to know that.'

A weight of Jurassic proportions rolled off my chest, making me almost dizzy with relief. In her unobtrusive, completely non-invasive, way, she has always been the eyes and ears of our family. I trust her implicitly. I find myself able to breathe at last.

'Yes, I heard. But only now do I really believe it. Thank You, Mama.'

She nodded. 'Now, tell me a little about him.'

'He's a good guy. Honest. Makes an honest living, I mean. He's not as successful as dad, but…' I'm stuttering like a fifteen-year-old confessing about her first crush.

'I did not ask you about his work. Tell me, why you see him. Why he is important to you. You can be straight with me. I'm not dad or your brothers.'

'All right. I'll try.' And suddenly, I find my voice.

'When I first met him, I thought that he was lost. This country, Mom, this land of expats, it can make or break you. On my way to work, I see some of these people, young and smart and full of hope, rushing about like little kids hunting for Easter eggs. *Where's the prize, where's the prize*... and over the years, some win, like Dad, but many fail. And the ones that fail, I see the way their shoulders slope, and their eyes don't leave the ground, as if therein lies their fate.'

'Samir,' I swallowed, 'came to the Agency for his work papers. He took a long time over his resume as if his own life was a conundrum, and as I watched him, just for the sake of amusement, I gentrified him -gave him a haircut, stripped off his faded black pants and white sneakers, and swapped the shapeless, *Bedoon* tee shirt he had on for a light pair of slacks, suede loafers and a silk shirt, the color of butter cream. It was quite a mental exercise. And after it was done, I thought, hmmm, dressed like a dapper dude, he could look quite hot. Worth showing off a little.'

'Then I asked him a question or two and realized there was more to him than meets the eye. A lot more. Despite his humble status, he has a sort of stubborn confidence, bordering on arrogance. Even the way he walked belied his situation, as if the agency was simply a transit station, a gateway to a brilliant future. In his own environment, he was probably a bit of a rake. I dare say, if I was some girl he'd met in a pub in Mumbai, he would try to pick me up and easily charm his way into buying me a drink.'

'In any case, I called him, after I helped him find a job, and we met now and again. And each time we met I felt as if I knew a little bit more about him, but also a little less. He is so full of contradictions, you see – his language is crude but his hands are gentle, he has very little money and a great deal of pride, he is street smart but still without cunning, reckless but also painfully shy and when at last he kissed me, I just knew.'

I've never felt this way before, Mom. I love him. I love him the way I love Father, who can do no wrong, even when he is wrong. I can count on him. He will take me in his fold, the way a peregrine takes the geese, and he will not abandon me, ever! I love him the way I love Munir, Adar and Galib, not one of them given to intelligent discourse. Can they even spell *discourse*? But they are street smart, and their childish antics performed solely for my benefit, are like yum, sticky taffy after a bland meal. I love him the way I love you, Mom. Your sadness feels like a knife in my gut, and your happiness is like listening to raga *Bilahari* in the light of dawn. And I love him like a woman. This is not an infection I will recover from or a passion that will fizz out in time, but rock-solid love, the kind I've always known and the kind I've ever dreamed of - coalesced and transcended into my Samir. We are two people with one strong beating heart,'

I tell my mother. We sit in silence for a minute as long as an hour. I feel light-headed and moved by my own words, the honeyed words I never thought I'd speak aloud.

Tall and elegant as a queen despite the casual housedress, Mother rises from the chaise lounge.

I tug at the tassels of her sash.

'Mom. Could you get my brothers to release him from the hell hole they are holding him in and simply let us love each other? I mean, please, tell me we're not living in medieval times!'

'We are not living in medieval times.' She bends down to kiss the top of my head. 'And, I promise I will do what I can, Uzma. Now, I must get dressed.'

There is tenderness in her eyes. But also fear.

Malavika

The call from Uzma Habib left me feeling a little out of sorts, anxiety wheezing out of my chest. I tried to hide it as best as I could, peppering them with questions, moving constantly, setting the table, snipping cilantro, and half listening. Poor Adi, caught like a raft between shifting winds - the pallid reserve of his wife and the forced animation of his sister-in-law -moored himself to the table at last, suggesting gently, that we have an early dinner.

There was no time to roll individual rotis or make cumin rice, so, with a sheepish smile, I dished out the biryani instead. Surprisingly, we all ate with gusto, even Anika, licking her fingers pensively.

'May I pack some chicken for you? Some cauliflower?'

'Wow, that would be...'

'No, Adi. Your aunts might think we don't like their cooking!'

'Oh, alright. If you think...' he said, with the harried look of a man in a woman's world.

At the door, I attempted to explain. 'There was something I needed to discuss, with you, both of you, but I'm afraid, I'm feeling a bit off, today.'

'It's nothing. I think you are both nervous, and understandably so. We will see you again before we leave,' said the good man and let it go. I stood a moment longer, watching them tread carefully down the poorly lit stairs.

He called the next day, suggesting a walk by the beach. 'Let's meet by the juice stand across the street from the bus stop,' he said.

'Okay, but don't have the juice there. It's not as sanitary as it should be,' I warned.

Despite the carnivalesque atmosphere - hundreds of people were out, (therefore, hundreds of hawkers as well) taking advantage of the slight drop in temperature. It was a tranquil evening. The ocean was in a state of rest. A waning sun took a final bow, bathing the skies in roseate light. A spittle-white foam licked the rocks, waxing them to a high gloss. I looked at the illusory line where the ocean ended, wondering for the millionth time, what Uzma Habib (*a Muslim name. Samir, must you always choose the thorny path?*) could have possibly meant when she said, she had reason to believe my son was "safe". How could she suppose he was safe and tell me in the same breath she did not know where he was? And under what circumstances would he leave behind his cell phone? Samir was a lot of things, but he was not careless. He never left home without patting his front pocket to make sure he held his cell phone close to his heart, as if afraid some mythical god, residing in the SIM card, might chime a message that would miraculously change his future, and he must answer it at once or lose the opportunity.

I turned my eyes from the horizon to find Anika staring at me in her astute way.

'So, Anika with two ns, you are quite the American now, ain't ya?' I quipped in, what I thought was a western accent. She grinned shyly and took my hand. *A head taller but still a little girl afraid to let go.*

Then Adi, with perfect timing, broke it to me that he planned on returning home as scheduled, but he'd changed Anika's return date. 'Actually, I've made it an open ticket, so she can stay as long as she wants. It's time you two got to know each other again,' he said.

'You are a sensitive soul, Adi Sharma,' I sighed.

Anika leaned sideways, butted him with her shoulder.

He grinned sheepishly, stopped before a vendor, and asked, 'And what lovely treats do you have in that basket of yours?'

'Boiled or masala peanuts, Sahib.'

'Where are they? All I see is onion and those very hot peppers.'

'Oh no, Sahib, they are right below.'

And so, we strolled up and down, with our paper cones of spiced bliss. Just another family enjoying a day at the beach.

Samir

They are here. All of them. It does not seem to matter that I am bound to a bed in a dank room, the stench of shit worse than a bloody lavatory, a single light bulb flickering over my head, the water in my lungs suffocating me. *I want to sit up, please, just help me sit up!* It's as if they don't hear me, my parents.

'Ouch, this old age business is killing me,' Mother grimaces, clutching at her arthritic knee.

'Not the worst way to go, dying of old age,' he laughs.

'You would know, you've been old ever since we met, you rooster!' she giggles.

The jokes go on and on. I cannot breathe. How is it possible, my parents don't see me?!

Uzma is here too. 'Samir spoke about you often. I feel as though I know you. May I stay with you? We loved each other, you know.' She is hugging my mother. My father is staring at her arse. He is drawn to her like a bee to a honey pot. He puts a hand on her spine, slides it lower and almost inadvertently cups one cheek. She turns to look at him and smiles dreamily. Her mouth is slack. What is she doing! And why is she referring to me in the past tense?

Principal Spencer is making the light bulb flicker. She's whipped out her hose. Oh my God, I can't take it anymore. No, don't touch me, ugly bitch!

I am under a tree. No. I am a tree - two hundred feet tall, bleached of color, and completely bare. Pinned on my chest is a scrap of paper. It reads, "The Standing Dead".

Do you see me, Uzma?

Those goons at the door, holding their noses, for the smell, they look like my bookies, come to collect. Is the past catching up with me?

Blood everywhere. I am dying. Or maybe I'm already dead. Someone covers my face with a sheet.

27

Annika

We are seated on the bed, Malavika and I, bolstered by pillows. She has spread a blue vinyl cloth to protect the bedcover. And on the vinyl table cloth, a little picnic of tea, pound cake, onion fritters and ground lamb samosas. Green and red chutney in clay bowls begging for a dip.

A house lizard, attached to the wall above my head, looks as if it has always been there, just like this house, this picnic, the two of us on this bed, comfortable with the silences between conversation.

There is an almirah and a bookshelf in a corner with Father's books. A week ago, it would have made me hyperventilate. Now, I give it scarcely a glance. The room looks cozy, reminding me of a private coupe on the Deccan Queen (train), the absence of furniture actually liberating. I think guiltily of our accumulations, Adi and mine. How many afternoons over the years have we spent paying homage to industry? Surely, there is something to be said for the Thoreau-like simplicity of my sister's home?

On the other hand, maybe it has nothing to do with having a monastic attitude. With apartments like pigeon holes, where is the room for furniture! I yawn, lazily.

I take a sip of the steaming tea she pours, with a *ta... da*! It's a special blend that takes over thirty minutes to brew. Laced with cinnamon, cloves, nutmeg and other spices, it fills me with a strange nostalgia for something I haven't ever experienced before.

'I used to add a spoon of my tea to your milk when you were little. It made you feel grown-up.' Malavika smiles at the memory.

I do remember that. 'Except, you wouldn't let me drink out of the china teacup. I had a horrid little stainless-steel glass.' I make a face.

We are quiet for a moment, sipping the tea, sipping from the past.

'You have over three hundred friends on Facebook,' I grin.

'Ha! Like three hundred sweaters one does not need, but holds on to, *just in case.*' She grimaced.

'Do you cook a lot? Are you writing regularly? Haiku?' I ask, suddenly hungry for any information. As if the Malavika, sitting inches away, was still blurry at the edges, needed definition.

'Not if I can help it. Cooking, I mean. Haiku, now and then, when I'm inspired.'

'What inspires you?' I ask.

'You do.'

She leans forward to tweak my nose.

'I had to cook when his ma was with us, but now she's gone, I guess I'll take it easier,' I sigh.

'Salil's father visited us once, briefly, but I've never lived with in-laws. What was it like? Having her around?'

Salil. She usually called him Captain. I give her question some thought.

'She could not fill the hole left in my heart, after Gone-Mother,' I say, treading carefully,

'Still, she was the only mother I got to know and I will miss her.'

We were both silent for a while, lost in our own thoughts.

Then she smiled, 'Gone-Mother! Why the prefix? It sounds so strange.'

I shrug. 'Father always referred to her that way when he was lecturing me: Your gone-mother never slept without cleaning the kitchen. Your gone-mother did not bother with lipstick. Your gone-mother was a saint. I guess it stuck.'

She bit her lip.

'I shouldn't have left you with that mons ... with him, alone. You were just a child. I'm sorry, Anika, I was... immature, self-absorbed.'

I balled my fists. A lifetime of rage, hoarded and honed for just such a moment, dissipated like fizz, leaving me flattened.

'Yes. You certainly were. But it's okay, I guess.' I shrugged. Her lips twisted in a rictus.

'I always wondered, why didn't you just leave?'

'Where would I go? I left when I met Adi. With my head held high. Besides, why would I want to repeat your mistakes?' I retorted sharply.

She turned red. I wanted to soften my last words, regain the sweet serenity of the past few hours, but I did not know how, so I was silent, letting them resonate, the warm and fuzzy feeling now out the window.

'I'm so sorry he struck you, you know. Father,' I finally said.

She looked startled.

'It's fine. It was almost a relief, sometimes,' she added ruefully, 'It actually cleared the air. For a few days after he broke my face, he was almost nice. No verbal abuse or anything.'

Is that how she saw it! 'It should never have happened. I wish we could've prevented it.'

She shook her head and shifted uncomfortably. 'Anika, after today, let's never talk of him again. Promise me.'

'I do. I promise.'

'He let you marry Adi. There is that,' she added, contradicting herself, pensively.

'Bina auntie made it happen. I was to pretend I'd never set eyes on Adi in my life. She spoke to Father, and in the end, he thought it was all his idea.'

We giggled at that. And suddenly the air was light again, twirling with the conspiracies of childhood.

Then, I saw the lone portrait on the wall – Samir, leaning

forward with a cricket bat, his eyes intense, the collar of his shirt turned up, ready to strike. He must've been around ten at the time, I imagine. I pointed my chin to the wall,

'He called me, you know, Sammy. Did you ask him too?'

'He called you? My son?' There was a look of wonder on her face, 'Did he… was he…?'

'Yes. Your son. My nephew. We had a nice little chat. He was concerned about you, didi…Malavika.'

'He was concerned about me!' she repeated and paused between each word, as if its specific placement in the sentence was foreign and remarkable.

'Uh, why didn't you call me sooner, Ana-banana? I almost gave up, waiting.'

I bit my lip.

'I don't know. I have abandonment issues.' *Damn. Why did I say that?*

She digested the information in silence.

Then she tapped her head as if remembering something.

'Speaking of abandonment,' she rose from the bed with a wry smile, 'I have something I need to show you.'

She went to the shelf, and from between the pages of a book, pulled out a sheet and dropped it in my hands.

'What's this?'

'I found it one day, when I was tidying up. Read it. It's why I've been trying to reach you, so urgently. I have to sort out a few things, based on your decision. Adi should see it as well. I will send him a scanned copy.'

The sight of Father's handwriting made me break out in a sweat. I had to read the scribble a few times to make sense of it.

'Is this Father's will?'

'It appears so, yes.'

'I don't want any part of it. Burn it!' 'Anika!'

'No! Besides, it isn't even signed. You can contest it and win.'

'It isn't about winning, Ana-banana, it is about doing the right thing,' she said, sounding tired.

'You know, I thought we had made our peace with each other towards the end, Father and I.

I took care of him, when there was no one else, but apparently, he didn't feel the same way. Now, years after he's passed on, I find this! I cannot live here, knowing he hated me to the end, knowing he would rather have *you* own his property.' Her voice shook as if saying the words out loud made the outcome definite.

'*When there was no one else,*' her words went through me like an ice pick. But she was right, wasn't she? Where was I?

'Father died *ages* ago, Malavika! He has no say in the matter anymore, does he?' I said, hotly. 'I went halfway across the world to get away from this place. You, on the other hand, came full circle! This is where you belong. And Gone-Mother, if she were alive, she would have something to say about that scrap of paper too, wouldn't she? It was her home as well! She loved you. You know it. All she ever wanted was to see you settled, giggling and dancing into the sunset as only you could. Our mother rests, now because you are here, on this little plot she scrubbed and shone and made as comfortable as she could, for her two flowers! (*She called us by a different flower every night*) Do you know the first thing I felt when I stepped inside your apartment? Her absence, yes. But without the accompanying feeling of heaviness. It is as if she let the sun in, made the very air lighter for you.'

Exhausted, I offered my hand.

'Tear up the will, Malavika.' She took the will in her hand, finally nodding in agreement.

Malavika

Those last words, her gift to me. Little Ana-banana, with her heart of gold, knew exactly how to strike the right chord. I will keep the apartment for now. From my upper deck, I will watch the waters change from season to season and light to ephemeral light. I will listen to the endless rhapsody of the waves as they move from shore to shore, and I will bow to Varuna, god of the oceans.

They will come down more often. My sister and Adi. We will sit at this table. I will add a leaf to accommodate my Samir and his Uzma. *How shy and tentative she sounded on the phone, so unlike his previous girlfriends.* And between slices of pizza and bowls of Mulligatawny, the children and (someday) their children's children will recount their plans for the future and vanquish the past with their smiles.

And when he is ready, my Samir, perhaps I will let him have this place and move to the Nilgiri Hills, a step closer to Him, closer to His forgiveness. With the money his father has left him, and a girl like Uzma by his side, he will have that which has forever eluded me, that which I sought in all the wrong places: balance - the seed mantra of happiness.

Come home, Samir.

Samir

In the middle of the night, or at least, I think it is the middle of the night, I'm picked up like garbage and flung in the back of a pick-up truck. At some point, the juddering stops, and my arse says, 'Thank you.' Too soon, of course, because then the tailgate is lowered, some heavy breathing ensues, I'm grabbed by my legs and dropped to the earth. Before I can muster a shocked, whoa! They are gone.

It must have been an hour, maybe more, before I realize that they have neglected to consider my sleeping arrangements, making it someone else's business, I suppose, now that I am no longer in their custody. Fuming silently – too weak to shout, brought to my knees with pain and claustrophobic in the inky blackness, I am suddenly nostalgic for my sagging bed situated conveniently beside a latrine and the reassuring sounds of my phlegmy watch dogs. At least there, I was tethered to something, not splayed out in the center of the street like a welcome mat for oncoming traffic.

I inch myself into a crawling position, losing precious breath, impressing myself with my extensive repertoire of swear words, when I saw headlights in the distance. Scrambling like a crab, if crabs can scramble, I somehow landed out of harm's way, and ended on my back, legs in the air, yelping like a girl.

The vehicle, also a truck, seemingly, the preferred mode of travel for night warriors, miraculously stops. A giant in plaid appeared out of a cloud of diesel fumes, took one look at the heap of rubbish writhing between gravel and asphalt, clicked his tongue and muttered, 'I'll call you an ambulance.'

'Ah! No. Please,' I managed, trying to peer into the holes behind the facial hair.

'I can't take you in my truck, son. This is a meat truck. I have a delivery scheduled.' I continued to shake my head frantically. He pulled at the hair, tapered to cotton wicks on his upper lip, trying to think.

'Isn't there someone you can call?' he finally asked, sticking his hand under his shirt to retrieve a cell phone from the money belt he flashed.

I nodded. *Uzma*, I thought. I opened my mouth. I drew a blank. I also realized, with some alarm, that I needed to take a piss, not in itself a matter of concern, unless your hands are bound.

He was getting restive, glancing uneasily at his truck as if it was not a 3000–pound freight carrier but a demanding mistress, tapping her heels, waiting to be gone.

'Uhm, yes,' I gave him my own cell number, stalling for time, trying frantically meanwhile to recall Uzma's. 367 no 368…, I had the first three digits, *so at least it's not brain damage.* I rocked back and forth, trying to pry loose the digits out of my brain, roll them out like balls in a lottery machine. No luck. My bladder was about to burst.

He dialed the number and held the phone to my ear. It rang. "Hello."

The voice at the other end trilled and I could swear I heard angel music at my shoulder.

'Uzma.'

As always, it was the sound of her voice that spurred me on, that perfect decibel, delicate as a bird, pregnant with feeling. I convinced my roadside friend to carry me to his truck and drive me to the nearest gas station. En route, he fiddled with his two-way radio, giving and receiving instructions to a robotic voice. When he dropped me, he had driven full twenty miles off course. After what I'd been through, it was almost impossible to wrap my arms around such kindness.

'Here,' he said, sticking a tenner in my pocket, after I jumped out of his truck with an impressive groan. I had nothing to give him for his trouble except an awkward hug. It actually felt good in his meaty arms. He accepted it with awkwardness of his own.

'Be careful,' shot the man of few words without a backward glance and raced back to his revved-up mistress.

At last, in the safety of the owner's back office, nursing a pot of scalding coffee, blotting out blood and dirt with damp lavatory towels, I waited to be rescued.

28

Annika

It was the thought of him, casting a shadow in her heart, like a terminal patient in the next room. Attuned by now, to her every mood, I lead my big sister to a low, wind-chapped building, unadorned except for a single wooden cross mounted on the steeple.

We walk past the southern perimeter of the church, where a privacy wall serves as a natural backrest for the Friday Market vendors. How mesmerizing the colorful displays to the eyes of a child. How pathetic the gaudy displays, to the eyes of an adult. A malnourished boy, sitting on his haunches, is blowing and twisting balloons into animal shapes. Some of the artist's work, pink dogs and green swans, yellow snakes and aquamarine fish, rub noses in the air. The strings of the balloons are secured to a rock. I watch him briefly, resuscitating each balloon, cheeks puffing out alarmingly, eyes lengthening to slits.

I want to buy every balloon. Malavika forges ahead, oblivious.

In the far corner, closer to the entry and, therefore, hard to miss, stood a solitary kiosk. A living version of Our Lady of Sorrows, not so much sold, as presided over, candles, soaps and wax objects that looked like decapitated body parts. I take a pair of slim candles and slip all the money in my purse into her gnarly hands. She nods inscrutably.

Through the open doors we walk to stare wordlessly up at St. Jude, The Patron Saint of Desperate Causes. Despite the flame crowning his head, the apostle's eyes look gentle.

Malavika's eyes fill with tears. I give the candles to my sister and dip my fingers into the stoup at the door to make a sign of the cross. It feels like a tunnel inside the church. Adjusting to the cool darkness, I go toward the points of light, trembling on a tabernacle, and light a few votive candles, snuffed out by occasional air, gusting through invisible vents. Silence, laced with burning incense, makes me shudder with an intensity of feeling I had not expected. Not wanting to weep, I take a sharp intake of breath. A hand rests on my shoulder, grazes my head.

Gone Mother draped in beauteous light!

'Wait!' I hold out my arms. Shadows everywhere.

It's Malavika, smiling tenderly.

After a few moments, she makes her way to the pew, lowers herself to the kneeler in front of the seating bench rubbed white by suppliants, and sends out a prayer for her only son. There are only two other parishioners in the entire church. I look at the time. It is 12.00 p.m. As if on cue, startling the hallowed quiet, the church bells peal, piercing sweet. A single shaft of sunlight falls like a blessing on my sister's head, suffusing her face with a numinous glow.

And in that modest, self-effacing building, dimly lit, like most houses of worship, I feel utterly certain that her prayers are received.

Adi

The thing about grief is it cannot be pressed and folded away like mourning clothes, to be used as needed. It has no sense of protocol, comes in unannounced. It is a boozy, drugged-out wreck of a relative that won't be ignored and casts a pall wherever he shows up.

You could be sitting with a bowl of chips watching reruns of The Big Bang Theory when it grabs you by the throat, knocking the canned laughter right out of the box. Or maybe you are tapping on your brakes at a school crossing, watching the shiny-faced woman in pink boots directing traffic, when it hits you in the gut, this death you thought has lost its sting.

Or you are finally getting into rhythm, arms entwined around your lover's neck, a tongue of Merlot licking the bedspread, one whisper away from sweet, shuddering relief, when it slithers in on all fours drags you by the balls and brings you to your knees.

Everybody dies. I know that. What I did not know – grief is a mother that knocks you for six, despite a lifetime of slow disappearing.

Epilogue

'We need your mother. Call her, Samir.'

'Huh! Why?'

'Because I need her. Tell her to come. My water just broke.'

He stares at her, uncomprehending.

'Dude! Get your act together. I'm having the BABY!'

He calls his mother on the way to the hospital. His palms are damp from wiping his forehead, the back of his neck. A rush of static, before her breathy voice fills the receiver.

'Samir! Is it time? How is Uzma?'

'Yes. Yes, please come,' he says, and hangs up exhausted.

'Shall we stop for a quick bottle of Mango Lassi, Samir? I'm so thirsty!'

He looks at her, bewildered once again, what happened to the sense of urgency, the panic of the last hour? Then he sees her eyes crinkle.

'I thought you could do with a joke.'

For Samir, the five and a half miles from Cuffe Parade to Breach Candy Hospital do not go by in a blink. He grips her hand until she squirms and shakes it off, and mutters darkly to the driver, 'Hurry up, are you driving in your sleep, arsehole?'

'Shhh! The baby will hear you!'

This time she is not joking.

To his horror, Uzma wants him with her in the delivery room. It is not an easy labor, but relatively quick, the contractions coming closer and closer, her body roaring for relief, the nurses cooing encouragement, as he, Samir, dripping like a faucet, ready to pass out, inches as far back from her bed as he dares until the last contraction, when there are suddenly too many white coats in the room, and what with the bright lights and the uproar, he almost does not see the baby slip out, covered in what looks like shit, and becomes a father.

⌛⌛⌛

Malavika arrives on the next flight, stopping on the way for balloons and cake and all the pink finery she can carry. Both mother and child are fast asleep, but her son rushes out to greet her. She hugs him, and he hugs her back, breathing in the smell of her, warm and comforting as breast milk.

They sit side by side in the lounge.

'I'm so glad it's a girl!' His smile is wide, infectious.

'Why?'

'I wouldn't know how to take care of a boy. But girls! Girls are soft. Forgiving. Lovely.'

His breath catches.

'Yes,' she says. 'Yes,' a little woozy, what with the flight and the rushing around and the surges of joy.

'Listen, Samir. Can you get me some honey?'

'Huh?'

'Yes. Honey. Can you get me some? It's important. For the *baby*.'

'Okay. Hey, Ma?'

'Yes?'

'You will help us, won't you? Uzma and I need you, at the flat in Cuffe Parade for at least a month. Or we can come and stay with you.'

'Of course, I will help.'

'Maybe down the road, we can live together. We'll come to you.'

'You can't give up Cuffe Parade, son. It's prime property. Now, about that honey?'

A nurse with a self-important air, motions them in. Uzma, still flat on her back, legs numb from the epidural, looks both dreadfully tired and blissfully happy as the baby chirrups in her crib.

'Welcome to the world, my Shireen!' whispers Malavika. 'Look, Uzma, she is smiling.'

Then Samir takes the infant in his arms. Shireen, wrapped like a mummy and wiggling in her cotton sheet, stares up at him, eyes like slits, and sticks her pinkie into her mouth.